1746580 TV

JAN 1 9 2011

D0781213

Corporate Governance

VT

JAN 1 9 2011

SAGE has been part of the global academic community since 1965, supporting high quality research and learning that transforms society and our understanding of individuals, groups, and cultures. SAGE is the independent, innovative, natural home for authors, editors and societies who share our commitment and passion for the social sciences.

Find out more at: **www.sagepublications.com**

Corporate Governance

Principles and Issues

Donald Nordberg

Los Angeles | London | New Delhi
Singapore | Washington DC

© Donald Nordberg, 2011

First published 2011

Apart from any fair dealing for the purposes of research or
private study, or criticism or review, as permitted under the
Copyright, Designs and Patents Act, 1988, this publication
may be reproduced, stored or transmitted in any form, or
by any means, only with the prior permission in writing of
the publishers, or in the case of reprographic reproduction, in
accordance with the terms of licences issued by the Copyright
Licensing Agency. Enquiries concerning reproduction outside
those terms should be sent to the publishers.

SAGE Publications Ltd
1 Oliver's Yard
55 City Road
London EC1Y 1SP

SAGE Publications Inc.
2455 Teller Road
Thousand Oaks, California 91320

SAGE Publications India Pvt Ltd
B 1/I 1 Mohan Cooperative Industrial Area
Mathura Road, New Delhi 110 044
India

SAGE Publications Asia-Pacific Pte Ltd
33 Pekin Street #02-01
Far East Square
Singapore 048763

Library of Congress Control Number 2010923779

British Library Cataloguing in Publication data

A catalogue record for this book is available
from the British Library

ISBN 978-1-84787-332-3
ISBN 978-1-84787-333-0 (pbk)

Typeset by C&M Digitals (P) Ltd., Chennai, India
Printed by MPG Books Group, Bodmin, Cornwall
Printed on paper from sustainable resources

Mixed Sources
Product group from well-managed
forests and other controlled sources
www.fsc.org Cert no. SA-COC-1565
© 1996 Forest Stewardship Council
FSC

Contents

List of case studies

Agenda point boxes

Preface

Corporate governance is a difficult subject to circumnavigate. No one quite knows where it starts and ends. Moreover, it is a moving target. The subject has been at or near the centre of serious public policy debate in many countries around the world – and with increasing vigour – for more than a quarter of a century, for reasons this book seeks to make clear. Corporate governance has developed into a kind of social experiment, at least if we think of 'society' as pertaining to the *société anonyme* in French-speaking countries, the *Gesellschaft mit beschräfter Haftung* and *Aktiengesellschaft* in German-speaking ones, the *sociedad anónima* in Spanish-speaking ones, the *società per azioni* in Italy, or the mounting calls around the world for corporate social responsibility.

Moreover, people – practitioners and theoreticians alike – see corporate governance from a variety of perspectives, perspectives almost as wide as the corporation itself.

- *Law and regulation:* Corporations must comply with the legislation that allows them to exist at all, and staying within and amending law sets the stage for everything else that happens in a corporation. Understanding the legal obligations of the corporation is part of the reason why so many members of the community of corporate secretaries in the US – who administer the work of boards of directors – are lawyers and why an increasing number of their counterparts in other countries are too. Shareholder rights, too, are enforced through law, and lobbying organizations seeking change in corporate practices press for changes in law to suit their purposes.
- *Accounting and reporting:* The corporation has obligations to its shareholders – under law and regulation – to report on its financial affairs and increasingly on a host of other matters as well. Doing so requires people to collect the data, and that also requires systems to hold, sort and make sense of them.
- *Finance:* Corporate governance is deeply tied into the complex of issues that connect the providers of capital – equity and debt – with its uses, and therefore with financial control. Within this perspective, corporate governance is also about internal control and risk management, and with it about the auditing function that creates the link back to accounting and reporting.
- *Economics:* The corporation exists, in the view of many scholars, as a mechanism of economic utility. It costs less to conduct business if the people engaged in its processes sit together in an organization, rather than contracting with each other every time there

is work to be done. Moreover, the corporation is a construct whose aim, more often than not, is (or should be, many would say) the maximization of profit for a given amount of resource. The role of the board is then to oversee these processes and ensure the greatest possible value creation.

- *Financial economics:* Here the focus is on how capital markets themselves function and influence the ability of the corporation to achieve the resources necessary to run the business. Some scholars even argue that this is the very centre of corporate governance: without capital markets the corporation as an organizational form would never have achieved its prominence or created nearly as much value as it has done. A minority view adds another interpretation: the corporation exists to meet the needs of savers for a vehicle of investment; production of goods and services is a secondary consideration.
- *Organization design:* Boards of directors form a part of the design of the corporation. Lessons learned from organizational behaviour concerning hierarchies and group dynamics come into play with boards as well. And boards decide, ultimately, on major changes to the structures of the rest of the organization as well.
- *Management and leadership:* In this view, corporate governance is the top layer in the management of a corporation. The work of the board is to guide, motivate, develop, reward and punish their executives and plan for their departure and succession. The board leads the corporation.
- *Marketing:* Even marketing makes a modest claim to be the focus of corporate governance. It is a minority view, to be sure, but if the value of the corporation is the net present value of future customer relationships, then designing corporate governance to help customers is not quite so far-fetched an idea.
- *Strategy:* Strategists would claim the corporate governance is the culmination of strategy-making. It involves allocating resources, monitoring their use and controlling the outcomes, and deciding on corporate direction: why else do we call board members directors?

Corporate governance might also be considered a subset of ethics. The decisions of the board cover all those matters that are not prescribed by law and regulation, by accounting principles and capital market dynamics. Boards decide, fundamentally, the question: What's the right thing to do?

These perspectives overlap, of course, making the task of understanding corporate governance all the more complex. Following each thread inevitably leads to pulling on the tangle of threads that make up the corporation and the study of business and management. This book attempts to do this, but we may encounter knotty problems along the way. As the final chapter seeks to demonstrate, the one thing we can be certain about is this: there may be more unanswered questions about this subject than certainties.

The idea for this book has been germinating for many years, but it was only by moving from business life to academia that I found the mental space and intellectual stimulus to pull as many of the threads as I have first out and then together. A lot of people helped along the way. Bernard Taylor's invitations to me to attend conferences of the Centre for Board Effectiveness at the old Henley Management College in Oxfordshire – not to mention his enthusiasm for everything in life – brought me into contact with both academics and practitioners for lively debates. My occasional conversations with Robert A.G. Monks have always been enlightening. Recollecting his encouragement for my journalism and academic writing on these themes – and his own boundless energy – kept my energy levels up. Georges Selim let me to take part in his discussion forums at Cass Business School, part of City University London, where again academics, corporate officers and officials of major institutional investors compared ideas. Terry McNulty demonstrated the value of considering corporate governance from managerial and strategic perspectives. John Sedgwick and Photis Lysandrou, in different ways, pushed the project forward, too. The editors at Sage Publications deserve special mention for tolerating this sometimes unconventional approach to the subject. Those who read various drafts led me to think I was moving in an interesting direction. Thanks to Roger Tooze, Lisa Day, Luca Enriques and the anonymous readers who reviewed for Sage. Many, many people at what we used to know as Reuters Group stimulated my personal debate about what a corporation is for.

Thanks, too, to all the directors, senior managers, company secretaries, investor relations officers, investment analysts and fund managers I have met over the years and who have shared their insights and frustrations. Mistakes, of course, are my own.

Donald Nordberg
London, November 2010

ONE

Introducing corporate governance

Case: Lehman Brothers and the subprime crisis

In November 2008, Richard Fuld was called to testify before a US Congressional committee investigating the sudden collapse of Lehman Brothers, the investment bank he had headed for many years. Its deep involvement in the markets for asset-backed securities – bonds developed from what were called 'subprime' mortgages and derivatives contracts associated with them – had brought the bank to a crisis two months before. When the US government refused to bail it out, credit markets around the world seized up, accelerating the growing slump of the world economy. The next day, perhaps realizing the mistake of allowing Lehman Brothers to fail, the US Treasury pumped money into the American Insurance Group (AIG), a company that had become the biggest player in a gigantic global market for credit default swaps – tradable securities that initially served as insurance against corporate borrowers, individual mortgage-holders and the banks who lent to them being unable to meet their commitments. As credit dried up around the world, almost any credit default swap might have to pay out. There was insufficient money to pay them all at once. The US Treasury saved AIG, but it proved too little and too late to prevent a string of calamities of varying degrees of severity in Italy, France, Japan, Thailand, Germany, the UK and even Switzerland.

By the end of November, several major commercial banks in a variety of countries had, in effect, been nationalized. Citigroup, the world's largest bank, had been propped up with new equity supplied by US taxpayers, and the entire banking system of a whole country – Iceland – was on its knees. Investments made by Icelandic banks – especially in the retail sector across Europe – were threatened as other banks refused to lend the retailers money to pay their suppliers for merchandise in the run-up to the busy Christmas sales.

The problems in the system were not entirely of Lehman Brothers' making, of course. It had been only one of many intermediaries in the complex web of transactions that collapsed in on itself that month. In the preceding months, Britain had been forced to nationalize a mortgage lender, Northern Rock, after other banks had lost confidence in its ability to repay loans it had taken from other banks to fund its activities. America's biggest stockbroker, the venerable Merrill Lynch, had been impelled into a takeover by Bank of America, the country's second largest commercial bank. Wachovia, the fourth largest, was salvaged by Wells Fargo. On Wall Street, the model of investment banking that had dominated capital markets – from mergers and acquisitions advice, to stock and bond trading, commodities futures and lending to the burgeoning hedge fund industry – had come to an end. After Lehman filed for bankruptcy, its rivals Goldman Sachs and Morgan Stanley, the last two large investment banks, turned themselves into commercial banks, subjecting themselves to a myriad of new regulations in exchange for the right to borrow the money they needed to stay afloat directly from the Federal Reserve, America's central banking system (for background, see Economist, 2008a, 2008b, 2008c).

The legislators wanted to hear from Fuld just what he had done to earn the $500 million he had taken home from Lehman Brothers over the last nine years. (It was not that much, he protested, something closer to $250 million.) But they also wanted to know: How did the board of directors – the people charged with watching over the policies and practices of the company known as Lehman Brothers Holdings Inc. – how had they so completely failed in their duties to the shareholders, that is, the owners of the business they had pledged to serve? How had they failed to see that the business had gone bad, that the assets of the bank had become so 'toxic' – the word that had become an emblem of the banking crisis – that it had afflicted with global financial system, spreading the discomfort throughout the world economy? Were they simply asleep on the job? And what of the directors of all the other banks, brokers and businesses now threatening the wealth of their shareholders, the jobs of their employees, the pensions of their retired workers and of all those whose savings were locked up in other pension funds that invested in stock, debt and property markets now threatened with one of the greatest collapses of value in the modern history of finance? How could these smart people get things so catastrophically wrong?

This was not, to be sure, the first time that directors of public companies had presided over massive destruction of value, despite widespread use of mechanisms of corporate governance – ranging from auditors to credit rating agencies, voluntary codes of conduct to stringent laws on liability and listing requirements of stock exchange – to prevent just that. In the first few years of the twenty-first century, the Italian dairy company Parmalat failed under allegations of fraud and misdealing, and Ahold, a Dutch supermarket group, reeled under a scandal of false accounting. In America, the names of Enron and WorldCom, once among the largest and most respected companies in the country, became synonymous with corporate greed, arrogance, fraud and deception. Aided and abetted by their auditors, the venerable firm of Arthur Andersen, these two colossuses proved to be only two of a string of companies that had exploited every loophole in the US regulatory system to pump up their financial statements well beyond a true reflection of the state of the business. The first wave of internet-related euphoria in financial markets – the dot-com bubble – burst at about the same time, wiping trillions of dollars off the nominal value of stock markets in America, Germany, France, Italy, the UK and just about every developed economy in the world.

A decade earlier in the UK, major three companies failed in spectacular fashion, the Bank of Credit and Commerce International, better known as BCCI, Polly Peck International, a trader in fruit and textiles, and Maxwell Communication, a newspaper publisher run by a larger-than-life proprietor and one-time member of parliament whose apparent suicide led to the unravelling of his business empire in the US and UK alike.

These were massive failures in the practice we know of as corporate governance. But the lessons we learn from corporate governance extend into almost all areas of life in organizations. How do family-owned companies cope when the founder of the business retires? How do small, private companies deal with the interests of people who provided capital – the initial funding – to get the business started in the first place? When a business floats shares on public markets, how do its directors look after the interests of those outside shareholders, those not directly involved in the business, too numerous and perhaps too widely spread around the country and the world to consult individually for their views and whose interests will not, anyway, all be the same? How do other organizations – charities, government agencies, clubs and trade associations – look after the interests of their donors, taxpayers, members and beneficiaries? What structures and processes will help the people entrusted with running them remain accountable to their interests? While this book will focus on the affairs of quoted companies drawn mainly from the major western economies, it will do so knowing that readers will be seeking lessons as well about the affairs of other organizations in other parts of the world whose aim is to create value for those whose interests they represent.

Questions arising

Let's remember, for the moment, that the subprime mortgage market benefited many people in society, before the system crashed. Poorer people got a chance at home ownership, by virtue of the way this market – initially, at least – held the promise to distribute risk more widely than ever before. And remember that Lehman Brothers was only one of many banks and corporations that become entangled in the crisis.

1 What approaches might the Lehman board or the US government have used to prevent a disaster?

   a) Which are external to the company?
   b) Which are internal to the company?
   c) Which external to the profession/industry?
   d) Which internal to the profession/industry?
   e) Which have force of law?
   f) Which have force of custom and practice?
   g) Which have ethical force?
   h) Which draw their force from politics and power?

2 What power did Richard Fuld have to prevent a disaster?
3 What power did the board of Lehman Brothers have?
4 To whom were they responsible?
5 To whom were they not responsible? What were the limits of their responsibility?

What is corporate governance?

Seeking a tidy definition of any subject presents difficulties, but few are less tidy than corporate governance. Corporations create employment for many if not most people in the advanced economies around the world. Their profits fuel wealth creation, through the payment of dividends they pay to their shareholders or the money they invest in research and development to create new products or to reduce the costs of creating the goods and services that people around the world want to buy. Much of the improvement we have seen in living standards in the last 200 years can be attributed to corporate activity, since the industrial revolution made mass production possible and with it made products available to the masses. Governing such entities involves overseeing strategy, human resources, financial accounting, marketing, external communications, factories and organizational structures and deciding how they all fit together.

Corporations – the large businesses operating on a scale that one individual person could easily control and only a few could ever dream of owning – also operate in ways unlike other entities, other 'economic actors'. Unlike individual people, corporations are difficult to hold to account. You cannot imprison a corporation. Their owners claim property rights over them, but in a very peculiar way. Owners' rights over the corporation scarcely justify using the term 'ownership' at all.

Corporations occupy an odd place in the political systems in which they reside. Even the word 'reside' is odd: to create the structures we know of as corporations, nineteenth-century political and legal theorists decided to treat them as though they were people. Companies – groups of people working as an economic unit – were allowed to incorporate and in so doing become 'legal persons', entitled in law to enter into contracts with people and other corporations, and given the protection of law as though they were people. But unlike people – or, until the past few decades, partnerships between people – corporations, received in law the recognition that their members, that is, their shareholders or 'owners', were not personally liable for their debts or if something went wrong. This protection in law allowed corporations to amass the large amounts of capital needed to build large enterprises using large machinery and employing large numbers of people. Through that protection, they grew throughout the twentieth century into the enterprises we know today (for background, see McCraw, 1997).

Many large corporations, the ones we sometimes call multinational enterprises or 'transnational' companies, have more income and produce more wealth than many countries. Their employees may well be citizens of a country – or of more than one – but their expatriate managers may have a greater sense of allegiance to the corporation than to any single nation-state. Their actions – if nothing else through threatening to move their legal seat from one political jurisdiction to another – can prompt governments to change policy. A few have conspired to overthrow governments, so great is the potential of their power (for the case of ITT and Chile, see Sampson, 1973).

Most corporations, of course, do not enjoy such power let alone use it. But neither are they easy to subsume under law in any one jurisdiction. Particularly in the liberal democracies that fostered the growth of corporations and the economic welfare they allowed, governments claim legitimacy through their right to govern the people who live under their jurisdiction. Corporations cannot claim such legitimacy, yet they can govern, in many ways, the lives and activities of the workforces and the companies and individuals who supply them or buy the products and services they create. The scope of this power sits ultimately but uncomfortably under the jurisdiction of law and society. But the power they possess puts them and the managers who lead them in a position to do much damage as well as much good.

How, then, do we govern these corporate entities? In the narrow sense, corporate governance looks at the mechanisms put in place inside companies to guide their actions and monitor their performance. Most writing and thinking about corporate governance focuses on the role of the board of directors, the group of people who sit at the top of the enterprise, deciding what direction it should take, what strategies it should adopt, hiring a team of managers and then holding them to account for the performance they deliver. Another aspect of corporate governance looks at how those boards of directors relate to their owners, the investors who bought shares in the corporation and claim, through the legitimacy of their property rights, to have some sort of say over the affairs of the corporation. These two areas – the relationship between boards and managers and the relationship between investors and boards – form what we will call the classical agenda of corporate governance, which has dominated the thinking and writing about corporate governance (Cadbury & Millstein, 2005;

Charkham, 1994; MacAvoy & Millstein, 2003; Millstein & MacAvoy, 1998; Monks & Minow, 2003). Despite the difficulties associated with looking into the private and often highly confidential affairs of private entities, scholars have attempted to describe how these processes work, in part so that other directors on other boards can see, if only through a glass darkly, how they might conduct their business. Even more scholars have attempted to prescribe how boards ought to conduct their relationships – with managers and investors – even in absence of definitive information about how the complex interaction of all the factors that come together at the board really works.

There is, however, another range of issues that have increasingly come to be seen as forming a new agenda in corporate governance: how corporations relate to their broader society. Whether we call it corporate social responsibility, sustainability, ethics or just corporate responsibility without the 'social', this stream of thinking (Benn & Dunphy, 2007; Crowther & Rayman-Bacchus, 2004; DesJardins, 2007; Elkington, 1999) involves a consideration of how boards and the top management teams they employ relate to their employees, suppliers, customers, and even their competitors and those who might seek to compete against them. It seeks to take into account as well how the corporation relates to the community in which it operates, the people who live near the factories and office buildings the corporation operates, local governments, and even national governments and supranational organizations. It seeks as well to examine how and even whether corporations have a responsibility to non-governmental organizations, even those that are not particularly part of a local community in which the global corporation just happens to work. It seeks to identify the role of the corporation and its board in preserving the environment in which we all live, a larger and more prominent part of the agenda as the consensus of scientific opinion has built around the impact of global warming and the role corporations play in it. This second agenda has been widely studied in descriptive ways as well, often with even less access to definitive information that would lead to conclusions we might consider robust. It, too, has developed a large academic literature of a prescriptive nature, and one with perhaps even more vigour of opinion than we see in the literature of the classical corporate governance agenda.

Both streams of thinking seek to address simultaneously two issues:

- How are corporations directed and monitored, and what mechanisms can we use to make them perform better?
- What mechanisms can we put in place to ensure that corporations, their managers and directors do not destroy the value that the corporation was meant to create and destroy the value of others with whom it conducts its affairs?

Inside corporations, however, corporate governance has another aspect: How can we create value? That was, after all, why the corporation was formed; indeed, why society created the institution of the corporation in the first place.

In that sense, running a corporation is a bit like sailing a ship or driving a car. The term governance traces its roots to the Latin word *gubernare* – to steer – as in directing a ship towards its destination, overcoming whatever vagaries the wind and tides might inflict on the crew's intended course of action. Governance is, therefore, the job of setting the direction. When kings were truly sovereign, governance referred to the instructions that the leader had set out for his subjects to follow, come what may. But over the centuries other definitions have come into play. Democracies govern not by edict, but rather by systems of checks and balances, by negotiating a settlement between competing interests. The role of governance is not merely to set direction, but rather to mediate between the various parties contesting for control of resources.

Agenda point 1: Operating the controls

Governance involves steering, yes, but in a modern economy, one powered by engines rather than wind, it also involved stepping on the brakes and limiting the throttle. In mechanical engineering, a governor prevents engines from generating too much power, from propelling the mopeds faster than a speed limit deemed appropriate to keep their riders and other users of the road safe. Corporate governance also concerns slowing things down, avoiding disasters, protecting something of value, preventing one party from scaring others off the road.

Strategy, when the driver uses the steering wheel the accelerator pedal, is also a part of corporate governance. But both the classical and the new corporate governance agendas involve thinking about how we should apply the brakes. People who drive use all three controls – the steering wheel, the accelerator and the brakes – hopefully at the right time and in the right circumstances. We use brakes, as the presenter of a British television programme on motoring once said, *to make the car go faster*.

Agenda point 1 suggests we can think of governance as involving three controls: the steering wheel, the brake and the accelerator. This book considers all three and their purpose. We will look a bit at direction, though it more often than not is the subject of books on strategy and its use tends to be specific to each company. We will look at the importance of speed in creating value, too; how corporations innovate and bring ideas to market quickly to remain competitive and to add value. But the main focus of this book is examining the brakes, not because they should be applied at all times – quite the contrary. This book is intended to help us be sure, when we do go into a sudden change of direction or we're just gaining speed as we cruise straight ahead downhill, so that we can take the actions necessary to avoid a crash and get to the destination faster.

How this book is organized

Chapter 2 explores some of the background to the two questions that have dominated the corporate governance agenda: 1) the disasters that have led to massive destruction of wealth and of trust in the role of corporations in society, and 2) the smaller, day-to-day grievances that are piled at the doorstep of the board of directors, whether in complaints about excesses in executive pay, the role of corporations in philanthropic activities, or any of a variety of other issues the board may need to decide. The three sections that make up the rest of the book explore the principles of corporate governance, the governance issues facing boards of directors, and how companies account for their activities and what that holds for the future.

Principles of corporate governance

Chapter 3 examines those issues through the lens of theory, showing how *agency theory* can help us understand the actions of managers and boards and their relationship to owners. We will look at alternative views as well: what scholars call *resource dependency theory* concerning the way boards facilitate access to key resources, contributing to the company's creation of value, and how that invokes *stewardship* and its implication for board performance. We will look as well at what has come to be called *stakeholder theory* helps illuminate competing claims to the resources that the corporation controls, whether they come from workers, suppliers, customers or the public at large.

Chapter 4 sets corporate governance in a wider context, looking at the range of mechanisms that constrain how corporations function – from the ways that markets and competition play a role in applying the brakes to corporate greed and personal ambition, to the role of law and regulation in setting a framework that prescribes what corporations, their boards and managers must and must not do.

This leads us, in Chapter 5, to a discussion of the approaches taken in different countries to the way corporations are organized, the roles boards of directors play, and the tensions that result. We will also see how that situation is changing, in large part under pressure from markets themselves: global markets for products and services and the increasingly global market for capital and investment.

Chapter 6 brings us to the attempts to reconcile these pressures: the ones that led to disasters in corporate governance like those sketched out in the opening section of this chapter, and the ones that look at those smaller, day-to-day issues that confront corporations of all sizes, industries and nationalities – if corporations really can be said to have nationalities any more. We will look at how codes of conduct have developed around the world, though with a heavy focus on Europe and the United States, whose measures came first and were copied in many other parts of the world, whether or not they were appropriate to local conditions.

Issues on the board's agenda

The next four chapters explore the key issues on the classical corporate governance agenda of monitoring and control, those examined in the main through agency theory. Chapter 7 considers how codes have sought to address these issues through the structure and composition of the board. The chapter also looks at the limitations that formal measures have. That leads to a discussion of board processes and how the characteristics of board members can work against the twin aims of corporate governance – performance monitoring and value creation.

In Chapter 8 we look at the issues of executive pay (which can involve paying too little as well as too much), its more sinister extensions into fraud and self-dealing by top management, and how accounting has been used to cover it up. The solution to these types of issues rests in increasing the independence of the board of directors and in modifying the structure of the boards.

Chapter 9 considers the relationship between boards and their owners, and in particular two aspects: the role of founding families and other large shareholders who can exert decisive power in board decisions, and how institutional investors, like pension funds, insurance companies and the companies that create collective investment vehicles like mutual funds, seek to influence corporate affairs.

Chapter 10 explores the trend in these ownership issues, and in particular the role that non-traditional investors – like hedge funds, private equity houses and sovereign wealth funds – are changing the investment landscape, raising new issues about the nature of the classical corporate governance agenda.

Chapter 11 then turns to what we have called the new corporate governance agenda, looking first through the lens of a particular type of specialized investment activity: the growth of what is sometimes called *socially responsible* or *ethical investment*, approaches that can in some ways challenge the assumptions which underpin traditional institutional investment, and indeed the non-traditional world of hedge funds and their kindred spirits. In this context we will also consider issues of sustainability in the face of the uncertain science of climate change as well as the uncertainties of markets for goods and services and the resulting uncertainties about the sustainability of strategy and the profits it aims to create.

Reporting, rebalancing and the future

Chapter 12 revisits the some of the issues raised about *how* we conduct corporate governance, but with a special focus on the roles of transparency and disclosure as alternatives to detailed rules, regulations and enforcement.

Chapter 13 makes a modest attempt to link these themes to the debate over what private companies, charities and public sector bodies have to learn from the emerging consensus – as we will see, even orthodoxy – about what corporate governance entails.

The book concludes in Chapter 14 by returning to the question of whether all this attention to the brake pedal means that we have slowed the enterprise down too much and lost momentum towards value creation. We consider the board's role in strategy and provision of resources, before ending with a few tentative thoughts about the issues we are likely to face in these unsettled and unsettling times, when global economic integration is proceeding even as the banking and regulatory issues rised in the discussion at the start of this chapter pose questions about whether the governance mechanisms we have implemented so far are capable of doing the job we designed them to perform.

Further readings

IFC (2005). The Irresistible Case for Corporate Governance. *International Finance Corp.* Retrieved April 26, 2009, from http://ifcln1.ifc.org/ifcext/corporategovernance. nsf/AttachmentsByTitle/The_Irrisistible_Case_Text/$FILE/IrresistibleCase4CG. pdf.

Leblanc, R. & Gillies, J. (2003). The Coming Revolution in Corporate Governance. *Ivey Business Journal, 68*(1), 1–11.

Millstein, I. M., Gregory, H. J. & Grapsas, R. C. (2008, Jan). Rethinking Board and Shareholder Engagement in 2008. Retrieved March 22, 2008, from http://www.weil. com/files/Publication/5c443ec5-4732-4988-bb2c-b757c207d291/Presentation/ PublicationAttachment/a9c9ed8e-f7b1-4b87-8010-c58e024c2834/Corporate_ Governance_Advisory_Memo_Jan_2008.pdf.

Zahra, S. A. & Pearce, J. A., II. (1989). Boards of Directors and Corporate Financial Performance: A Review and Integrative Model. *Journal of Management, 15*(2), 291–334.

TWO

The problems of corporate governance

Case: Robert Maxwell and the recurrent crisis

'The achievement at the end of it is that I feel that my life, which I continue to live to the full and will do until the day I die, I will have left the world a slightly better place by having lived in it, and have influenced a few things and people in the right direction, rather as if it hadn't mattered that I had been born, lived or died,' Robert Maxwell once said (quoted in Langdon, 2008).

But then late in 1991 the body of a very large man washed ashore in the Canary Islands, an apparent suicide, though we will never know. He was cremated within 24 hours in Israel. Robert Maxwell's UK and US publishing empire was in ruins. The former Labour member of the British parliament had been born in Czechoslovakia and was rumoured to have served as a spy for Mossad, Israel's renowned intelligence service. At first he used loans, then profits to build his business empire. But he ended up raiding the pension funds of his workforces to keep alive his ambition to become the world's most influential publisher, not merely the proprietor of the *Daily Mirror* in Britain, the *New York Daily News* and a collection of academic journals. The scandal that led to his death – suicide, or was it murder? – changed the way corporations around the world are governed.

Maxwell's two main companies, Maxwell Communication and Mirror Group Newspapers, were both listed on the London Stock Exchange. A fierce executive, Maxwell was notorious for bullying members of staff and any journalists who might write stories about him taking a critical tone. As chairman and chief executive of his company, he reigned supreme. His boards of directors were largely hand-picked by Maxwell himself. His sons Kevin and Ian served on the boards and in senior executive roles. After his death, the companies collapsed and his sons were made personally bankrupt with debts of £400 million.

Robert Maxwell had built his companies by acquiring one property after the next: an academic publisher called Pergamon Press, the *Mirror* newspaper in Britain and the *New York Daily News*, the book publishers Collier and Macmillan, and various interests in broadcasting and professional sports. In the court proceedings after his death, it became clear that the empire had been a house of cards, built up on debt raised in part by manipulating the share prices of his listed companies and by draining capital from the pension funds of his workforces (for a fuller account see Wearing, 2005). With the bankruptcy, many of the workers lost all their pension entitlements. In death Maxwell was vilified as the epitome of the all-powerful chief executive, running rampant without any checks or balances on his actions, treating shareholders' money as if it were his own. How did he get away with it, and for so long? And what, many people wondered after the fall, were his boards of directors, and auditors, and all the other bodies that had dealings with the companies, doing all the time?

Maxwell's death and the rubble of a business empire he left behind represented only one of a string of corporate disasters that the UK faced that year. A fruit and textiles company, Polly Peck International, had skyrocketed into the ranks of the largest companies in the country – the FTSE-100, often called the 'Footsie' – just a few years before. By the end of 1990 it was in ruins and its chief executive had fled to the Turkish part of his native Cyprus, where he could avoid extradition to face charges of fraud and false accounting. A privately controlled bank, the Bank of Credit and Commerce International, had crumbled as well. It took the courts more than 15 years to clear the Bank of England, its sometime supervisor, of liability in the failure. With roots in Pakistan, BCCI was formally incorporated in Luxembourg though most of its operations were in Britain. (Wearing, 2005, gives a detailed account of all three cases.)

Losing one big company in a year might have been an accident and two just bad luck. But losing three big corporations at almost the same time suggested that something serious was wrong. Something had to be done.

Ten years later, Kenneth Lay was called back from his semi-retirement to return as chief executive of an energy company in Houston, Texas, that had become the fastest growing and most admired company in the world. The workers had even been encouraged to invest their self-managed pensions in the company's own stock. Lay had 'retired' as CEO but took over the chairmanship, in keeping with a separation of powers he had learned from the lessons of the Maxwell affair. But then his protégé, Jeffrey Skilling, became even more aggressive than Lay had been in promoting the growth of the company, and the board lost faith. Lay's task would be to rebuild the company's reputation. Within months it was insolvent, and within a few more months its auditors, one of the largest firms in the world, had imploded. Enron and Arthur Andersen are now symbols of greed and deception.

And Enron was not alone. WorldCom, Adelphia, Tyco and other prominent US corporations joined it in the Hall of Shame. In Europe Ahold, a Dutch supermarket group, suffered an accounting scandal centred on its US operations. The problems of the Italian dairy company Parmalat had a US link, but the core of the problems was located at its headquarters. These scandals further changed the way corporations around the world are governed. (Wearing, 2005, again has details.)

Six years later, a little bank in Germany known as IKB sought a rescue from the government when money got tight. Then a state-owned bank, Sachsen LB, had difficulties. More followed: Northern Rock, Bear Stearns, HBOS, Lehman Brothers, AIG, Wachovia, Citigroup, Merrill Lynch, Royal Bank of Scotland, UBS, and a string of others, all with problems stemming from the proximate cause of mortgage lending by US banks to borrowers they had deemed to be 'subprime' (Nordberg, 2008b). This convulsion – the most serious since the great Wall Street Crash in 1929 – is sure to bring about changes to the way corporations around the world are governed.

When are we going to get it right?

Questions arising

Imagine yourself in charge of a government panel ordered to draft new legislation to prevent a recurrence.

1   What aspects of the Maxwell case would be different had he been the sole owner of the companies?
2   How does the governance of his enterprises affect public policy?
3   What recommendations would you make?
4   What is at risk in altering the way companies work?
5   What alternatives are there to changing company law?

Corporate malfeasance

That corporate governance has grown in interest is obvious from even a modest analysis. The *Financial Times* newspaper has been concerned with the topic for many years, even predating the scandals of the early 1990s. Indeed, its categorization used by the Nexis database includes stories labelled with the topic code 'corporate governance' even when individual stories may not contain the phrase. While the difficulties at Maxwell, BCCI and Polly Peck provoked a lot of interest in the field, it was not really until 2001 and Enron that we see a big expansion of news on the subject.

The data in Figure 1 suggest that it was not until thinking began to coalesce around the phrase 'Combined Code' in 1996 that readers of the *Financial Times* would have been offered something close to daily coverage. News coverage is often a lagging indicator of the concern about new topics, as journalists initially feel their way into new fields. Once a topic is hot, however, coverage ramps up. It then wanes, perhaps before an issue has really gone off the boil, as the journalists come to believe that their readers have had enough. Absent major

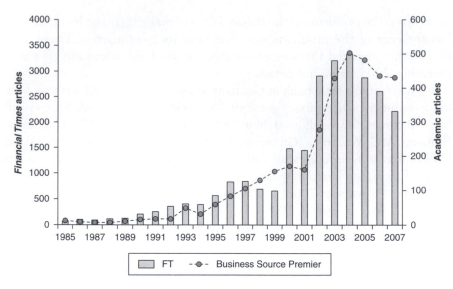

Figure 1 Corporate governance in the FT and academic journals

corporate scandals or substantive revisions of governance codes, it is not surprising to see some decline in treatment of governance issues in 2007 and the first half of 2008 (FT data sourced from the Nexis database).

Remarkably similar is the trend in interest among academics for the corporate governance theme. Given the lead time for academic journal publication (often 18 months to two years from the time the article is submitted and perhaps a year or more from the time it is conceived to the point at which it is written), these data suggest that the academic community was ahead of the journalists in sensing the development of one of the biggest corporate policy stories in history. (Academic journal data come from searching for the phrase 'corporate governance' in abstracts from the academic journals indexed by Business Source Premier.)

Since 2002, corporate boards have been preoccupied with the governance agenda. In Europe – to an even greater degree than the United States – governance codes have proliferated, focusing attention on the work of board committees and the question of the independence of mind directors need to show. In reaction to corporate scandals – first in the US, then in Europe – boards have been faced with external demands for greater accountability and transparency. The bursting of the internet bubble, the collapse of Enron, WorldCom and accounting scandals at Ahold, Parmalat and others understandably created a climate in which the actions of corporate leaders came under much closer scrutiny from investors, regulators and legislators around the world. Hundreds of billions of dollars in valuation were lost, exposing a looming pension crisis that had lain hidden in part by the implausibly high asset values of the valuation bubble. These circumstances conspired to create a climate in which trust between consumers and companies, between investors and directors, reached perhaps the lowest ebb since the 1930s. 'Restoring Trust' became the watchword.[1]

With each new incident of corporate malfeasance, attention to corporate governance intensifies – among academics, business journalists, policymakers and the general public. We look to find out what went wrong, who was responsible, and what lessons we can draw to prevent it happening again.

- What should government have done? Government establishes the basis on which economic activity takes place and looks after the interests of the public. Law establishes the basis of the contractual rights of the various parties to economic transactions and provides mechanisms for enforcement through civil and criminal courts.
- What should regulators have done? Regulation, usually set in the context of law, provides a way to judge the fairness of transactions. Most have enforcement mechanisms; those that lack enforcement power can appeal to higher authorities.
- What should trade associations have done? Members of such associations can be bound by standard contracts, codes of conduct and ethical principles. Many have the ability to exclude members from the association's benefits if they fail to comply.
- What should stock exchanges have done? Although many stock markets around the world have lost their direct regulatory powers, they maintain some elements of control over the behaviour of the companies that seek to have their shares trading on the exchange.
- What should industry as a whole have done? Absent any formal mechanisms for enforcing good behaviour, moral suasion comes into play.
- What should companies themselves have done? Companies have in their internal organization a number of ways to protect themselves, their owners, employees, customers and suppliers from malfeasance. They have structures, processes and systems. They give their owners, employees, suppliers and customers certain rights and pledge to them certain obligations. They have managements empowered to use their best efforts to fulfil those obligations, and they have a board of directors to ensure that management uses that power wisely.

A brief history of the corporation

The first concerns about how corporations are guided date back to the very beginning of corporations themselves. In the South Sea Bubble in the early eighteenth century, a frenzy developed among investors seeking to participate it the vast profits promised as sailing vessels found ways to navigate from Europe to distant parts of the globe in search of spices, precious metals and stones (Mackay, 1852/1995). It was the first great scandal of what we have come to call the 'modern corporation' with its shareholders distant from the managers who ran the business but it would not be the last (Temin & Voth, 2004). The experience made Adam Smith, one of the founders of modern economic theory, deeply suspicious of the value of 'joint stock companies' (A. Smith, 1776/1904).

The invention – in Britain during Queen Victoria's reign and other countries at about the same time – of limited liability for shareholders in such companies solved the problem that had arisen a century earlier, in the collapse of the South Sea Company in 1720. Now shareholders could speculate but would not be liable for any losses that the enterprise might incur beyond the capital they had invested. This invention made the industrial revolution and the expansion of railways possible. It allowed companies to raise large sums of money from the small investments of a large number of people to buy the machines that allowed new products to be built and new processes exploited. Investors, wealthy individuals in the main, could invest in a variety of companies, spreading their risk should one of the ventures fail. But that dispersion of interest meant that investors were now not directly engaged in the business of the company, and with investments in a variety of businesses they lacked the resources individually to keep track of how well the companies were performing (for a good overview see Micklethwait & Wooldridge, 2003).

Investing in a company became less risky with the development of stock exchanges, through which investors could find a way to realize the value of their shares without waiting for dividends to be paid or for the company to be wound up and its assets dispersed. This facility created the scope for what we now call insider trading, where a knowledgeable investors sell (or buy) shares knowing that bad (or good) news is about to come out. To create fairer markets, exchanges like the London Stock Exchange or the bourses around continental Europe added *disclosure requirements* for any company that wanted its shares to trade on the exchange. We shall return to the role of disclosure in Chapter 12.

These developments did not immediately lead to the capital markets we have today. Indeed, capital markets in continental Europe remain quite different in structure from those in the UK and the United States. Ownership varies as a result, and with it approaches to corporate governance: Italian corporations make wide use of pyramid holdings, the Swedes of unequal voting rights, the Belgians of family controlled enterprises, the Germans of bank-led businesses until the very end of the twentieth century. In America and Britain shareholding tends to be widely dispersed, with few companies having a dominant shareholder. We shall examine these examples and their implications in greater detail in Chapter 4.

But whatever the approach, these systems all share an issue for the investor who sits outside the boardroom, removed from knowledge of the inner workings of the company and lacking personal knowledge of the executives and their passions. Outsiders suffer from restricted access to information and limits on how they can exercise their voice on matters of corporate policy.

Value destruction

The separation of ownership and control that made Adam Smith wary of corporations became recognized after the Wall Street Crash of 1929 as perhaps the biggest problem in the topic we would come to call corporate governance. It was a system with great virtues in terms of mobilizing capital for productive ventures, but it was also one open to abuse of investors who lacked the time, information and access to shape what happened in the boardroom. It was one that two Americans scholars, Adolph Berle and Gardiner Means, worried might threaten the ability of capitalism itself to survive the destruction of the Great Depression (Berle & Means, 1932/1991).

Value destruction on a massive scale affects the wider economy and even confidence in financial markets, in the leadership of corporations, in the degree of freedom that we permit them to have. One of the worst cases was the 1929 Crash and the subsequent Great Depression in countries around the world, when massive speculation fuelled by cheap credit and exploded by certain cases of fraud and deception led to misery for millions who never engaged in the speculation nor had the chance to benefit from its excesses. That case led many to question the value of capitalism itself. It contributed in no small measure to the events that precipitated the Second World War.

Corporate misalignments

As dramatic and economically significant as they are, such cases of massive malfeasance are quite rare and constitute only one of the issues on the corporate governance agenda, and probably the least common even if its impact can transform how we live. On a more mundane level, corporations seem by their very structure to encourage minor fraud and self-dealing. In some cases it comes in the form of employees using the company's resources as though they were their own. That is a managerial issue, and managements seek to monitor petty fraud and enforce internal rules. But not all such self-dealing is so petty. When it concerns the top level of management, where individual employees have substantial power over budgets, the problems need attention from boards. And in many cases the self-interest of the employee – especially when he is also the chief executive officer, with wide discretion to write his own ticket – can become matters of contracts. The size and structure of CEO remuneration has been a topic of debate for decades, as executive pay leapt by orders of magnitude in proportion to that of the average worker. Attempts to control executive pay and align it with the interests of shareholders led to the widespread use of stock options, under which executives would have a strong incentive to act in a way that also was of direct benefit to shareholders. But here, too, executives seem to be able to rig the system to their own benefit, many observers including some shareholders have charged.

Executive pay

What level of pay is 'excessive' for the top management of a large corporation? This is not at all a straightforward question; nor have scholars and practitioners settled on any formula to prevent excesses from arising even when we can agree on what 'excess' means. Its role has been central, though, in focusing attention on the board of directors as a mechanism to keep senior management working towards corporate aims, rather than their own. One reason often cited for the escalation in executive pay has been the strong role that the CEO often plays in selecting people to join the board, who will then go on to determine how much the CEO gets paid. The process of board nominations is, therefore, a highly contentious area between *executive directors*, the top managers who sit on the board, the outside directors we call *non-executives*, and shareholders themselves.

Agenda point 2: What should we do about bankers and their rewards?

The subject of executive pay is never far from the lips of corporate governance specialists. The subject of paying bankers never comes up these days in ordinary life without a few expletives inserted. But solving either the general or the specific problem isn't easy. That said, big names in corporate governance research have offered a more than tentative set of recommendations. Lucian Bebchuk and Holger Spamann (2009) have produced a paper to help the authorities around the world speak with authority when they address the issue, as they must.

'Although there is now wide recognition that bank executives' decisions might have been distorted by the short-term focus of pay packages, we identify a separate and critical distortion that has received little attention,' they write. It involves a switch of focus between equity and debt. 'Because bank executives have been paid with shares in bank holding companies or options on such shares, and both banks and bank holding companies issued much debt to bondholders, executives' payoffs have been tied to highly levered bets on the value of the capital that banks have. These highly levered structures gave executives powerful incentives to take excessive risks.'

Current legislative and regulatory attempts to discourage excessive risk-taking fail to address this distortion. Even issuing restricted common shares in these companies and introducing 'say on pay' votes by these shareholders do not eliminate the divergence of interests between executives and all those with a stake in the bank. Common shareholders of bank holding companies – especially at today's lower valuations – would favour different strategies than those the government as shareholder and guarantor of some of the bank's obligations would want the banks to pursue.

Their solution is something like asking a junkie to go cold turkey. 'Beyond banks receiving governmental support, we argue that monitoring and regulating bankers' pay should be an important element of banking regulation in general,' they write. (*The BoardAgenda*, 4 July 2009; http://www.edgevantage.co.uk/categories/article.asp?i=4679.)

One of the few property rights that shareholders actually have is the ability to elect directors to the board. But in many countries, the trappings of shareholder democracy are undone by laws or conventions that make it difficult for shareholder to vote. For many years and in almost all of the United States, shareholder votes on candidates for the board were all but meaningless, except in the most extreme cases.

The level of pay and the way in which directors are selected are perhaps the two most central issues over the way corporate governance is applied in the normal operations of companies. If shareholders had greater say over the appointment of directors, and those directors had greater influence over how executive pay was determined, perhaps the structure and level of pay could be brought in line with shareholder interests. That was, at least, the theory. We shall return in Chapter 8 to the vexed question of whether we can determine what level of pay is excessive and what is not only fair but necessary to provide the incentives to focus managers on how to create value.

Self-dealing

Executives might engage in self-dealing in other ways, however. Studies focusing on mergers and acquisitions involving US companies, for example, show that CEOs of larger companies tend to earn more money, irrespective of whether the acquisition increases profits – or indeed destroys value. In corporate governance, the size of the corporation matters. It is often said that executives at large corporations earn more than those in charge of smaller ones, though the view can be difficult to substantiate with precision (Baker & Hall, 2004). Top executives of big companies certainly figure more prominently in newspapers and magazines and get invited to a join a more prestigious range of charities and join in a more exclusive range of parties. So executives would seem to have an incentive to pursue major transactions whether or not those deals are good for shareholders – as long as those executives remain in charge of the combined companies. A more complex and nuanced view emerges from empirical studies, however (Balkin & Gomez-Mejia, 1990; Kroll, Wright, Toombs, & Leavell, 1997; Wright, Kroll, & Elenkov, 2002). Given the common view that most business combinations destroy value for the acquiring company, the incentives in M&A would seem to be perverse, though here too the view may be more subtle (Graham, Lemmon, & Wolf, 2002). Whatever the subtleties, however, giving shareholders a right to vote on major transactions has long been an item on the traditional corporate governance agenda.

Executive directors and non-executives alike could also enter into other transactions with the company in its normal line of business. Senior bankers sitting on the board of another company can be very valuable assets. Their knowledge of finance and capital markets can point non-financially minded directors to interesting solutions to business problems and even facilitate access to loans or underwriting of new bonds or equity issues by the company.

As such, their expertise can allow the company to reduce its transaction costs, lowering its cost of capital and in so doing increasing its profitability and competitiveness. But those bankers may well also be more inclined to point the company towards their own banks, and even if not, then to their own preferred form of funding, rather than the funding that would be best under an objective scrutiny of the alternatives.

Executives on the board have other avenues of self-dealing open to them. They might use patronage to place members of their families on the payroll and even on the board. They could form private corporations in businesses that could act as suppliers and then direct business towards those companies to their private benefit. With almost unrestricted access to corporate funds, they can arrange personal loans from the company to pay for private acquisitions – for example, owning a house near to where the company has operations in various parts of the country or the world might seem a sound idea. But if the loans are at anything other than a commercial rate of interest they involve transferring shareholder funds from the company directly to the executive. Even if the loan is made at a fully commercial rate, there is still a transfer of value: first, the loan represents an additional risk for the company to manage; second, it uses up credit resources that the company might have used for business purposes – for the purpose of increasing shareholder value.

Personal use of company assets is a nebulous yet problematic area. For a CEO to use a private jet often makes economic sense. The time a highly paid executive spends in an airport is costly. Assuming a CEO worked even 80 hours a week – twice the level of normal employees – for all 52 weeks of the year and earned as little (if we dare say that) as $1 million a year in salary, an hour waiting in an airport for a commercial flight costs $240. But that is just the time costs. If the CEO is indeed adding value to the corporation, the opportunity cost – the cost of other profitable uses of that time – could be a multiple of several times that. But when he uses that same corporate jet to fly off for a skiing holiday, the question becomes blurred. And if the family flies along with him, the question of private versus shareholder benefit becomes rather more problematic.

Corporate control

A more problematic area – intellectually and morally – is the question of how control over corporations changes hands. Here the competing interests of a wide range of people can come into conflict. Let's take the abstract situation of a company engaged in ordinary economic activity, making products for customers, paying dividends to shareholders, growing in line with the economy. It is a good performer, but nothing special. It is not so large a company that it poses problems about the degree of competition in the industry. That is, the market for its goods and services performs a useful function in preventing managers from abusing their position. Another company – a competitor – offers a premium of, say, 25 per cent over the average share price of the past three months. The board of directors needs to make a recommendation to shareholders. How should it decide?

Agenda point 3: 'Shine light on derivatives' or risk 'new darkness'

This issue has recurred in several places over recent years: a financial institution secures a stronger position in a company than the share register indicates through the use of derivative contracts. The UK and Australia have moved to force disclosure of such positions when a takeover bid is underway, and Britain's Financial Services Authority also added temporary measures to force disclosure of short positions during capital-raising exercises. In the US, meanwhile, something odd happened, pointing in the opposite direction and raising the ire of one of America's most prominent governance scholars. John Coffee of Columbia University was furious with the US Securities and Exchange Commission over its inaction in a hotly contested struggle for corporate control involving a UK-based hedge fund and a US corporation.

The Children's Investment Fund, famous for its 2005 assault on Deutsche Börse, took a large stake in the railroad operator CSX. The position it accumulated involved total return equity swaps. CSX tried to prevent voting of the 14 per cent stake linked to the swaps because the holders had failed to disclose who the beneficiary owner was. The SEC might have forced disclosure – the judge clearly wanted it to – and in so doing set a precedent that others could use. But the SEC staff demurred. 'While the SEC has vacillated, other securities regulators have recognised the necessity of addressing equity derivatives,' Coffee railed in a column in the *Financial Times*. 'Until it joins the growing consensus a new darkness is about to descend over the market.' (*The BoardAgenda*, 30 June 2008; http://www.edgevantage.co.uk/categories/article.asp?i=4170.)

There are three types of decisions: recommend, reject or do neither. Each has several possibilities. The outcome of that decision will depend on the circumstances of the specific case. We are looking here for the underlying basis of the decision – how the board goes about the process of deciding, whose interests the board considers in coming to its conclusion. It could decide, for example, on the basis of a simple economic rationale, by estimating, say, the net present value of its strategic initiatives and comparing that with the bid price. A bid premium in excess of what's planned is, by this definition, value-creating and therefore valuable for all shareholders. That suggests that shareholder value is the driving concern for the directors.

But boards might decide that other interests are at stake. A takeover will almost certainly result in job losses – what the people who write the press release will call 'synergies' – and from experience, the losses will fall dispropor-tionately on the workforce of the acquired company, not the acquirer. If teamwork is a source of value creation – or if workers have a right, in some sense, to their jobs – directors might well judge the case a different way.

Boards might also consider the impact of the transaction on customers or suppliers, longstanding partners who have worked with the company to build its business. What is their stake in this decision? What role should their inter-ests play in the choice? They might even consider the impact of takeover on the community in which they operate. Corporations formed of mergers or by acquisitions do not need two headquarters. They may have overlapping capaci-ties and wish to close entire factories, relocating the work to other locations. That could affect tax revenues in the places vacated and with it the level of public services available to the former members of the workforce, and to their friends and families left behind.

Board members may well also consider their own interests, and in particular the interests of the senior managers who sit as executives on the board. Do they keep their jobs after the acquisition? Do they get better jobs in the com-bined organizations? Do they get a sufficiently handsome payoff that it does not matter that they have to seek work elsewhere? They might be approaching retirement, however, and not care about their own status in the new organiza-tion or even about getting another job. The non-executive directors may also have something to lose, or gain.

Directors could well solicit the views of shareholders. But what if there is a single, large shareholder – a founding family, for example – that values tradition, ties to the community or workforce, more than do the other shareholders, the distant asset management firms interested only in profit? What if that single large shareholder wants to sell and take cash out of the business, and those other, distant asset managers consider the 25 per cent premium to be too low? Which shareholders' views does the board solicit?

Directors could also decide to let shareholders vote on the bid, in effect abdi-cating responsibility for making a recommendation. (In some countries deals above a certain size must be approved by shareholders of both companies.)

These types of questions all concern the operations of what in corporate governance we call the market for corporate control (Becht, Bolton, & Röell, 2002; Thompson & Davis, 1997). From the point of view of creating share-holder value, a free market for corporate control – including the freedom from government interference in the process – is a value check on the potential abuse of power by managers. From other vantage points – those of the work-force, the community, the supply chain, the shareholders whose views do not correspond to the ones the board follows – this market can appear to be a cold, calculating, unfair way of making a decision, even a decision that is in its heart an economic choice.

Corporate contributions

Perhaps a smaller but no less problematic area is how companies use their resources on things that are not, in any direct way at least, related to the business. Gifts to charity sound like a good thing, but perhaps the money could have been better used in paying higher wages or higher dividends, so that the workforce or the shareholders could decide for themselves which charities to support or whether to support them at all. Gifts to political parties and candidates sound less like a good thing. But gaining influence, or at least gaining access so you can make your case, could have an impact on the corporation's ability to operate in the market. The legitimacy of corporate philanthropy and political donations has come under question by asset management firms and trade unions, as well as governments and non-governmental organizations.

Corporate purpose in question

As the case of Robert Maxwell showed, the purpose of a corporation can mean different things to different people. Maxwell regarded his corporations as his property, ignoring the interests of other shareholders and even the moral rights of employees to the benefit of their pension savings. But in so doing, he was acting within powers formally conferred upon him by the board of directors, who were themselves elected by shareholders. Maxwell's position as dominant shareholder made it possible for him to appoint boards of directors that could scarcely be called independent, and who provided no brake against his headlong attempts to push the companies into ventures with limited potential and then his failed attempts to pull them out of the resulting problems.

While the issues of corporate malfeasance and corporate misalignment differ in the level of value they destroy, they share a common theme. In what Berle and Means (1932/1991) called the 'modern corporation' the interests of shareholders can easily fall out of line with the interests of the managers they entrust with running the business. The imperfect solution to this intractable misalignment is to have a board of directors in charge of the executives who are then in charge of the business. But this concept is based on the premise that corporate executives should be working in the interests of shareholders to the exclusion of all other interests, a concept that is not shared by all the people and organizations with which the corporation comes into contact. Their concerns also figure heavily on the board's agenda. Perhaps the board's purpose is not just to pursue shareholder value. Perhaps there are other interests that directors should consider in overseeing the actions of senior management in leading the day-to-day operations of the business or taking the decisions we might consider to be of corporate life and death.

Corporations come into existence for a variety of reasons, and those reasons can change over time. Entrepreneurs may set out to make a fortune, or they may simply have a product idea they think will help customers. Perhaps they enjoy working with certain friends, or being their own boss. The situation changes once the company asks other people – or other corporations – to provide equity capital to the business. Now the freedom of the entrepreneur receives the challenge from the obligations of the business to its providers of capital, at least. But as we have seen in some of the questions raised so far, many scholars and commentators on corporate affairs contend that corporations face other demands on the resources at their disposal. Directors face calls to decide complex cases in the favour of entities other than those that can claim to be owners. We will see in Chapter 10 just how difficult it can be to determine where the interests of shareholders lie. First, though, we shall need to explore the legitimacy of the claim to shareholder value and other claims on the corporation as we consider theoretical perspectives on corporate governance.

Notes

1 The theme of 'restoring trust' was the underlying context of the Sarbanes–Oxley Act in the US and gave the title to numerous newspaper and magazine articles and several books. It was also the title of an investigation into the functioning of the UK capital market by the Centre for Tomorrow's Company, a London-based corporate think-tank whose members include many of the top business people in a country whose governance practices were used as a model for many of the attempts worldwide at reform.

Further readings

Bebchuk, L. A. (2005). The Case for Increasing Shareholder Power. *Harvard Law Review, 118*(3), 833–914.

Berle, A. A. & Means, G. C. (1932/1991). *The Modern Corporation and Private Property* (rev. ed.). New Brunswick, NJ: Transaction Publishers.

Bhagat, S. & Bolton, B. (2008). Corporate Governance and Firm Performance. *Journal of Corporate Finance, 14*(3), 257–73.

Bogle, J. (2003). Owners' Capitalism. Speech to the National Investor Relations Institute annual conference. Retrieved 28 June 2009, from http://www.vanguard.com/bogle_site/sp20030611.html.

Coffee, J. C., Jr. (2005). A Theory of Corporate Scandals: Why the U.S. and Europe Differ. Retrieved 7 Nov. 2007, from http://ssrn.com/paper=694581.

Fama, E. F. & Jensen, M. C. (1983). Separation of Ownership and Control. *Journal of Law and Economics, 23*(2), 301–25.

Finkelstein, S. & D'Aveni, R. A. (1994). CEO Duality as a Double-Edged Sword: How Boards of Directors Balance Entrenchment Avoidance and Unity of Command. *Academy of Management Journal, 37*(5), 1079–108.

Pettigrew, A. & McNulty, T. (1998). Sources and Uses of Power in the Boardroom. *European Journal of Work & Organizational Psychology, 7*(2), 197–214.

PART 1

Principles of Corporate Governance

In this section we examine how the problems in corporate governance have led to principles that boards of directors are either required or expected to follow.

Theories of corporate governance: Concerns over corporate governance have led to a variety of ways to understand how and why boards do the things they do. Most prominent among them is agency theory, the notion that left unattended the managers of a company – the agents – will work in their own interests. To keep their actions aligned with those of shareholders – the principals – companies put various mechanisms in place to monitor their activities. But this is far from the only view. Stewardship theory comes to quite different conclusions, working from the presumption that most people, most of the time, seek to do a good job. Resource dependency theory looks at the other aspect of the board's role: helping the company get access to the resource that will lead to better performance. Stakeholder theory suggests a different notion of the purpose of the board and the company, according to which shareholders' interests are rather less prominent.

Mechanisms of corporate governance: Arising from these perspectives is a variety of ways that corporate governance can be enforced. Although they are often ignored in discussions of the field, markets – for goods and services and for employment – constrain the freedom of action of corporate managers and therefore their ability to be self-serving. But other mechanisms have been put in place: law and regulation; a host of 'gatekeepers' and 'watchdogs', including credit rating agencies, investment analysts, headhunters and news organizations; industry codes and practices. But there is still a large gap where the board of directors plays a role.

Corporate governance in a global economy: Law and regulation, as well as cultural considerations, play a big role in governing the corporation. This chapter explores how corporate governance works in different countries with different histories and different modes of operation. It also examines some of

the pressures leading to a growing convergence of approach – not least the globalization of investment markets.

Codes of corporate governance: The failure of existing mechanisms to control the problems in corporate governance together with the rise of institutional
investors active on a global stage have led to development of codes of conduct
for boards, with many common elements across different jurisdictions.

THREE

Theories of corporate governance

Case: Percy Barnevik and the board of ABB

For more than a decade, Percy Barnevik was one of the world's most highly respected, even revered, businessmen. He presided over the company known as ABB, formed in 1987 from the merger of Asea of Sweden with Brown Boveri of Switzerland. Both companies had extensive operations around the world, not just in Europe. But the market for their goods and services – heavy engineering services, power generation equipment and the like – was hugely complex and the industry required both large capital investment and a great degree of responsiveness to the demands of customers, often on a local basis. Its competitors included American giants like General Electric and Honeywell, whose own merger would be blocked by the European competition authorities more than a decade later. These powerful rivals put both companies under pressure, making it hard to raise the capital required to fund research and fulfil contracts to stay competitive over the long term. The boards of both companies saw little hope that either business could continue to operate independently for very long. Barnevik not only had to merge companies with different nationalities and languages, he had to impose the version developed by one company on the other, or shape a new way of operating.

His solution was to create what we now call a 'transnational' corporation, using a loose–tight approach to structure and processes, both highly integrated globally and highly responsive on a localized basis, which a complex but flexible management matrix. He also adopted English as the company's language, setting a trend that would sweep through major companies around continental Europe. ABB became one of the world's most favourite companies to work for, and Barnevik's face adorned the covers of business magazines in many of the countries in which ABB did business. His performance at ABB became the subject of business school case studies in strategy and business policy. In eight full years under his direction ABB saw revenue grow by a compound annual rate of about 8.5 per cent and net income rise by nearly 16 per cent a year, despite a downturn during the global recession of 1990–2. When he retired as CEO in 1996, the board of the joint company awarded him an extra bonus of 148 million Swiss francs (worth $120 million at the time), in recognition of his extraordinary accomplishments, and he went on to guide the merger of the Swedish pharmaceutical company Astra with its British rival Zeneca and work his magic again, this time as chairman.

But at ABB did not fare so well under its next two chief executives. By 2002, the accounts were heading for a second annual loss in excess of $700 million, in part owing to costs of liabilities for asbestos injuries suffered by workers at a US company acquired during Barnevik's tenure as CEO. The adoring press and public turned against him. The board's decision took valuable capital out of the business to fund a glorious retirement for someone who had now finished contributing to the value of the business. By weakening the company's financial position, the move may have contributed to the later destruction of shareholder value. In the face of public attacks throughout the financial media at home and around the world, Barnevik agreed to repay half his retirement bonus and to step down as an adviser to ABB.

Barnevik's payoff was not particularly large compared with what some departing corporate executives would earn, even those whose companies had fared rather less well than ABB. In the 2007–8 banking crisis, Charles Prince of Citigroup and Stanley Neal of Merrill Lynch would be forced out of their positions as CEO of the two large US financial services firms after a vote of no-confidence from their boards and after just a few years in charge. Each received a departing settlement similar in size to Barnevik's, even though the Swede had served for a combined 17 years and led Asea and then ABB to very much better performance.

Questions arising

The ABB board clearly valued the work that Barnevik had done in his long tenure at the company. His leadership was central to the success of the merger. Upon his retirement, they clearly thought him worthy of a generous extra reward.

1 What are the allegiances of directors in practice?
2 Who should they be working for?
3 How can we understand the way they work?
4 How can we use that information to decide how directors ought to work?

Agency theory and shareholder value

Percy Barnevik had been a strong CEO, for which he had received a salary, bonuses and other forms of financial reward in line with his contract. His success no doubt gave other members of the board reason to value his service. It gave shareholders reason to be grateful, too, at least until 1996 when he stepped down as CEO and accepted the retirement package. Had not Barnevik already been paid for his performance, through his salary, bonuses and stock operations? Whose interests did the board have in mind when it approved the payment of 148 million Swiss francs – shareholders' or those of their friend and close colleague for all those years? Under what we will call the classical corporate governance agenda – the point of view strongly advocated by investment institutions – the focus of the work of boards of directors is to keep the company focused on creating value for shareholders.

The problem that Berle and Means had identified in the 1930s as central to modern corporations was the separation that had developed between ownership of a company and control of its resources. Forty years later other scholars would call it the *agency problem* (Jensen & Meckling, 1976), a view that would come to dominate discussion about the work of boards of directors and the nature of corporate governance.

Agency theory has wide implications for the affairs of a company, but it is in essence a very simple idea: people will tend to do what is in their own interest. Managers placed in charge of a business that is not their own – with access to the bank accounts of the business and the ability to choose how to spend the company's money – will spend it in ways that best suit the managers themselves. Human beings will act in their own interests. Ordinary employees will do the same, so we require them to get the approval of a manager before they spend the company's money, even often for quite trivial sums. Managers will do the same, so we put senior managers in charge, and then we employ accountants to examine what the senior managers authorize. But when it comes to the top layer of management – to the people at whose discretion all the managers and accountants work – how can we make sure that they will not regard the company's money as their own?

In agency theory, the owner of the business is considered the *principal*, the person with moral and legal rights to the property we call the company and indirectly to the assets the company controls. We think of the manager as being an *agent*, charged to act in the principal's best interest, in exchange for a fee. If people are naturally greedy, a proposition that is not universally accepted, the top managers need to be watched or other mechanisms found to prevent them from exercising that greed. Depending on their structure, the fees that agents receive may be able to channel that greed in ways that motivate the agent to keep the principal's interest in mind.

Agency costs

Agency has a cost, like any other aspect of doing business. Self-dealing by a manager, however problematic it may be from an ethical point of view, is in economic terms one of those costs. The cost of monitoring and controlling for greed may exceed the benefits in stamping it out. It certainly is more costly for each individual shareholder to monitor management, and if some shareholders do and others do not, then those that bear the costs are, in effect, subsidizing the others. When those shareholders are asset management institutions competing with each other for the right to manage the investments of, say, pension funds, those costs, taken across a whole portfolio, could make the careful investor seem much less productive, even on portfolios containing exactly the same shares.

For these reasons, many of the recommendations of agency theory focus on the board of directors, as we shall explore at greater length in Chapter 9. But it should be borne in mind that directors themselves create an additional layer of agency relationship between owners and those in control of the company's resources. Boards of directors represent a cost, too, through their fees, but also through mistaken judgements about when to apply the brakes and when to step on the accelerator.

It is useful to remember, however, that eliminating cost may sometimes not be in the interest of owners; it could even be in the principal's interest to increase them. If an investment – including the investment in a good agent – produces a return in excess of the cost of capital, theories of corporate finance and economics tell us they are investments worth making. As with many aspects of management, however, we cannot easily determine whether the investment in the agent has paid off. As a result, the principals of the business will seek to minimize the agency cost while monitoring the agent's performance. For large corporations employing senior managers, however, there is a problem: the separation of ownership from active or even arm's length involvement in the business.

Before the development of the 'modern corporation', that is, before the development of active trading of shares in companies on stock markets, the owner of the company was usually the manager as well. In a family-owned business, Dad was often in charge. The children, and sometimes the wife, would sit as directors. Board meetings were as easy to convene as Sunday lunch. When the company took out a loan from the bank, the bank manager would demand to see the accounts and would exert pressure on the company, on Dad, to conduct its (his and the family's) affairs in such a way as to protect the company's ability, first and foremost, to make interest payments on the loans and, secondarily, to repay its capital. A commercial bank is not generally interested in whether the family grows wealthy, though if they did, it would be happy to help them with other banking services. The bank is primarily worried about its own business, and that means receiving interest payments in good time so it can pay its depositors interest with a little to spare. Commercial banks want to see a cushion of capital behind the borrower – of collateral – to protect the bank's interest in case the business does not perform as well as expected. Banks are, therefore, supposed to be cautious about large expansion plans.

That's why companies seek outside investors and sell them shares in the company. But the manager – Dad – does not really want to give up control, and the outside investors do not really want to manage the business on a day-to-day basis. But investors also do not want to give the manager the ability to spend the company's money – including their money – as though it was all his own. To square this circle, investors have, since the invention of the modern corporation, demanded two mechanisms to prevent abuse, approaches often described through the shorthand of *voice* and *exit*.

'Voice' as a mechanism of control

Shareholders in a company have surprisingly few rights. Owning a stake in a company is unlike owning almost anything else. Property rights usually allow the owner control over the property itself. Owners can use the asset, sell it, even destroy it. They can modify it, too; change the way the object looks or functions. Shareholders do not enjoy many of the rights of property ownership, however. They have no rights to use any of the assets of the business, no *right* to any repayment, not even in the form of a dividend. Should the company fail or otherwise need to be wound up, shareholders have a right only to what is left over after everyone has been paid off – banks, lawyers, accountants, trade creditors, workers, bond holders, anyone who might have sued the company, and of course the tax collector. The economist Oliver Williamson has remarked that while labour, suppliers, customers and lenders all have a chance to renegotiate terms at the end of their contracts with the company, 'Stockholders, by contrast, invest for the life of the firm, and their claims are located at the end of the queue should liquidation occur' (Williamson, 1985, pp. 304–5). It is a wonder that anyone would choose to become a shareholder, so limited are their rights. When companies fail, workers may lose their jobs, but they take away their ability to work in the future together with the knowledge they have gained by working in the company. Suppliers may well suffer, but they can try to find other customers to replace the loss of business; customers can find a new supplier, a comparatively easy task in competitive markets for goods and services. The shareholder has to make do with what is left over, and that is often nothing at all. In corporate failures, lenders often seek to recapitalize the business, converting old loans into equity and providing new loans to get it going again. The old shares may be declared worthless or diluted to such an extent that they have next to no value.

Agenda point 4: The value in voting rights, 'ownerless' corporations

British asset management firms have in general been among the most vocal proponents of the concept we know as 'one share, one vote'. Shareholder democracy demands it: votes at shareholder meetings should be taken in proportion to the capital at risk. It's, well, fair. Their lobbying failed to win over the European Commission in 2007, even though the commissioner in charge, Charles McCreevy, strongly shared their view. So it came as a bit of a surprise when one of the 'grand old men' of the City of London, as the financial district is known, came out in favour of giving some shareholders more votes than others. Paul Myners was once chief executive of the asset management firm Gartmore and later chairman of the retailer Marks & Spencer. He wrote reports for the government along the way, too, concerning institutional investors and their role in corporate governance, and on the issue in the pensions industry. Having been made a member of the House of Lords, he joined the government in September 2008, just in time to play a role in the messy rescue of the UK banking system, including the tempest over the pension awarded to the chief executive of the Royal Bank of Scotland, whom the government forced out of office.

Reflective thinking: Lord Myners, now a Treasury minister, took up an invitation to be interviewed by the BBC's business editor, Robert Peston, who himself played quite a controversial role in the banking crisis. Peston's news report on Northern Rock's problems triggered a run on the bank by retail investors. In the interview, Myners mused about his boyhood as a butcher's son, how he was in the City but never of it. He even spoke earnestly about retiring to study theology, perhaps to become a priest. But what hit the headlines was a different sort of morality, a different sort of fairness. He asked how we make banks and perhaps all companies pay more attention to shareholder interests, and along the way make it more likely that shareholders and the entire system of capital would focus more on the long term, rather than on short-term targets.

Voting rights: Lord Myners told the BBC that 'companies are too important' for big shareholders to trade in and out of them 'willy nilly'. He worried about 'ownerless corporations that float out there, in a vacuum', left to the vagaries of markets and takeover bids. 'We've lost sight of the fact that a share certificate – in fact we don't have them now, it's all recorded electronically – but a share certificate is a right and entitlement of ownership which carries with it certain responsibilities,' he said. 'It's not a piece of paper to be traded, to be bought and sold.' In France, company law reforms in 2001 gave shareholders of two years' tenure a double right to vote. Each share held by a single owner for two years or more gets two votes, all others just one.

'Can of worms': Peter Montagnon, head of investment affairs at the Association of British Insurers, then told the BBC owners had to be able to retain the right to sell and differential voting rights was not the answer. 'If you discriminate between

types of shareholder, that's not good for confidence in the market.' Montagnon and the ABI had been forceful advocates of 'one share, one vote' in the European deliberations, and when the European Union's Takeover Directive failed to outlaw differential voting rights in its tortuous journey from idea to EU law. The proxy voting adviser PIRC, whose clients include many local government pension plans, said Myners had 'opened a can of worms' in his 'crusade to encourage institutional shareholders to act like owners'. PIRC itself is known for crusading, too, and on points not far from the activism that talk of 'share ownership' has in mind. But violating 'one share, one vote' is one step too far. David Paterson, head of corporate governance at the National Association of Pension Funds, was more restrained. He told the *Financial Times* that Myners' view 'fails to take into account the need for managers to buy or sell shares based on external factors. What is needed is better dialogue between companies and shareholders.'

The record: The EU issue in 2007 turned on an independent report that McCreevy commissioned, which showed that differential voting rights didn't harm competitiveness: 'control enhancing mechanisms have advantages and drawbacks,' it said. 'How CEMs operate in theory depends on the context in which they are utilised, in particular the current and future shareholder structure. The same CEMs can be beneficial in companies with widely dispersed share ownership, but harmful in a company with a dominant shareholder.' The language was hardly a ringing endorsement for the idea of making the rest of Europe adopt the way shareholding works in the UK or McCreevy's native Ireland.

What's the problem? What Myners advocates is a situation in which corporate boards would be more inclined to pay attention to the wishes of one class of shareholders – the long-only, long-term oriented asset management firms, like Gartmore in his days there – rather than the 'noise' of traders, including hedge funds. That stance ought to favour investors like those in the ABI, not to mention PIRC's clients and members of the NAPF. But it also points, at least in theory, to boards becoming more entrenched, more difficult to oust, more difficult to persuade of the need for change. It put even more power in the hands of management, by giving those sensing a greater potential under new direction less of a chance to effect the necessary change. Ultimately, it makes it less likely that any other company would be willing to mount a takeover bid, making those long-term shareholders less likely to earn a premium from a hostile bidder willing to pay more to gain control. And many of the long-only, long-term oriented investors are also the low-cost, index-tracking funds with low interest in corporate governance, low use of proxy votes, and low turnout at shareholder meetings. (*The BoardAgenda*, 6 Aug. 2009; http://www.edgevantage.co.uk/categories/article.asp?i=4744.)

The entrepreneur seeking additional finance to expand the business must, therefore, offer would-be investors some form of protection for the money they put at risk. To secure the investment, the business must, therefore, offer investors a say in how the business is operated, a system of corporate governance that gives them a voice in determining corporate policy and monitoring the entrepreneur's performance.

In the typical joint-stock company that means the shareholders are given the right to elect the board of directors. Particularly large shareholders often make it a condition of their investment that they are allowed to name one or more members of the board. Those large investors will expect these members to look after their investor's interests first and foremost, even if that is at odds with the law of the land. To be able to exercise that oversight, boards need to have access to information about the company, and the right to decide crucial matters. Investors, too, may demand direct access to information, to ensure their new agents – the board – are doing their job properly. They may demand the right to question the directors about their performance and the performance of the company, which often takes the form of an annual meeting of shareholders and special – sometimes called *extraordinary* – meetings if important and unusual matters need a decision, things like takeover bids or major transformations in the nature of the business itself.

Different countries – and in the United States, different states – give shareholders a different range of ways to exercise *voice*. In Germany, for example, shareholders vote at the annual meeting to discharge the management of their responsibility for the accounts. Before that point, members of the management board remain legally liable for errors and omissions. After the vote – assuming shareholders agree – comes what is known as *Entlastung*, which translates as 'lifting the burden'.

In most European countries, votes by shareholders are binding on the board of directors. If shareholders reject a motion that management and board have put forward, the company is obliged not to pursue it. If shareholders approve a motion that the board has opposed, the board is obliged to adopt it, though in practice board members may well choose to resign rather than adopt policies they do not favour. Taking something to a vote is, therefore, quite a serious matter. In practice, however, few votes go against management. Investors, especially the distant investors who lack a controlling shareholding, have little reason to oppose the direction that the board recommends. Often they lack the information to make an intelligent choice over specific policies. They lack even the time or inclination to monitor the boards they appoint. But investors, especially some of the large investment institutions who feel they have no choice but to remain a shareholder, jealously guard their right to elect directors and will use the right to lobby for other changes in policy they see as problematic.

The situation is different in the United States, where company law is exercised, in the main, at the level of the individual state government. Companies have a choice about where to have their legal seat. As a result, individual states found themselves competing to offer the most generous terms to the managements and boards that would make that decision. About half of all the corporations in the United States that issue shares or bonds to the investing public have chosen to incorporate in Delaware, second smallest of the 50 states, where traditionally shareholders have enjoyed the most limited rights. To avoid a wholesale erosion of the corporate tax base, most other states have chosen to follow the key elements of Delaware law, among them provisions that can reduce shareholder voice to a whisper.

In most of the United States, for example, shareholder votes are not binding on management, but merely advisory. The so-called *business judgement rule* means that shareholders cannot challenge in the courts many of the actions that boards, working as the agent of shareholders, take on the shareholders' behalf. Even electing new directors is a less than straightforward affair. This became an area of considerable dispute in the mid-2000s, but for most companies shareholders are not allowed to vote against a candidate for the board; they can merely abstain from voting. Moreover, shareholders are not allowed to nominate candidates without engaging in a costly exercise of communicating with all the other shareholders at their own expense, meaning that they rarely face a contested election for new directors. The consequence is that a candidate for director may well get elected to the board as long as only one shareholder votes for him – provided that he can secure a nomination.

Nominations are controlled by the board, and if the chief executive has great sway over other members of the board, in effect only candidates suitable to the interests of top management will ever get the chance to monitor the performance of those managers. These things are changing, in part because of the concern that lax boards of directors may have failed to take action to stop the most egregious malfeasances of managements in cases like Enron, WorldCom, Tyco, Adelphia and others. We will return to this theme in Chapters 8 and 9.

In Britain, shareholders have won the right to another way to exercise voice. Since 2002, shareholders of companies listed on the stock exchange have a chance to vote each year on the policies under which directors and senior management are paid. This does not give them veto power over remuneration packages for specific individuals. But it does provide a chance to voice displeasure at the pay awarded to an individual and ultimately to force the board to rethink the policy under which the award was made. It is a move that many countries, and not just in Europe, have made efforts to copy. Even in the United States, where as we have seen shareholders have very limited voice, a groundswell of action has led to some companies permitting shareholders a 'say on pay'.

Even in European countries where votes are binding, shareholder voice may not be all that loud. Many countries, including the large and well-developed capital market of the Netherlands, allow companies to issue what we call *bearer shares*. These give the person physically in possession of the shares the right to vote them. Bearer shares are in some ways a relic of a less comfortable part of Europe's past. At a time of great racial discrimination, bearer shares became a way Jewish investors could shield their identity from discovery. Bearer shares, lodged with trusted banks in Switzerland, Luxembourg, Liechtenstein or Andorra, became a way for many wealthy Europeans to hide money from the tax inspector, behind the protection of banking secrecy.

Having the physical shares and transporting them to the company annual meeting was, however, a dangerous affair. As the shares have no registered owner, even someone who steals the share certificates can vote them, although it is more likely that they would instead sell them to another investor. As a result, bearer shares tend to stay in the vault, and their holders forgo the right to exercise voice.

Some countries in Europe have built impediments with the effect of discouraging investors in other countries from exercising their right to vote. For many years, France, for example, demanded that holders of shares lodge them for safe-keeping for a time before and after the company's shareholder meeting, if the holders wanted to exercise their right to vote. As a result, many foreign institutional investors opted not to try to vote their shares and risk the possibility that they would be unable to sell them should market conditions require it. Such restrictions on the rights of shareholders to exercise their voice have led to efforts from the commission of the European Union to consider legislating new rights for shareholders.

But some investors will remain uninterested in voting. Voting usually occurs only once a year, and perhaps not at the time that the investor grows dissatisfied with the performance of management and the board. For those investors, capital markets offer another option – exit.

'Exit' as a mechanism of control

One of the problems facing investors in nineteenth-century corporations was that their money was trapped in the company. If the business was flourishing, profits would allow dividend payments, providing a yield on the investment often in excess of what an investor might achieve from investing in government bonds. There was a chance for an extra benefit if someone else, perhaps another corporation, bought the entire business, giving all its owners a capital gain. But if the business was not doing well and the 'voice' of outside investors was insufficiently strong to force a change in direction, an outside investor had little choice but to sit on the sideline and hope (Micklethwait & Wooldridge, 2003).

This situation still affects many small and even quite large private businesses today. Individuals who invest in a private company – perhaps they are friends or relatives of the founder, 'business angels', wealthy people willing to back speculative ventures, or a venture capital fund, whose business is to identify early-stage businesses – often do so in the hope that it will become a large corporation. Often, it does not. They too have investments trapped in the company until and unless someone is willing to buy it.

These demands from investors to create a mechanism through which they could turn such investments into cash again was the driving force in the second half of the nineteenth century for the development of stock exchange that focused on company shares. The prospect that a private company might list its shares one day on a stock exchange through what is called an initial public offering, or IPO, makes private equity investment a far more attractive proposition. That attraction means investors can treat the investment as less risky, which in turn means they can lower their expectations on the return needed on the investment, leaving the other owners with a greater percentage of the business for the same cash infusion. Financiers speak of this as lowering the cost of capital, which improves the likely profitability of the business by making it more competitive because of its improved access to funding. This in turn helps to explain why companies with shares widely held and trading on stock markets can often outperform rivals, both among private firms or other listed companies that still have a single large shareholder that abuses its power over corporate decision-making and as a consequence find it more difficult to convince new outside investors to provide capital.

The ability to sell shares in an active market gives investors another mechanism to express displeasure with the direction of the company: they can sell their shares – the exit. In America there is even a name for it: the Wall Street Walk (Admati & Pfleiderer, 2009). Selling pressure on the shares lower its market price, making remaining investors more worried about the value of their holdings, creating internal pressure for a change in policy. It also discourages outside investors from buying new shares or even providing loans or other forms of debt, which in turn weakens the company's profitability, putting outside pressure on management for a change in direction.

New investors will demand access to information about the company before they are willing to invest as a means of assessing the risk, and then demand ongoing information to monitor performance. As a result, stock exchanges from early on required companies with listings to disclose financial information not just to owners but to all potential owners of the company's shares. As markets expand to embrace not just wealthy individuals but also the wider public, disclosure became a matter of public interest, and the demands for disclosure became matters of law. We return to this theme in Chapter 12.

Implications of agency theory for corporate governance

Taken together, 'voice' and 'exit' form important mechanisms of corporate governance to address the agency problem. Shareholders demand voice and once they have it they demand a greater voice. Managements demand, to a greater or lesser extent, freedom in decision-making, and top managers may well elect to use their 'exit' – through the job market rather than the stock market – if they do not get it. This tension between the demands of investors and the demands of managers leaves the people in the middle – the board of directors – with the job of acting as buffers. The agency problem in corporations with widely dispersed shareholdings arises because individual shareholders have insufficient voice to influence decisions and insufficient knowledge of the business to give it detailed direction. The board of directors, as a intermediate agent of shareholders, can play that role in much the way that the financiers of the nineteenth-century did by demanding a seat on the board in exchange for their investment.

This classical view of the role of the board, with its focus on representing the interests of investors, leads to a variety of logical conclusions about its role, structure and composition, conclusions that are central to how corporate governance has come to be viewed in most countries around the world:

- *Board composition*: The board of directors should consist of people who are willing to challenge the views of managers. In practice, therefore, a majority of the board should be independent, non-executive directors – people who have no ties to the managers and no significant business dealings with the company.

- *Board structures*: Board committees that have authority over crucial functions should be controlled by these independent directors: auditing the company's accounts, nominating new members of the board, deciding on how much to pay the top managers and what structure pay should take.

- *Board leadership*: The chairman of the board, whose role is organizing its meetings and thereby determining which items come to discussion, is of central importance. This has been and remains one of the most hotly contested areas in the debate over corporate governance and one that will arise repeatedly throughout the book. It is probably fair to say, however, that among investors – especially the asset management institutions, pension funds and insurance companies that dominate investment in most large economies – the consensus that has emerged is that the power concentrated in the hands of the CEO needs a countervailing force in the boardroom. That argues, in this view, for the chairman to be someone other than the CEO and someone independent of the top management team.

This view of the board, its structure and composition, is built around the notion that the board purpose is to look after the interests of shareholders, to strive for shareholder value, and to pull the levers of its remuneration policies, audit of finances and control over budgets, to direct the energies of their agents in top management to advance shareholder value. That is not, however, the only view of what boards are supposed to do.

Resources and the board

As we have seen, agency theory asks questions about the board in its role of monitoring the performance of management and keeping it under control. But that is only part of the task facing directors. Investors want more than control when they call for shareholder value. They want value to be created from the company's activities.

Directors can contribute to what we have called this accelerator function in a number of ways. With its roots in a long-overlooked aspect of the management literature from the 1950s (Penrose, 1959), a new approach to strategic management developed quietly for many years before becoming what many see as the dominant way of considering strategy today: the resource-based view. There have been many views of how companies work, and why they exist at all, as we have seen. In what had long been the central view arising from industrial economics, corporations exist because they are a more efficient way of working than dealing with each individual transaction a business needed to conduct as a separate contract (Coase, 1937; Williamson & Winter, 1993). This notion of efficiency runs deep in business. Managers seek to organize the corporation in such a way that it delivers the greatest output per unit of input. Competitive strategies arise, in this view, from matching the organization's operations to the requirements of customers in ways that are more efficient – providing goods at a lower cost and therefore potentially at a higher profit margin than competitors can do. Those that cannot achieve the lowest cost are forced to choose a different strategy, one that differentiates the product from competing ones in ways that some customers will prefer. This, too, provides an efficient outcome, but with its efficiency defined somewhat differently, based on the different preferences expressed by different customers. Efficiency thus underpins much of the development of approaches to value creation, ranging from theories of growth promoted in the 1960s by the major consultancy firms like McKinsey and Boston Consulting Group, through to the work of Michael Porter and his famous Fives Forces and generic strategies approaches (Porter, 1980).

What Penrose observed in the 1950s and what became apparent to many other scholars later on was this: corporations were not really all that efficient, despite their professed intention to become so. What we now see as the acceleration in the pace of change in society that began with big oil prices rises the 1970s and then surged with technological progress, especially in computing, made many managers realize that another way to create value came through having preferential access to the resources you needed, when you needed them, to cope with changes in the nature of demand. Birger Wernerfelt (1984) called this the resource-based view, and soon many other scholars and strategists in corporations starting to recognize how managing resources, capabilities, competencies or the 'value chain' give a company flexibility in coping with rapidly changing markets. Supply chain management became an important part of operations, too, as companies came to appreciate that they did not have to own all the resources that contributed to their production, as long as they could achieve some sort of preferential access.

Directors have long been one of those flexible resources. Most directors of companies – ones listed on stock exchanges and even small, family businesses – come to the post because they have special knowledge or access to external resources. Financiers who sat on the boards of corporations in the nineteenth and early twentieth centuries were there in part to look after their investments – monitoring and controlling management. But they also gave management preferential access to capital, through loans or new equity. Having retired executives from other companies in the industry, or from organizations in different industries, can be a low-cost way for managers to get valuable advice about strategic decisions without having to ask a consulting firm to undertake a study. Directors often come to the post with networks of contacts – in industry, in government, in regulatory bodies or from other interest groups – who can provide advice or even join the company in an executive capacity. Someone who has already been CEO or finance director of a major corporation will bring experience to the board of the issues that arise when the company is undertaking a major acquisition or facing a takeover bid. What the strategy scholars only recently came to recognize has, therefore, been a part of corporate governance from the earliest of days: the right directors can give managers preferential access to some of the resources the company needs to be competitive.

This view of value creation is sometimes called *resource dependency theory*. The company is dependent on access to key resources. Directors can contribute to that in at least four ways (Pfeffer & Salancik, 1978):

- *Advice and counsel*: They advise managers about alternative approaches and answer questions about management's own ideas. Whether their background is industry, government, or even non-governmental organizations or charities, successful people can provide useful advice.

- *Preferential access to channels of communication*: Companies need to tell the outside world about their activities, whether it is informing and attracting, customers, locating suppliers, or dealing with regulatory bodies.

- *Preferential access to finance, people, equipment*: Directors can facilitate access to the tangible and intangible resources that make up a company's operational requirements.

- *Legitimacy*: Directors provide both credibility – 'if she (a famous person) is on the board, it must be an important company' – and legitimacy, the broad sense that this business will be responsible about how it conducts its affairs.

The two roles of the director – monitoring and control on the one hand, resource provision on the other – can sometimes conflict. The CEO of one company who sits on the board of another may be an excellent person to provide advice and counsel, help with communications, help to find key business partners, or help to demonstrate the legitimacy of the business. But if he identifies strongly with the role of 'being a CEO', how mindful will he be of the need to monitor the CEO's performance, challenge his decisions and constrain his freedom of action? A banker sitting as director of a company may be an excellent adviser on financial affairs, perhaps even having the strong technical skills needed to lead the audit committee. But she may be culturally inclined to support management's decisions to raise new debt, rather than to advise caution about an investment plan (for a good discussion of these issues, see Hillman & Dalziel, 2003; Hillman et al., 2008).

Juggling these different requirements – of monitoring and control, of providing access to resources – would be challenging enough if the only demand on the board was provision of shareholder value. But that is not the only item on the board's agenda these days.

Stakeholder theory

Corporations affect the lives of a wide range of people, some directly and often many more indirectly, not to mention the affairs of other corporations. Scholars in the field of strategy often speak about how the corporation relates to its environment. Indeed, one school of thought about strategy takes an ecological perspective, viewing the company as part of an organic system in which the environment may even largely determine what the company does, and very often the limits what it can do.

While adherents to neo-classical economics view the corporation as an engine of profits working in a market, political economic theory places this creation in a force-field of other political actors. The 'legal person' has responsibilities to the rest of society set out in law. Its board of directors, the real people behind the 'legal person', must take those considerations into account. But another view – part political, part ethical – has emerged, holding that corporations should be accountable to all the people and the other corporations with whom they have dealings. Many adherents to this view hold that the accountability goes beyond that of the contracts that govern the formal relationships between the legal person and those with whom it conducts its business. Some hold that corporations have obligations to those with whom the company has had no direct dealings, perhaps to society at large. As a result, boards of directors have an obligation, this position holds, to take into account a wide range of interests when deciding how to use the company's resources – not just those of creating shareholder value. This approach – or perhaps better put, these approaches – can be viewed through a lens often called 'stakeholder theory'.

The word 'stakeholder' is one we use here with considerable reluctance. It is a made-up word, a neologism of the 1980s, at least in this context, and one chosen for its rhetorical and perhaps even deceptive power. In history, a 'stakeholder' was a neutral party in a wager, the person selected to hold the monies put at stake by the gamblers.[1]

Use of the term in the corporate governance context arises from 1984, when R. Edward Freeman, a US academic, broke with the common view about the purpose of companies by articulating a view of strategy and accountability that put relationships with employees, suppliers and customers at its heart. Freeman based his adoption the word 'stakeholder' on the fact that it sounds like 'stockholder', the usual term in America for owners of shares in a business.

Words, he writes, 'make a difference in how we see the world. By using "stake-holder" managers and theorists alike will come to see these groups as having a "stake"' (Freeman, 1984, p. 45).

In his view, which grew in importance over the next two decades, the interests of these stakeholders were central to a company's business. This sociological view of the corporation was deeply at odds with the mechanistic view of the corporation as a machine to make profits, or the economic view of the company as a legal institution comprising a 'nexus of contracts' and drawing on the theory of transaction costs (Coase, 1937; Williamson, 1985).

A 'weak' approach to stakeholder theory

We can think of shareholder theory as having two varieties: strong and weak. The 'weak' view holds that employees, suppliers and customers – indeed, others with whom the company has dealings – are important to the company's success. It rejects an antagonistic approach to contracting parties as the right way to do business. It is not business versus labour. Instead we recognize that a contented workforce, one that contributes ideas and motivation to the processes of production, adds value to shareholders as well. We do not seek to charge customers the highest price we possibly can, but rather view customer relationships as important, and customers as the source of ideas for new product development, perhaps even as being directly involved in creating them. Suppliers are not selected simply on the basis of offering the lowest price, but instead for their likely contribution of a system of supply chain management that shares information, yielding better profits for all. This weak form of the theory holds, then, that the company benefits from regarding its stakeholders as partners rather than opponents, and its business as relationships rather than merely a string of transactions. This thinking is broadly in line with theories of strategic management being developed at the same time, including customer relationships (Berry, 1983; Gummesson, 2002), core competencies (Prahalad & Hamel, 1990), and a balanced scorecard approach to accounting (Kaplan & Norton, 1992). Good relationships lead to better profits.

In this weak view, stakeholders have legitimacy because they can affect the direction of the company; it is legitimate for management to spend time and resources on them. In the view of the financial economist Michael Jensen, enlightened value maximization involves and is even identical to enlightened stakeholder theory (Jensen, 2001). That is, however, still some way from arguing that these people and groups are 'ends' of corporate purpose, to which corporate boards owe a duty, rather than just 'means' to the end of shareholder value.

The 'strong' form of stakeholder theory

The 'strong' view takes a harder approach: stakeholders have intrinsic value, irrespective of how they contribute towards profitability. As a result they have 'rights' that go beyond the ones specified in contract. While Freeman's (1984) book argues for a stakeholder largely on weak grounds, he and his many followers soon move beyond it to views that impose on boards of directors an approach to corporate governance that involves shareholder interests as being only one of many legitimate claims on the resources of the business (see Boatright, 2002; Bowie, 2000; Donaldson & Preston, 1995; Evan & Freeman, 1993; Freeman, 1994; Freeman & Evan, 1990).

Instead of arguing the economic case – that a contented workforce, cooperative suppliers and happy customers lead to greater shareholder value – this view takes an ethical stance based on what philosophers call a *deontological* approach: that stakeholder interests represent in some sense an *a priori* good, not merely because taking their interests into account leads to the good *consequence* of higher profits. From this arises notions based in part on the idea that any company requires, in effect, a licence from society to operate, and as a result has obligations to society that go beyond those of making profits and distributing dividends to shareholders. This approach is echoed in what is often called *corporate social responsibility*, a theme to which we will return in Chapter 11.

Implications of stakeholder theory for corporate governance

Viewed from the board of directors, the implications of weak and strong stakeholder theories may not be particularly large, most of the time. Most of the time, having a dedicated and productive workforce makes it worthwhile – in profit contribution – to pay them more and give them better working conditions. Most of the time, good supply-chain practices pay for themselves in terms of profit. Customer satisfaction has well-known benefits for value creation.

But some of the time – and importantly when operational matters become matters for the board's consideration – the implications of weak and strong stakeholder theories diverge. When a company faces a difficult economic climate and sales are falling, the interests of shareholders may be very different from those of employees, suppliers and customers. If conditions are bad enough that the survival of the business itself is threatened, the board may face the need not only to ignore the soft rights of these stakeholders, but also to breach or seek to alter their contractual rights. When the company is liquidated, the call on any residual assets will be the subject of a contest pitting each stakeholder against the others. In that case, the strong form of stakeholder theory provides no guidance, suggesting that it is at best a rather incomplete theory, and perhaps an unworkable one.

Agenda point 5: Residual rights?

The question of residual rights has long been considered central to the share-holder value approach to corporate governance. If other stakeholders are protected in contract but shareholders are not, perhaps it is rightly the role of both law and ethics for boards to place the interests of shareholders above those of other claimants. This view is implicit and often explicit in both academic and practitioner discussion of corporate governance and the obligations of boards. But it is not without challenge. Margaret Blair and Lynn Stout (1999) advanced the case that many stakeholders in a company have at best incomplete contracts and that their relationships with it are not simply contractual. Under their 'team production' theory of how such organizations work, boards of directors act as a 'mediating hierarchy' to settle those claims. The existence of boards with this mediating role is what encourages various parties to make 'firm-specific investments' essential to the production of the company. We can think of these as including the investment in time and thought that workers make in learning aspects of the business they cannot use with other employers or the development by employees of the company's know-how. 'In other words, boards exist not to protect shareholders *per se*, but to protect the enterprise-specific investments of *all* the members of the corporate "team", including shareholders, managers, rank and file employees, and possibly other groups, such as creditors' (Blair & Stout, 1999, p. 253). Blair and Stout argue that a team production approach suggests not that boards should be accountable to a wide range of stakeholders, but rather that they should not be under the control of shareholders or stakeholders.

Luigi Zingales (2000, pp. 1634–5) went further: 'In fact, once we recognize the existence of implicit contracts, then there are other residual claimants besides equity holders who may need to be protected (the famous stakeholders, often mentioned in the public policy debate). It then becomes unclear whether control should reside in the hands of shareholders, because the pursuit of share-holders' value maximization may lead to inefficient actions, such as the breach of valuable implicit contracts.'

These views contributed to the development of a stakeholder-based view of corporate governance, though they remained a minority voice in the literature. With the financial crisis of 2007–9, however, Bernard Sharfman, a corporate governance attorney, suggests that the full scale of implicit contracts and residual risk has become apparent and the need for a mediating hierarchy in the board has been substantiated. 'This understanding of corporate governance provides corporate law with another compelling reason to maintain its approach of not locking itself into an inflexible shareholder wealth maximization norm,' he argues (Sharfman, 2010, p. 2).

Similarly, when faced with a takeover bid – one that puts a value on the company's success by offering a substantial premium to the current share price – in whose interest should the board act? Stakeholder theory in its strong form places an obligation to consider the welfare of employees and suppliers over and above what the law requires. The acquiring company may well decide to cut employment, move production to different locations, change supply contracts and make other operational changes in the interests of achieving economies sufficient in scale to justify the premium it is willing to transfer to shareholders in the acquired firm. In some cases like this, owners of private companies have been known to forgo the premium and keep the company independent for the sake of their employees' and suppliers' welfare. Some may choose to share that premium with the workforce in terms of enhanced severance pay, or with suppliers in terms of extra payments to help them make commercial adjustments to their businesses. They can do that because they are, under agency theory, the principal of the business. Their example is, however, rather less instructive for the outside, independent directors of a public company. In whose interests should they decide?

Stewardship of the board

A third way – neither shareholder value, stakeholder claims, nor halfway in between those irreconcilable approaches – provides another theoretical basis on which directors might choose to act. Some writers on corporate governance and practising directors think that *stewardship theory* holds valuable insights. In this view, directors and managers alike are motivated less for personal gain than for the sake of doing a good job. This challenge to agency theory is based in part on evidence that not all people working in companies – whether as employees, managers or directors – seek only personal gain. In many of their decisions, they strive for 'the good of the company' so as to strengthen its competitive position, or just to do a good job of work (points elaborated in Donaldson & Davis, 1991).

This approach has been central to the discussion about how the trustees of charities act. Charities do not have owners in the conventional sense of the 'modern corporation' of Berle and Means. Many people on their workforce are not employees but rather volunteers. Their key suppliers are, in fact, donors, who do not expect to make a return on 'sales'. Their consumers, if we can call them that, are recipients of aid, not paying customers. In whose interests, then, do the trustees of charities act? This is a theme to which we will return in Chapter 13, but perhaps it can also provide guidance to the wider range of organizations in the commercial, for-profit sector as well.

Agenda point 6: Stewardship of the news

Many important news organizations operate on a narrow stewardship principle, often sacrificing profitability for the sake of the integrity of their reporting. While we could argue that integrity contributes to the brand, which attracts customers and generates profits in the long term, the financial results of a lot of news companies cast doubt upon the links. Like many other great newspapers around the world, the *New York Times* runs in effect as a family trust: it makes less money than it might because it spends more money on reporting and editing the news than it needs to. Unlike some other great newspapers, including *Le Monde* in France or the *Süddeutsche Zeitung* in Germany, the *New York Times* is operated by a corporation listed on the New York Stock Exchange, with the attendant demands on working for shareholders.

The UK-based news agency Reuters embedded in its corporate governance structures a separate board to overrule decisions that the main board might take that would endanger the objectivity of its reporting or alter its purpose to something more simply commercial. When it faced a takeover bid from the Thomson Corp. of Canada, that board needed to grant its approval before the deal could be completed. Dow Jones, the company that owns the *Wall Street Journal*, had family shareholders that controlled the votes and was able to elect directors who backed news gathering when it came into conflict with profitability, until, that is, the family fell out over the degree to which that faith in editorial integrity conflicted with the value on offer in a hostile takeover bid from Rupert Murdoch's News Corporation (for an elaboration, see Nordberg, 2007a).

Trustees of charities and some directors on boards of corporations see themselves acting as stewards of the company they serve. They may, however, view their stewardship role as applying to some aspect of the organization that they regard as of particular importance, to protect that value, add to it, and advance its cause. In a narrow sense, some directors are quite directly stewards of specific interests. When, for example, a family retains seats on the board of a company they founded but no longer control, those directors often see themselves as looking after the interests of the family and not necessarily of other shareholders, other stakeholders, or even the company as a whole, whatever that may mean. Directors appointed by banks as a condition of providing the company with cash will have the interests of the bank at heart, whatever the law might say about their duties to the company. That may mean advocating policies designed to improve cash flow rather than to invest in new production facilities, irrespective of which promised greater long-term profitability or offered more chances for expanding employment. In such cases their stance may lead them to choose to act in ways that put neither shareholder value nor other stakeholder interests to the fore.

In Germany, representatives of the workforce have a right in law to half the seats on the boards of directors of major companies (called the supervisory board). The interests those directors represent may seem clear in most cases, and they can be at odds with the objectives of profitability and even the expansion of the business, if that growth takes place by relocating jobs to other countries.

In other cases, directors may act as stewards of the assets and traditions of the business, wanting to preserve and enhance what has made it great. When those assets are less tangible and tradition begins to blend with reputation and reputation with brand, it becomes more difficult to establish precisely what basis they can use to make a contested decision, one in which the interests of the various parties diverge. We see this narrow form of stewardship in action in cases of companies where a strong ethos guides the business. When Anita Roddick created her cosmetics manufacturing and retailing business Body Shop, it was a private company responsive only to her concerns, and it built a loyal customer following of people who shared her views that companies should not test cosmetics on animals. When the company went public to raise funds to invest further, applications were invited on the basis that this principle was central to the business. Directors were expected to uphold that view even if the eventual owners of those shares decided this view was no longer the best approach for creating shareholder value. While we might see directors acting in 'stakeholder' interests – the interests of customers or perhaps in some vague sense of suppliers – the stance they were asked to take was that of stewards of an ethical principle.

As appealing as this stewardship approach can seem as an underlying principle for boards, it too presents directors with unclear guidance on which to base their decisions. When acting as stewards for specific individuals or organizations, directors may face choices that are simple enough: follow instructions. But it can often be less than clear what choice is in the interest of a specific constituency. Which is the right choice when an acquisition would propel the company into the forefront of its industry but the price is so high that the risk of failure looms? Knowing that you represent a bank, a family, a trade union or a principle does not make clear on its own which choice is in the interest of the values the steward is meant to guard.

Tensions in approach to corporate governance

What was the board of ABB thinking in 1996 when it voted to give Percy Barnevik a farewell present of 148 million Swiss francs? Did the directors believe that good service demanded a reward over and above that specified in contract? Were they being kind to a colleague of long standing? Did they think that by rewarding him they would create a sense of goodwill among the workforce about their generosity, motivating them, too, to work hard for the corporation in the future? Did they think that public gesture would help them to recruit the best managers in the future, so they could repeat the process? Did they believe that inclusive, open and rich corporate culture he had developed was such a valuable accomplishment that they were willing to put that extra price tag on it? One principle was not at work: shareholder value. Viewing through the lens of agency theory and focusing on the returns in earnings per share, shareholders were not happy.

Boards are where the tough issues come for decision. Where law is clear, corporations by in large obey the law. Where economic outcomes are easily predicted, managers in charge of operations just decide and get on with the job, rather than seeking guidance from the board. On certain occasions, board decisions have major consequences – mergers, acquisitions, appointment of a new chief executive, approval of a change in strategy, provision of budgets for all the operations, whether or not to raise new capital. All board decisions, even the most trivial, can have signalling value. A frugal board – one that chooses not to dine at company expense and to gather in an ordinary conference room rather than fit out a special room with oak panelling – sends a message to the whole corporation concerning its purpose and culture. Contributions to the local community can signal that the company is friendly to society, or – by focusing on donations linked to the business – that shareholder interests still prevail, even in charitable spending.

The basis of board decisions and of individual directors' own choices often leads to a confrontation of values: do shareholder interests take precedence over everything else? Where that is the principle, where do we need to make compromises? On what basis do we decide in whose interest the compromise is made?

Where governance in based in agency theory, the calculus may still be hard, but it has a clear focus. Moreover, in competitive markets many mechanisms other than boards exist that help to check the abuse that agents might make of their principal's interests. For that we need to consider the landscape in which corporate governance takes place. In so doing, we will see what space directors occupy, what leeway they have for control and monitoring as well as for decisions about how to create value.

Note

1 The word goes back centuries in English usage. It can be heard in the 1964 movie *Robin and the Seven Hoods* when a Chicago gangster with a heart of gold named Robbo, played by Frank Sinatra, first meets his sidekick Little John, played by Dean Martin, over a game of pool.

Further readings

Davis, J. H., Schoorman, F. D. & Donaldson, L. (1997). Toward a Stewardship Theory of Management. *Academy of Management Review, 22*(1), 20–47.

Donaldson, T. & Preston, L. E. (1995). The Stakeholder Theory of the Corporation: Concepts, Evidence, and Implications. *Academy of Management Review, 20*(1), 65–91.

Eisenhardt, K. M. (1989). Agency Theory: An Assessment and Review. *Academy of Management Review, 14*(1), 57–74.

Freeman, R. E., & Evan, W. M. (1990). Corporate Governance: A Stakeholder Interpretation. *Journal of Behavioral Economics, 19*(4), 337–59.

Hillman, A. J., Cannella, J. A. A. & Paetzold, R. L. (2000). The Resource Dependence Role of Corporate Directors: Strategic Adaptation of Board Composition in Response to Environmental Change. *Journal of Management Studies, 37*(2), 235–55.

Jensen, M. C. & Meckling, W. H. (1976). Theory of the Firm: Managerial Behavior, Agency Costs and Ownership Structure. *The Journal of Financial Economics, 3*(4), 305–60.

FOUR

Mechanisms of corporate governance

Case: Bernard Madoff

The Lex column in the *Financial Times* used the headline 'Madoff with ya money' but nobody was in the mood to laugh. In December 2008 one of Wall Street's finest financiers was arrested by agents of the US Federal Bureau of Investigations. Bernard Madoff, a former chairman of the Nasdaq stock market, owner of a brokerage house and operator of a hedge fund that bore his name, was charged with having defrauded investors of $50 billion. He was accused of running a giant 'Ponzi' scheme. They were not real investments, so the US Securities and Exchange Commission alleged. Instead Madoff had used money from new investors to pay returns to older ones. It was an investment pyramid, a house of cards that had to fall and would have sooner or later, even if the rest of the global banking system had not fallen victim to the subprime mortgage crisis. Among the victims of his failure were movie stars, children's charities, and even some of the world's most famous economists.

His biggest investors, however, were other financial institutions. HSBC, based in London and one of the largest banks in the world, lost perhaps $1 billion, and Banco Santander, a Spanish bank with major operations in Latin America and Asia as well as around Europe, was also heavily committed to the Madoff fund. Just weeks before, these two banks had received plaudits in the press about how their senior managements had largely avoided the errors afflicting almost all the world's other major banks in the credit crisis unfolding at the same time. Now they, too, faced write-offs against losses that would impair their ability to lend to customers and therefore to generate profits for shareholders and jobs for the workforce.

Another financial services firm, listed on the London Stock Exchange and famous for its mastery of the complex mathematics that lay behind the investment Madoff was supposed to be making, was caught in the web.

Case

Man Group, once a world-famous sugar trading firm, had grown from a family business trading commodity futures contracts on the London exchanges into a giant investment firm using its expertise in derivatives contracts – futures, options, swaps and the like – to hedge against losses, while allowing leverage in the form of bank loans to magnify any profits. A hedge fund itself, Man Group was widely considered to be astute in assessing risks and knew how other hedge funds, like Madoff's, worked. It also lost substantial sums.

Another UK investment firm, Bramdean Asset Management, also lost money. Its chief executive, Nicola Horlick, who had come to newspaper fame as 'Superwoman' while running another asset management firm while raising small children, said she had invested her investors' money with Madoff. She did so because Man Group had invested with Madoff, so she assumed it must be good. Man Group, after all, was always scrupulous in conducting due diligence about its investments and had expertise in hedge fund investing unrivalled in the industry.

After the arrest, it became clear that Madoff had used his own brokerage to place the orders for the hedge fund, raising questions of custodianship of the assets as well as accountability. Other hedge funds usually worked with outside prime brokers. Moreover, the auditor of Madoff's $65 billion fund was a sole practitioner accountant with just two employees. The fund's compliance officer – whose job involved assessing whether the activities met the requirements of the law and securities regulation – was Madoff's niece. Various would-be business partners had previously raised questions with the SEC about the fund's activities, which the SEC once investigated, but only in a superficial fashion. The scandal finally became public because Madoff had confessed to his sons that the fund was nothing more than a scam. The sons turned their father in to the authorities.

Postscript: Bernard Madoff pleaded guilty on 12 March 2009 and was sentenced to a maximum of 150 years in prison. Madoff's auditor, David Friehling, pleaded guilty to securities fraud and filing false audit reports on 3 November 2009. 'At no time was I aware that Mr. Madoff was engaged in a Ponzi scheme,' he told the judge. 'I never had contact with investors and never acted as a feeder to investors.' He faces up to 114 years in prison and agreed to pay back $3.2 million in fees he received.

Questions arising

1 What role can customers – i.e. markets – play in keeping companies in line?
2 Who benefits from scrutiny …

By regulators?
By auditors?
By lawyers?
By the media?

3 What role might industry standards play?

How corporate governance works

The Madoff story, in part a tale of financial traders operating within private companies, in part a saga that that widened to include some of the largest corporations in the world, illustrates how the mechanisms of corporate governance are meant to work – and how they sometimes fail. Boards of directors are one of many structures, processes and systems meant to protect people who have dealings with legal persons we call corporations.

Those mechanisms start on one side with the law, which tend to breed regulation, which sets the boundaries of what a corporation is allowed to do. They start on the other side with markets – for goods and services, for people, and for capital – which together shape the operating environment for the corporation and set the boundaries of behaviour its business partners will tolerate. The gaps between those mechanisms of governance form the areas that the board itself must monitor and control, while at the same time making use of the freedoms they allow to create value.

Markets

With corporate failings driving the corporate governance agenda, it is perhaps not surprising that the focus of policy has been on finding mechanisms, inside the company and outside it, to prevent recurrences. We will examine these in some detail, but before we do it may be useful to reflect on what perhaps remain the most effective means to halt excesses by the managers of corporations: the power of markets.

Markets have limited the scope of economic operations since long before there were corporations. The artisan or farmer needed to sell goods. When customers were free to choose between competing offers, markets prevented what economists call rent-seeking, the demand for excessive prices. Makers of goods needed to buy raw materials and semi-finished products, and were constrained by the economic realities of their suppliers. Labour also exerts market pressure: if workers consider the pay available for the work at hand as insufficient, they will seek employment elsewhere or perhaps work less hard than they otherwise might. Businesses need capital too, especially when undertaking expansion of their facilities or when the markets for their goods and services, for supplies and for labour, turn against them. Capital markets, too, can limit the scope of managers' freedom of action without the need for intermediate mechanisms.

Markets operate through the exercise of power, affecting all the individual decisions that businesses make, a fact acknowledged in the literature on strategy and economics, and synthesized in the influential work of Michael Porter (1980). To function smoothly, competitive markets need sufficient offerings of goods and services and sufficient bids for them; buyers need sufficient information to evaluate those goods and services; sellers need sufficient feedback from buyers to be able to adjust their offers. The 'efficient market hypothesis' – a concept developed in particular to help explain capital markets (Fama, 1970) but which has wide application – holds that markets will be efficient – achieving a balance of bids and offers at a price – when buyers and sellers are free to act and have all the relevant information available at no cost.

While the hypothesis is appealing in theory, it is difficult to find any market – even advanced capital markets – where these conditions apply. Privileged access to information accrues to those with power, and power builds with success. Left unchecked, the accumulation of power distorts markets. Monopolies over-charge for goods and oligopolies are tempted to form cartels to divide the spoils. Labour markets lack transparency about both price and quality, making it difficult for workers and employers to know whether they are getting a good deal. Even in capital markets, outside intervention is needed to ensure that everyone has access to similar information, and even then access to inside knowledge – confidential data that might be commercially sensitive if made public – gives insiders an edge over those looking from the outside. Such *asymmetric* access to information prevents markets from functioning efficiently and hence from acting efficiently as mechanisms of corporate governance. Inefficient markets may still help prevent excesses, to some extent. But inefficiency – as in the case of market bubbles – can lead to market failure. Even the most ardent of neo-classical market economists acknowledge that cases of market failure may require the intervention of government though law or regulation.

Law and regulation

Law is a blunt instrument. Governments and parliaments make laws to establish broad frameworks under which their citizens can act. In economic interactions, law establishes the basis for contracts and provides in the courts a mechanism to adjudicate claims. In *civil law* countries, like France, Germany and much of continental Europe, the law seeks to articulate what may and may not be done and judge whether cases are in compliance with those principles. In *common law* countries, and especially in the United States and England, courts pay greater attention to what previous court rulings have said. Common law often predates legislation on a topic. A complaint between neighbours might be resolved by a judgement which is then used by other courts to settle other claims. The substance of legislation is still important, but courts seek to interpret the law in light of the evidence of the case. As a result of these distinctions, common law may seek to articulate details to avoid specific interpretations, but the law stays at a rather high level. In civil law countries, by contrast, the law may become very specific on many points to reduce any uncertainty. But law cannot anticipate all the possible situations that could arise, especially not in the affairs of businesses that seek, through innovation and by other means fair or foul, to get an advantage over their competitors.

Law is also usually a slow instrument. It takes time to draft legislation, to secure the votes to pass it. In emergencies, governments and parliaments may act quickly, but when they do so, they run the risk of making large mistakes. Company law establishes general guidelines for how this 'legal person', the corporation, should be organized. Those guidelines can become quite specific. Governments will face pressure to make them more specific in response to corporate scandals, as the response in the United States to the Enron collapse showed. But law in general is not best suited as a mechanism of governance to deal with cases of market failure. For that, governments create another layer of governance – the regulators.

In competitive markets, where all the relevant information is freely available and customers have a choice of suppliers, neo-classical economics suggests that Adam Smith's 'invisible hand' should be sufficient to steer participants to a fair outcome of their bargaining (A. Smith, 1776/1904, IV.2.10). But markets are not always competitive, and all the relevant information is not available and is not free, so regulation becomes a powerful force in governing the affairs of corporations.

Markets for goods and services are regulated to a greater or lesser extent, even in the most liberal of liberal-market economies. Competition authorities hold in reserve the right to break up corporations that dominate markets and use that market power to damage the interests of consumers. Monopoly providers of goods are fewer in number now than they were in most of the twentieth century. Telecommunications and postal services, once state-owned enterprises throughout Europe, have been privatized since the 1980s, leaving the market to act as a mechanism of governance. Utilities – gas and electric power, water supplies and sewage – once thought to be natural monopolies, are increasingly competitive services. In the United States where the Postal Service is still a government-controlled enterprise, the post is a fiercely competitive industry, especially for parcels and business services. And where competition is insufficient or entirely lacking, governments create regulators to govern the contracts those industries create.

Regulators have a role to play as well in markets where information is lacking – or available asymmetrically. Governments have found reason to create regulators to prevent abuse by those whose market power is increased by virtue of their superior access to information. That might take the form of *disclosure requirements*, making more information more freely available to all market participants, or *market oversight*, actively observing market trading and intervening to halt suspected cases of market abuse and to impose sanctions on those who cause it. Financial services – banking, insurance and securities industries – are heavily regulated because of the potential for abuse of asymmetric information, as well as their central role in funding the operations of the rest of the economy.

But regulators, too, can fall asleep on the job. In the case of Bernard Madoff, the US Securities and Exchange Commission came under intense scrutiny for failing to pursue leads from some Madoff clients and counterparties that something was amiss in the way he conducted business. Regulators around the world seemed to miss the warning signs in the relatively new market of derivative securities based on residential mortgages that led directly to the collapse of Lehman Brothers and the global credit crisis that ensued.

Regulators also face criticism that they stifle innovation and creativity by intervening too much. Health and safety regulations and other employment rules are designed to protect the workforce from abuse by employers. But employers regularly complain that the rules can be so restrictive that they make it unprofitable to experiment with new products or impossible to introduce labour-saving technologies to cut costs.

The central difficulty with regulation as a mechanism of corporate governance is this: while regulation does offer protection from market abuse, it does not usually seek to protect everyone. Labour-oriented regulation protects the workforce, but not suppliers, customers or shareholders. Utilities are regulated because their customers might be hurt by unfair prices that can arise in markets where the cost of switching suppliers is high. Mining companies are regulated because their processes can cause significant damage to landscape, air and water. The costs of fixing that would otherwise fall to the taxpayer, sooner or later. Financial services regulation protects the counterparties of trades on financial markets. Some may be shareholders, but the protection they receive from regulators is mainly that of giving them a fair market in which to buy or sell their shares, that is, to be counterparties in a financial market transaction. In that sense they receive protection from the regulator in their capacity as customer of a financial services firm. As mechanisms of governance, regulators are not really there to protect the owners of businesses.

A secondary problem arises with regulation as a mechanism of corporate governance – the problem of *regulatory capture*. Regulators can become deeply involved in the businesses they regulate. They become sympathetic to the concerns of the organizations – the people – whose actions they are meant to control. Many regulators go on to take much more lucrative positions in the corporations they once supervised, and not always because they treated those companies less stringently than they might have done. Former regulatory officials will know how best to capture their successors, having seen what actions failed to capture themselves.

While heavily regulated industries and corporations are, by definition, more closely watched than less regulated ones, regulation does not in itself give full protection. It might be said that what happens in regulation is an attempt to make particularly risky businesses more careful – careful enough that they can compete for capital from investors on a more nearly even footing with other, less risky businesses. While regulation governs the affairs of a corporation to an extent, it does not look after everyone – and shareholders perhaps least of all. So what other mechanisms can help?

Gatekeepers and watchdogs

Investors rely on a wide range of other sources of information, advice and opinion as ways of monitoring their investments in corporations. These organizations play a variety of roles, looking at a variety of aspects of the company's affairs. Some are by their position and structure rather less effective than others at finding out about how the business is being directed and making that information widely available. Others are highly effective at learning what goes on, but not in communicating it. Still others know well what happens in a company and communicate it well but often have severe conflicts of interest in their business models. Welcome to the world of the 'gatekeepers' and 'watchdogs'.

The term 'gatekeeper' has become a catch-all for a variety of organizations and occupations that have the potential to monitor the activities of corporations and report on their dealings so that investors can get a view inside without having to be inside (Coffee, 2006). Some are better described as 'watchdogs' of the public's interest, however, as they have no connection to the company and are not paid by the company in any way.

By virtue of their access, gatekeepers can gather insights that can be a valuable check on the accuracy and truthfulness of the statements that the company itself makes. If nothing else, they can present another view, more or less independent of management and the board, potentially critical of corporate policy, to round out the picture that investors see. They range in nature from amateurs to professionals in the world of finance and with greater of lesser access to senior management. None is a substitute for having a seat on the board and seeing for oneself. But, faced with the agency problem and insufficient time to monitor investments, investors rely to a greater or lesser extent on what these gatekeepers can discover and report (see Coffee, 2006, for an extended look at some of these gatekeepers).

Auditors　Auditors were perhaps the first and remain the most important of the outside voices in corporate governance. As a solution to the agency problem, their role is central: an independent, external firm of professionals in the field of accounting and skilled in the processes for dissecting accounts examines in fine detail specific transactions and the principles according to which they are reported. This firm – the auditor – will then attest to whether the accounts represent an accurate record of the economic activity the company has undertaken. As professionals, they operate under an oath of honesty and integrity. If they fail to uphold that oath, they will be prohibited, by law and by other members of the profession, from working again. They can examine any records they want and take as long as necessary to come to their conclusions. While the details of their examination will be kept confidential, they will attest in public once a year that the financial statements of the company present a fair picture of the business and that the business can be viewed as a *going concern* for the next year. If they are unable to reach that view, they will say so.

External audit is an important concession that business owners make when they invite outside investors to provide capital to the business. In most countries, companies with revenues above a certain level are required to have an audit, partly to protect the tax collector, partly to protect the interest of others who might do business with them. In public companies, the corporations listed on stock exchanges, the audit is a crucial element in determining whether the company is worth an investment. Companies often employ internal as well as external auditors. The *internal audit*, despite its name, is often conducted by an external firm of accountants and used by managements and boards to check whether the financial controllers have kept an accurate record of the company's funds. It is a continuous process, undertaken throughout the year, to ensure the business stays on an even keel. The work of the internal auditors, and indeed all the finance staff, is then subjected to an annual examination by external auditors, whose report is then published as part of the annual report to shareholders. This careful scrutiny ensures that money invested in the business stays in the business or is used correctly by the business until the board decides to pay a dividend, buy back shares or otherwise give the money back to shareholders.

Agenda point 7: Audit – squaring the circle, or circling for the kill?

Ever since the accountancy practice Arthur Andersen collapsed in 2002, in the wake of the failure of several of its major corporate clients, including Enron and WorldCom, we've been looking for a better way to do audits. Corporate governance reforms – including the UK Higgs Review, the New York Stock Exchange and Nasdaq governance guidelines, the Cromme Commission in Germany and others – laid great emphasis on the importance of audits. The Sarbanes–Oxley Act in the US created a imposed new watchdog for the profession and imposed new reporting requirements on audit practitioners. How to create greater competition in audit services has been the subject of numerous reviews, without anyone asking the question about why greater competition means anything other than poor-quality audits when the buyer doesn't actually want good service.

While we've been waiting to see whether limited auditors' liability or some other mechanism can gain momentum, the market is perhaps beginning to tell us what a market solution would look like. Rentokil Initial is a UK-based global business known for extermination and disinfectant services. With its 2009 half-year results, it announced a change in how its own books would be inspected for bugs and beasts in the accounting. Out went PricewaterhouseCoopers as external auditors and Deloitte as a contractor for internal audit services. In came KPMG as external auditor, working alongside Rentokil's own financial staff to produce a lower-cost external audit, saving £1 million a year, about 30 per cent of the overall costs.

(Cont'd)

KPMG insisted the deal didn't mean that it would, in effect, be both internal and external auditor. That was one of the many failings we saw in Andersen's work with Enron and WorldCom. (*The BoardAgenda*, 6 Aug. 2009; http://www.edgevantage.co.uk/categories/article.asp?i=4743.)

This important service, conducted even before the invention of the modern corporation, has also been a contributing cause to some of the worst corporate failures in history and the larger lapses in corporate governance. In the notorious cases of Enron and WorldCom, the auditors were found to have colluded with management in creating financial structures that obscured how the profitability of the businesses was draining away. In the cases of Parmalat and Ahold, the auditors appear to have missed obvious signs that something was wrong and passed the accounts for presentation to shareholders.

The centrality of audit to corporate governance means that we shall return to this subject several times as we explore how the field has developed and the issues that it still presents. For now, let's consider the source of the problem that seems to have contributed to such large corporate failures: the conflicts of interest at the heart of the audit business. Auditors are employed by the company to report to the company's shareholders. They act quite specifically as agents of shareholders to keep senior management in line. Auditors have been feared over centuries as they stand guard at the company's metaphorical financial vault.

More often than not, over at least the past 30 or so years, the auditor was actually commissioned to do the work by the company's finance director. In a formal sense the shareholders may have voted to appoint the auditor, but the vote was indeed a formality. The decision to recommend the audit firm was in the hands of precisely the senior manager whose work the auditor would then inspect. As large companies grew further and their businesses became more international and complex, the task of the audit grew more complex as well and audit firms internationalized, grew larger in size and fewer in number. By 2000, the Big Eight firms in the United States and Britain had become the Big Five global accountancy networks, acquiring global rivals as well as the leading accountancy practices in many other countries. The second tier of firms struggled to compete for the audit business of any of the large multinational corporations with shares trading on any important stock exchange in the world.

Audit is a labour-intensive business and one which companies would do by choice. It acts as insurance for shareholders but adds little if any value to the business. Accountancy practices found, however, that their contacts with the company through the audit also provided them with insights into how the business could be run differently. Senior management was happy to pay high fees for such good advice, and the audit firms began to play the role of management consultants, too. Price Waterhouse, which had acquired Coopers & Lybrand in 1998, became a powerhouse in strategy consulting and information systems. It also operated human resources consulting and recruitment services. Deloitte, which had previously acquire Touche, built up similar businesses. KPMG, the product of a earlier merger, advised on accounting technology and strategy. Ernst & Young, which had digested a large number of smaller firms, did likewise. And Arthur Andersen, building on the reputation of its founder for scrupulous honesty, developed a strategy and technology consulting business that eventually dwarfed its parent. The company we now know as Accenture emerged as a separate entity, listing on the New York Stock Exchange, so that its principal consultants could break free of the shackles of being attached to a partnership that, by law in important countries, had to be owned exclusively by accountants. After the split, in 1998, Arthur Andersen started to compete with its former colleagues for lucrative consulting work.

Among Arthur Andersen's clients were Enron and WorldCom. Its annual consulting revenues from Enron grew to be larger than the audit fee, which by the end was itself a very substantial $25 million. Andersen gave Enron management advice on tax, accounting systems, structuring new subsidiaries, creating off-balance-sheet entities to allow the company to take on more debt to fund its growth. Andersen even provided Enron with assistance in the internal audit, which external audits – from Andersen – would then examine. It was a member of Enron's own financial staff, not the auditors, who eventually blew the whistle on the financial irregularities at the company.

Arthur Andersen imploded when Enron and WorldCom failed. The partnership probably could not have survived the lawsuits that followed from all quarters – shareholders, employees, customers, suppliers, banks and other lenders. But Andersen did not have time to fail. Instead, its partners in the networks of partnerships around the world simply quit, taking their clients to rival firms. The remnants were bought by one or another of the large accountancy firms. The Big Five had become the Big Four.

The aftermath led to legislation in the United States and changes in practice in many other countries that meant limiting the extent to which auditors could conduct non-audit business. Seeing the writing on the wall, PwC, as PricewaterhouseCoopers came to be called, shed its consulting business to IBM. Ernst & Young sold its consulting business to Capgemini. KPMG's consultants followed the example of Accenture and formed a new company. Deloitte also made plans to spin out its consulting business, but then hesitated just long enough for some of the questions over the value of such splits to be raised. What would happen if another audit firm failed?

The conflicts of interest in audit – never deep below the surface – became obvious in the Enron case. How audit had failed in its role as a gatekeeper, working in the interests of shareholders, had become an object lesson for all the advisers a board of directors might employ.

Lawyers The legal profession shares many traditional characteristics with accounting: lawyers are obliged by their professional oath to put the interests of their clients first. External counsel work in partnerships, not as corporations with shareholders, so they are principals in their business, not agents for anyone but their clients.

Unlike accountants, however, the advice they give clients is confidential and not for release to a wider public without their permission. Although the role of legal advisers differs between common law countries, like the US and Britain, and civil law countries in much of the rest of the world, the role of lawyers in protecting the interests of shareholders is problematic. Lawyers may be engaged in a formal sense by the company, but in practice they are appointed by people, and usually by the corporation's internal legal staff, who report to the CEO or CFO. This can lead to at least a perception that their loyalties may not be with shareholders when the interests of management get out of line with those of distant owners or even the board of directors acting on their behalf.

Credit rating agencies These watchdogs of corporate affairs send teams of analysts into companies to review financial information, assess the risk, and then publish their conclusions for everyone to see. Their analysts are usually more financially astute than financial journalists, and less motivated by the need to sell a story. They should, therefore, be excellent sources of independent monitoring of the affairs of the corporation. Moreover, investors interested in buying corporate debt instruments ensure there is ready demand for the information for virtually every corporation. For decades, credit rating agencies provided a hugely valuable service.

Credit rating is a business fraught with difficulties over conflicts of interest (Frost, 2007; Strier, 2008). For many years, it did not seem to matter, however. The firms went about their business of rating debt instruments – bonds, commercial paper and other borrowings – giving those investors a reasonable opinion about how easy the corporation would find it to fund interest payments and repay the principal on time. Rating firms also rated non-corporate entities, including governments, for their creditworthiness. In the United States, state and municipal governments were even required in law to use a rating agency officially recognized by the Securities and Exchange Commission, the so-called Nationally Recognized Statistical Rating Organizations, or NRSROs.

The difficulty of this approach became glaringly obvious in the immediate aftermath of the collapse of Enron Corp. in 2001. Here was a company with a fabulous reputation, often cited as one of the most admired companies in the world. For years its debt was rated among the most secure. Even four days before it filed for bankruptcy on 2 December 2001, after several months of growing concern about its financial position, the credit rating agencies still considered its debt 'investment grade', a classification that allowed pension funds and other major investors to buy and hold it (Borrus, 2002). Something had gone seriously wrong.

The issue was in part that almost all credit rating agencies receive their revenue from the companies they assess. The company's chief financial officer, or CFO, decides which agency or agencies to select and then pays them a fee to inspect the company's accounts and determine the rating. A favourable rating reduces the cost of borrowing, lowering its cost of capital and improving its competitiveness. Ratings affect the cost of new funding, but they can also have an impact on the costs of borrowings made in the past. Some debt instruments contain legal clauses that require the company to pay higher rates of interest if their credit ratings are lowered, so the company has a powerful incentive to get as good a rating as possible. They sometimes ask the rating firms to give them advice about how to manage their finance and structure debt issues to achieve as high a rating as possible, paying a fee for these advisory services, too. The closer and more valuable the relationship becomes, the more danger there is, at least in theory, that rating firms' judgements will be impaired by the commercial relationship.

A second issue is the perceived lack of competition in the ratings business. For many years two US-based companies – Moody's and Standard & Poor's – dominated the business around the world. Although other organizations arose in specialized niches, the two giants exerted considerable power. A third firm, Fitch, emerged as a reasonable force, but its success remained focused in the banking industry and in Europe, where its roots lay. In the aftermath of Enron, the SEC took action to widen the circle of NRSROs, but the new, officially recognized firms still found it difficult to break into the wider market. In the mid to late 2000s, the governments of France and Germany both suggested creating national champions to increase competition, and the European Union took action in 2003–4, and again in 2008–9 after the subprime crisis, to require registration and impose standards of conduct on the agencies. The International Organization of Securities Commissions, a global regulators club, drafted a code of conduct for the ratings firms' operations in international markets in response to the Enron fiasco and then moved to strengthen it after the credit crisis in 2008.

These fixes – codes of conduct involving greater transparency on methodology and limits on how the agencies and their personnel may interact with their clients – could not address the issue at the core: who pays? One ratings agency attempted to develop a business using a different business model, one in which it would rate corporate debt for free, but then sell the information to the users, the asset management firms considering investing in the securities. This approach has difficulties, too, particularly that the information would leak out, perhaps even from the corporations themselves. Subscribing investment firms would get no greater benefit than those which had not paid for the service. A further complication comes from the analysts. Credit rating requires a high degree of expertise and analytic skills, which means that the successful analysts will also be in demand in other, often more lucrative occupations: investment banking, commercial banking, asset management and corporate finance.

Moreover, credit ratings concern only one aspect of the businesses they rate – their debt. The risk of default on debt involves a particularly cautious view of a company's finances. It does not tend to assess the company's ability to generate wealth, its innovations and new product development, the quality of its commercial management or the competitive nature of its industry. These considerations are important for investors judging whether to invest in the company's equity, and important for existing shareholders in deciding how to exercise their voice or make use of their exit.

Securities analysts   One of the longstanding sources of advice to investors has been the investment bankers who specialize in studying the corporations – the securities analysts. These share with credit rating analysts a high level of understanding of the complexities of financial reports. Their focus is traditionally on understanding where the business is going, how it can achieve success, what it takes to propel the business forward. The purpose of securities analysis is, ultimately, to try to work out what value to place on the company's shares, and then to use that information to recommend whether the shares are currently worth buying.

Investment banks employ analysts so they can use that information for a variety of purposes. The most obvious one is to convince investors – whether individuals with their savings or large asset management firms with billions of dollars to invest – to buy shares. The investment banks earn a commission for helping the fund managers or private clients invest their money. The investors benefit from not having to pay quite such close attention to the business of the companies in which they invest, because the securities analyst is doing that job for them.

The *sell-side*, as investment banks are often called because they try to sell ideas for trading in shares, gives advice about how well companies are being run to those on the *buy-side*, as the investors are often called, for which the investor pays a fee. If investment banking were that simple, this would be a good system.

It is not. In the case of WorldCom, Jack Grubman, the star securities analyst on telecommunications for the Wall Street firm Salomon Brothers, also advised Salomon's other bankers on how to advise WorldCom about raising money to fund its acquisitions. He advised WorldCom senior management on the value of other telecommunications it might seek to acquire. If WorldCom followed the advice, Salomon Brothers would earn a commission from WorldCom for helping with the acquisition. If WorldCom wanted to issue shares to fund the acquisition, Salomon would help it find buyers for the shares from among its buy-side clients, earning a fee from WorldCom for placing the shares with them. If these conflicts of interest in the business were not enough to raise doubts about the quality of advice the analyst might give, the close personal relationships that can develop should.

The aftermath of the collapses of Enron, WorldCom and other companies in the US and elsewhere in the early 2000s prompted a thorough rethink of how investment research is conducted. Asset management firms hired more of their own analysts, choosing not to rely on the views of the sell-side. Sell-side firms set up new internal rules, in part in response to legislation in the US and strong regulatory guidance elsewhere, to prevent securities analysts from advising both investors and their firms' own corporate finance teams. Investment banks came to consider. The cost of maintaining large research operations too high their only use was to generate trading orders from traditional buy-side asset managers and private clients. So instead they directed analysts to work out more complex trading strategies and then sell those complex ideas to their new and very active clients in the burgeoning hedge fund industry. The role of investment analysts as gatekeepers on behalf of traditional, mainstream investors had largely vanished.

Governance rating firms   Although a much smaller business than credit ratings, governance rating services also play an important and sometimes controversial role. Agencies that rate the quality of corporate governance in corporations emerged starting in the 1970s, when shareholder activism developed in response to economic stagflation as a way to put pressure of corporate managements to perform better. It was a niche business that only gained prominence after the collapse of Enron in 2001 and WorldCom six months later.

These businesses do not face the same conflicts of interest as the credit rating firms. They gather and compile public data about companies to assist asset management firms in determining how they should vote on issues put before shareholders and company annual meetings, as well as any extraordinary meetings called to ratify important changes in the company's position. Some offer recommendations about which way to vote, others merely provide the information in an easy-to-use format, saving the fund manager time. Many provide a service to help clients with the process of voting, which can be a complex and labour-intensive job. Because users of the information pay for the service they receive, governance rating firms do not suffer the same conflicts of interest that credit raters do, but the role is not without controversy.

The oldest and largest of the services is RiskMetrics Group, which in 2007 bought the agency ISS Governance Services, founded as Institutional Shareholder Services in the 1980s by the activist investor Robert Monks. A few years earlier, ISS purchased the rating service Déminor, a Brussels-based firm that otherwise concentrated on advocating the interests of small shareholders in companies in continental Europe. For several years, ISS also operated the advisory service for Britain's National Association of Pension Funds.

The scope for controversy in this business was underscored in the $22 billion takeover bid that Hewlett-Packard made for its rival computer-maker Compaq in 2002. Dissident directors of HP, including Walter Hewlett, a son of the founder, tried to block management's plan. In a closely fought battle to secure shareholder approval, Barclays Global Investors let ISS vote its shares. As a result, the takeover was probably decided by a company, ISS, that itself owned no shares in either HP or Compaq. When ISS issued its recommendation, HP even wrote to all its shareholders and issued a news release publicizing the decision (Hewlett-Packard, 2002). This takeover also saw Deutsche Bank, Germany's largest bank, embroiled in the voting controversy. Its asset management subsidiary owned enough shares to tip the balance, and its investment bank was advising HP management and helping to finance the takeover. After discovery that HP's CEO had threatened 'extraordinary measures' if Deutsche Asset Management did not back the deal, Deutsche's investment bankers intervened with their fund management colleagues. The SEC eventually ruled that Deutsche Bank had broken securities law by failing to disclose its conflicts of interest (Listokin, 2007, gives an account of the case; see also Schmolke, 2006). At the time, DAM reportedly said it would let the ISS recommendation determine which way it voted (Monks & Minow, 2003, pp. 171–3).

If RMG is the largest, it is not the only firm in its industry. Governance Metrics International started up in the US in 2000, Glass Lewis a year later. In Britain, PIRC, an adviser to pension funds, looks at UK companies, and Manifest started in the UK before branching out to continental Europe. France, Germany, Scandinavian countries and other European countries have firms that help smaller shareholders exercise their voice in company annual meetings, and some Asian would-be competitors have emerged as well. The use of governance data is spreading beyond voting, as research accumulates suggesting possible links between good corporate governance and aspects of companies' financial performance (for further discussion, see Bhagat et al., 2007; Gompers et al., 2003; Sonnenfeld, 2004). As it does, greater possibilities for conflicts of interest could arise. In so far as governance ratings firms seek to advise corporations as well, a different type of potential conflict of interest can emerge, one in which they influence companies to change corporate governance practices in line with the standards they themselves set (Rose, 2007). Moreover, some credit rating agencies assess corporate governance as part of their main ratings; others have attempted to develop governance ratings as a separate line of business.

Headhunters Executive search firms, for many years important advisers to corporate human resources departments, have grown in prominence as advisers to corporate boards of directors. Calls by asset managers and others for good corporate governance have focused attention on the role that outside, *non-executive* directors play in nominations to the board, of both new non-executives and of new executive directors, including the CEO. One consequence has been that boards have turned to independent recruitment advisers to conduct searches for would-be new directors, rather than have it seem that nominations stemmed simply from other members of the board, and especially from the CEO. Because these headhunters often perform other services for the company, their independence from management can be somewhat suspect. The confidentiality of the work, moreover, means they can provide little guidance to investors or others outside the firm itself. Their presence in searches is seen as an indication of good practice, rather than as a source of information.

The media   News organizations – newswires, newspapers, magazines, radio, television or online services – ought to be good sources of information (Borden, 2007; Sherman, 2002). They are (mainly) independent in approach, interested in meeting the needs of their readers, listeners and viewers, rather than serving the needs of the corporations they write about (Miller, 2003). But they face serious limitations, too (Nordberg, 2007a; Tambini, 2008). The financial newspapers – and especially the *Wall Street Journal* and *Financial Times*, with their global operations and sophisticated journalists – provide strong stories and have discovered the sorts of malfeasance and misalignment that lies at the heart of the corporate governance agenda. But they face limits on how much they can publish.

Newswires like Reuters, Dow Jones and Bloomberg transmit directly to the computer systems of major investment houses and as electronic services have almost unlimited space for publication. But with the demand for instantaneous news, they face constraints on the time they have available to research and write. Broadcasters have to be even more selective in the range of information they transmit, and online services are hampered by a lack of revenue and by questions over the integrity of their editorial practices. And all journalists need to sell their stories, if not to their readers, then at least to their editors.

Industry standards and self-regulation

Governance of corporations also takes place in a myriad of other ways, less dramatic perhaps than what we have considered so far, but still constraining operational decisions and the scope of choice available to boards and senior management. Industry standards, codes of ethics and custom-and-practice can limit the range of choices open for board-level decisions. Self-regulatory bodies sometimes perform oversight of transactions to provide assurance to outsiders that the industry and the companies in it are working properly. Examples include the associations of house builders and holiday travel companies in various countries that require members to contribute to an insurance fund that will

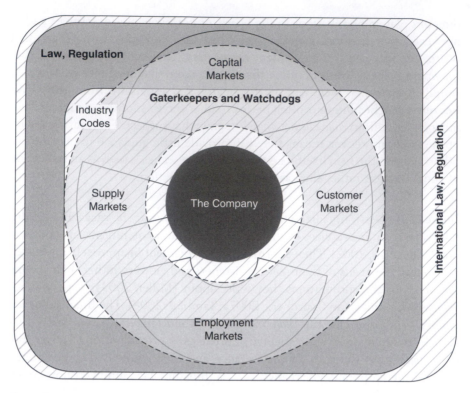

Figure 2   Layers of corporate governance

protect customers if a member company has financial difficulties. While not focused on shareholder interests, such self-regulatory devices can provide some assurance to shareholders, as the associations will often inspect members' businesses in a bid to correct damaging practices before they have a chance to damage the association's insurance pool.

The gap and the role of the board

With all these layers of governance mechanisms in place (see Figure 2), it may seem strange that so many lapses have occurred in the management of major companies and the monitoring of their activities by boards of directors. Bernard Madoff operated in an industry surrounded by law and regulation, and by intelligent and powerful customers able to conduct due diligence into his affairs. He was watched over by an auditor and to some extent by other gatekeepers. He was also a man much in the eye of the news media, those watchdogs of corporate integrity, even if he featured more in the celebrity and society pages of the newspapers, rather than in investigative journalism in the business pages. Though his was not a conventional listed corporation, he had dealings with such companies and pulled some into his orbit. The case of Madoff shows, however, that whatever the constraints imposed by the layers of governance outside the organization, it is still possible for someone inside it to do great damage to the company, to its investors and customers, and even to the wider society.

But total corporate failures and lesser corporate failings provide evidence that all these layers of governance do not entirely work. Company law is a blunt instrument, not suited for guiding corporate decision-making except at the highest level. Regulation helps, but it tends to be directed at the interests of customers rather than owners of businesses. Highly regulated businesses may not be any safer investments than lightly regulated ones, if the point of regulation is to bring down the level of risk to the norm of business as a whole.

The various organizations and occupations that surround a corporation and provide advice to it and to its investors often suffer from conflicts of interest that compromise their ability to do the job that shareholders might expect. Self-regulation within industries provides some succour, but it too is often focused on interests other than those of owners who, in the modern corporation of Berle and Means (1932/1991), may be quite distant from the seat of power and decision-making. For those reasons, the classical view of corporate governance holds: owners need the board of directors to act as a champion of their interests.

But how should a board be organized? What purposes does it serve? How do these practices work under the various legal structures and regulatory frameworks that exist in different countries and jurisdictions? And how are these changing as the corporation and the capital markets that provide its fuel in the form of funding grow increasingly more global and interconnected?

Further readings

Borden, M. (2007). The Role of Financial Journalists in Corporate Governance. *Fordham Journal of Corporate & Financial Law, 12*, 311–69.

Coffee, J. C., Jr. (2006). *Gatekeepers: The Professions and Corporate Governance*. Oxford: Oxford University Press.

Daily, C. M., Dalton, D. R. & Rajagopalan, N. (2003). Governance Through Ownership: Centuries of Practice, Decades of Research. *Academy of Management Journal, 46*(2), 151–8.

Donaldson, L. (1990). The Ethereal Hand: Organizational Economics and Management Theory. *Academy of Management Review, 15*(3), 369–81.

Edmans, A. (2009). Blockholder Trading, Market Efficiency, and Managerial Myopia. *The Journal of Finance, 64*(6), 2481–513.

Fama, E. F. (1970). Efficient Capital Markets: A Review of Theory and Empirical Work. *Journal of Finance, 25*(2), 383–417.

Frost, C. A. (2007). Credit Rating Agencies in Capital Markets: A Review of Research Evidence on Selected Criticisms of the Agencies. *Journal of Accounting, Auditing & Finance, 22*(3), 469–92.

Miller, G. S. (2006). The Press as a Watchdog for Accounting Fraud. *Journal of Accounting Research, 44*(5), 1001–33.

Rose, P. (2007). The Corporate Governance Industry. *Journal of Corporation Law, 32*(4), 887–926.

Sabherwal, S., & Smith, S. D. (2008). Concentrated Shareholders as Substitutes for Outside Analysts. *Corporate Governance: An International Review, 16*(6), 562–77.

Williamson, O. E. (1988). Corporate Finance and Corporate Governance. *The Journal of Finance, 43*(3), 567–91.

FIVE

Corporate governance in a global economy

Case: Allianz goes European

In the summer of 2005 the board of directors of Allianz AG, Germany's largest insurance company and one of the biggest in the industry worldwide, decided that the time had come to cease being, well, quite so German. Less than a year before that, the European Union had put into force legislation that allowed companies in any EU member state to conduct business in any other state without having to incorporate there. To make the process easier, the legislation, adopted by all member states, created a new legal form: *Societas Europaea* or SE, using a Latin term to avoid linguistic sensitivities. The European authorities found it rather surprising that most big enterprises did not immediately give up their 'plc', 'SA', 'SpA', 'AB' and similar such national monikers. But a handful of fairly large German companies took the plunge into becoming European Companies. Allianz was the biggest.

It probably did not matter much at large companies. They already operated in many member states, already had subsidiaries and financial reporting paths established. Changing to an SE might make things a bit simpler in the long run. In the short run, it would involve a lot of change, and with it a fair amount of disruption and cost. But for German companies, it was – at least – worth considering. German companies have usual corporate governance arrangements that can create unusual corporate governance issues. The SE offered a way out.

In explaining the discussion, the board of Allianz went out of its way to stress how little would in fact change. The conversion would affect its corporate governance, but the two-tier board, a feature of German law since the 1870s, would be retained. The management board would still report to a supervisory board. Both boards agreed that *co-determination* would continue on a parity basis: representatives of the workforce would continue to be entitled to half

Case

the seats on the supervisory board. But the size of the supervisory board would be reduced, to a more manageable 12, instead of the 20 people who needed to convene under its AG structure. At the same time – and one of the reasons for the move – Allianz would merge its partly owned Italian partner, Riunione Adriatica di Sicurtà SpA, into the new entity. Allianz had direct holdings in Italy, which could now be combined with RAS to give a stronger presence with a simpler structure (Allianz, 2005).

It did not need to convert to SE form to conduct the merger, of course, a fact the company's statements chose not to highlight. Indeed, to many observers the real reason for the change had nothing to do with the integration of RAS. It rested with the corporate governance implications: retaining co-determination, and reducing the size of the board.

Allianz did not highlight the fact that the German government fought with the European Commission over the SE legislation (Hopt, 2006). German company law required companies with more than 2,000 employees to have a supervisory board on which half the seats were elected only by the workforce (Enriques & Volpin, 2007). The government did not want to see companies free to adopt even more 'Anglo-Saxon' ways – becoming even more like the American and British companies – that trade unions said would make them less likely to respect workers' rights. Even for a conservative government, the electoral implications of big corporations abandoning this special privilege for the workforce would have been difficult. And Germany did not have a conservative government at the time: the Social Democrats were in power, with their strong ties to the trade union movement, and facing an election before too long. Further, Germany won the right to impose an 'exit tax' on any company that chose to move its headquarters to another country while keeping operations in Germany (IBFD, 2003).

So if the move to an SE was not going to allow Allianz's management and the supervisory board representatives of shareholders to get rid of unions on the board, why bother? Because an *Aktiengesellschaft*, or AG, required that half the members of the supervisory board come from the German workforce. As an SE, resident in Germany and working under the German version of EU law, Allianz could allow workers from Italy, France, the United Kingdom and all the other EU countries in which it operated to share in selecting the board. This manoeuvre had an analogy in military strategy: divide and conquer.

Questions arising

1 What might lead a board to refrain from changing corporate structure even when there are advantages?
2 What considerations might lead a board to reconstitute the company, even change the country of incorporation?
3 What factors argue in favour of persistence in established ways of thinking about corporate governance?
4 What factors argue for more uniform corporate governance? In Europe? Around the world?

Corporate governance in different settings

The notions of what constitutes good corporate governance are growing more similar around the world, but that does not mean they are identical, or that the differences lack a strong basis in law or historical reasons for the accountability they offer. If most of the studies of corporate governance have been based on agency theory, it is because most of the research has been conducted on companies operating in the large, liquid capital markets in Britain and the United States. Capitalism did not work quite that way, though, in other countries. We often find references to Japan and Germany as places where stakeholder capitalism is in evidence, and suggestions that these offer alternative models for how corporate governance can and should develop. But how did these differences arise? What problems did they seek to solve? What did they reflect about the society that developed them? And what implications do the changes in capitalism and capital markets around the world have for the legal or political basis for how corporations organize their management and control?

If dispersed shareholdings have led to one set of approaches to corporate governance, concentrated holdings might well point to others. Liquid capital markets, where 'exit' is an important mechanism of governance, may demand differing approaches than those where capital markets are less well developed and 'voice' is in effect the only mechanism available to shareholders. Markets for goods and services constrain the actions of corporations as well, and they differ between countries as well as between companies that operate locally in them and those that have a wide geographic footprint of activities. Employment markets also differ country to country, even if a small but elite market has developed for globally mobile top managers. Moreover, differing legal systems establish frameworks that are not necessarily quick to respond to changes taking place in the movements of either capital markets or the markets for goods and services and recruitment.

History as well as geography may play a role in determining the ways that companies are organized and how their activities are monitored and controlled. Indeed, history and geography may have determined many of the characteristics of corporations, and their influences can persist when economics and ethics point in a direction. Let's examine corporate governance, then, from a variety of directions to learn what lessons each has to teach, to see in what ways they may point to a common, mainstream approach for the future, and to see how they might persist despite strong reasons for convergence. Much of the discussion here draws upon the work of two scholars who have had a powerful influence on how we think about corporate governance. Jonathan Charkham, whose work for the Cadbury Committee in the UK contributed to its widespread influence around the world, described patterns of governance in different settings in two important studies (Charkham, 1994, 2005). Mark Roe, a Harvard economist, invoked a theory to describe the persistence of differences in approach called *path dependency*, that helps explain, in particular, the differing approach to corporate governance in America from those in continental Europe and in the UK (Roe, 2003). We will look first at the ways governance has been organized in different countries, focusing on four large markets – Japan, Germany, the US and UK – with shorter profiles of several other governance models. We then discuss the reasons for those differences and then reflect on how the landscape is changing to point towards an emerging mainstream, even an orthodox view, of how corporations ought to govern themselves. We will then question the basis for that emerging central view.

Japan

Japan has often been considered an example of a stakeholder approach to corporate governance. Employees could expect a job for life, a system that generated loyalty and a sense of shared culture that has all but vanished in western economies. The *keiretsu* system, in which families of unrelated businesses developed, encouraged trading between members of the 'family' on terms that were perhaps more favourable than might have been possible on the open market. Even end-customers for goods and services in the domestic market could be expected to be loyal to the products and services of many of the *keiretsu* companies. The intense loyalty involved some costs for each member, of course. The bank that may have served as the hub of the transactions might not offer the most competitive rates on loans. Supply relationships would bring with them expectations of cooperation beyond that specified in contracts. The companies would be expected to look after workers who were perhaps not pulling their full economic weight. Businesses elsewhere in the group might have to find a job for employees in another who had failed to stay up with changing technologies or practices.

Against these costs, though, were benefits: greater stability of markets for goods and services, and lower labour costs as workers stayed with one employer rather than seeking to maximize their value through the job market. During the 1980s, when Japanese car manufacturers and electronics companies led an invasion of US markets for consumer and industrial goods, many people wondered whether this stable core – based on respect for stakeholders sometimes at the short-term cost to providers of capital, both shareholders and lenders – was the way forward.

The system of corporate governance in Japan, which had a strong influence on South Korea and some other Asian countries, has historical roots in the ownership of corporations, their relationship with the state. As in many parts of the world, businesses in Japan started in real families. But unlike many of the families in western cultures, those in Japan and Chinese-related cultures around Asia maintained a strong hold on the ownership of the business. Francis Fukuyama, a US political economist, traces the difference to what he calls the low level of trust in Asian societies for outsiders. With family members, even the weaker members would feel bound by the bonds of kinship (Fukuyama, 1995). When they needed new capital to expand, they turned to the banks to borrow money, and only with great reluctance did they approach non-family-members to provide equity capital. Other Asian countries – Taiwan, for example – persisted in corporate forms that relied on internal capital from retained earnings for their growth and have perhaps been hampered by it.

In Japan, however, industrialization in the nineteenth century came in the form of *zaibatsu*, or 'money cliques', encouraged by the imperial government as a way of aggregating capital to fund growth, but with banks and loan capital as the centrepiece. After the Second World War, the occupying American forces banned *zaibatsu* as a threat to civil authority with imperial ties. But the need for capital – the economic rather than political imperative – won out and *keiretsu* quickly took the place of *zaibatsu* as the engine of economic growth. The result was that Japanese groups were able to grow to a size capable of competing with the American giants and the British companies that had grown large on the back of Empire. Private-sector enterprises in Japan are still much larger than those based in China, Hong Kong and Taiwan, even though Japan's equity capital market, while important, is smaller and less active than the stock exchanges in New York and London. The *keiretsu* – with their networks of interlinked companies, cross-shareholdings and reliance on bank finance – permitted enterprises to grow to great size while diminishing the need for equity capital to fund the expansion. By the time they came to challenge American companies for dominance on US soil in the 1980s, Japanese companies often operated with equity capital ratios of perhaps only 5 or 10 per cent, with 90 to 95 per cent debt. By contrast, investors in American corporations grew wary of excessive risk if the debt – equity ratio went much higher than 50:50. Without the 'family' of companies, the Japanese structure would have been risky, too (for a range of perspectives, see Aoki et al., 2007).

These financial arrangements led to governance structures to match. High levels of debt meant that bankers played a central role on boards of directors, as did representatives of other *keiretsu* companies, which might also have supplied some of the equity capital. Outside shareholders, by contrast, had little influence. Lacking influence – lacking 'voice' – meant they were less likely to want to provide capital without quite a lot of confidence that the businesses would grow. And the thin market for shares – with many held by other *keiretsu* companies – meant that outsider holders also faced a problem if they wanted to 'exit'. These governance arrangements worked acceptably well when Japanese companies were growing strongly and taking market shares from American and European rivals. But when the downturn came, as it did in the early 1990s and the subsequent 'lost decade' of falling asset prices and the collapse of large parts of the banking system, the viability of Japanese corporate governance, with its supposed shareholder orientation, came into doubt as well. The failures and forced mergers of banks upset the bank-centric approach to corporate finance and to some extent the protection that being part of a *keiretsu* brought to Japanese companies. But Japan remains a somewhat hostile place for foreign investors and the shareholder activism they have come to expect.

Germany

Corporate governance in Germany is also called stakeholder-oriented, but its structures and purpose are quite different from those in Japan. It is often held up as an example of how different continental Europe is from the British or American approach (Bassen et al., 2008; Charny, 1997; Cioffi, 2002; Dittmann et al., 2008; Fiss & Zajac, 2004; Lane, 2003), though none of the larger countries in Europe has a system quite as different from the Anglo-American approach as the Germans. The focal point of the system is its reliance on a dual-board structure, in which a board of management heads up the day-to-day operations of the company, reporting to a supervisory board charged with major decisions and policy. No manager may sit on the supervisory board, although many 'retire' from a management board post to a part-time role on the supervisory board. In that sense, Germany is a model for other countries in Europe, where company law either requires or allows dual-board structures.

What makes Germany different, however, is the composition of the supervisory board. Almost since the foundation of the country in 1871, when Bismarck brought the various Germanic states and principalities together, company law has provided a special status for the interests of the workforce. The principle of *Mitbestimmung*, or co-determination, has led to the practice under which any company of a reasonably large size, public or private, must reserve half the seats on its supervisory board for the workers. In Bismarck's time, it was a balancing power aimed at preventing companies from becoming more powerful than many of the politicians, who had lost power to the new federal government in Berlin (see Fear, 1997, for an account). The practice survived Germany's defeat in two world wars and the division and then reunification of the country in the decades afterward. Workers have had a say over all important policy decisions, and a right to be consulted over actions of management that might lead to job losses. With the chairman of the supervisory board allowed to break tie votes, the system includes a mechanism to avoid deadlocks. And Germany, like Japan, became a formidable industrial power in the world economy after the 1960s, so the system was not obviously a poor one.

Criticisms of *Mitbestimmung* include that it is clumsy and bureaucratic. Important decisions go to the supervisory board, but managements become skilful at developing policy in a way that avoids having to consult the supervisory board. The slowness of German companies to react to rapidly changing markets, compared with American ones for example, is sometimes ascribed to how co-determination has made bold responses more difficult.

But the most important issue about it is funding. Giving workers half the vote on the board means that outside investors, as in the case of Japan, will be wary of contributing new capital to the business and demand the prospect of higher returns than they would in a system more focused on shareholder value and rights. This has the effect of raising the cost of capital and lowering the profitability of the business. Together with structural rigidities imposed by the emphasis on worker rights, this higher cost of capital should in the long run damage the ability of German companies to compete on world markets against more nimble competitors, including ones with easier access to new capital to fund expansion and greater flexibility in laying off staff when needed.

Mark Roe (2003) argues that *Mitbestimmung* is not just an inefficient relic of a bygone era, though history plays a role in its preservation in the face of emerging global competition. He traces the decision to retain its worker-friendly features after the Second World War to the need to keep the workers in West Germany united behind a capitalist approach to business at a time when it was facing the threat of domination from the Soviet Union and its allies, including those in East Germany. *Mitbestimmung* gave German capitalism a social legitimacy, a sacrifice that providers of capital made – including the American, British and French capitalists who invested in Germany and whose countries and their armies were defending West German freedom. For capitalism to work, you need freedom; and for freedom to exist, you need peace, including peace in labour relations. Owners of companies were willing to cede power to the workforce to ensure harmonious labour relations, rather than risk having the country fall to Soviet domination, and with it lose all their investments. The path taken in the past then continues to determine the options available in the future.

No German government – conservative or social democratic in orientation – has even considered taking away the rights the workforce won initially as a prize for supporting the unification of Germany in the nineteenth century, or that sustained its freedom in much of the second half of the twentieth century, irrespective of the disappearance in the twenty-first-century of the threats that made them necessary.

One of the implications of co-determination is that it can frighten away equity investors, which was why German companies became heavily reliant on banks for new capital throughout the twentieth century. Immediately after the Second World War, banks provided a channel to route new capital – loans and equity – to the industrial companies struggling to re-establish themselves amid the ruins of defeat. The banks took shareholdings in large industrial companies often in excess of 25 per cent, the threshold in German law granting them a blocking vote in matters the supervisory board put before shareholders. These blocking minorities became an extra layer of protection against the possibilities that the workforce might have too great an influence on corporate policy. But they also meant that non-bank investors might have even less rights. As a consequence, German companies relied more and more on bank loans rather than equity capital to fund their expansion. And bank representatives on the supervisory boards might, therefore, be tempted to worry first about the company's ability to pay interest on the loans and less interested in shareholder value. This was a sacrifice worth making during the time when the Soviet Union posed a threat to West Germany, even if it meant German companies would be less able to respond to competitive pressures. But with the global economy expanding throughout the post-war years, German companies could ride a wave of economic prosperity.

Towards the end of the twentieth century things here began to change, as they had in Japan. The collapse of the Soviet Union and the reunification of Germany changed the political dynamics. German banks themselves needed to become more nimble to compete against expansion abroad by US, Swiss, French and other banks. They wanted to engage in global investment banking, taking over British merchant banks and using their capital market experience to build new global businesses. They pressed for and received tax changes in Germany to make it advantageous to dispose of their blocking minority stakes in industrial companies, and sought to make new fees from getting companies to raise capital by issuing shares rather than through bank loans. In short, the banks led a move that was transforming corporate finance and capital markets in Germany to look rather more like those in the US and UK. Early in the twenty-first century, the German stock exchange company, Deutsche Börse AG, even attempted to take over the London Stock Exchange, a plan beat back by US and UK activist shareholders, as we shall explore in greater length in Chapter 10.

With all these changes afoot in the market landscape in which corporate governance operates, it is less than clear that Germany's peculiar governance structures will continue to contribute value. The code of corporate governance adopted in 2002 and then revised in 2004 included many features modelled on the Combined Code in the UK, which we examine in more detail in Chapter 6. The increasing prominence given in US and UK governance to the role of independent, non-executive directors and their control of board committees has faint echoes of the separation of powers seen in Germany's two-tier board structures. But changes to *Mitbestimmung* may well prove to be a bridge too far.

United States

It was the US capital markets that Berle and Means had in mind as they considered the importance of the separation of ownership and control in the 'modern corporation' in the 1930s (Berle & Means, 1932/1991). It was US corporations with their growing international power in the late twentieth century operating in political and legal structures from the late nineteenth century that Jensen and Meckling had in mind when they articulated the agency problem inherent in separating ownership from control (Jensen & Meckling, 1976). Because so much of corporate governance thinking arises from the work of these scholars and from analyses of US corporate practice, it is useful to reflect on just how different the US is from the rest of the world, including from those of the economies of Germany and Japan that the US refashioned at the end of the Second World War.

Company law in the US rests, in the main, with the legislatures and courts of each of the 50 American states. Responsibility for banking supervision is split between federal and state agencies. Watching over trading in capital markets is a federal responsibility, or at least it has been since the Wall Street Crash of 1929 set off the Great Depression, bringing about the circumstances where individual states were powerless to resist centralization of some of the levers of control. But even then, the regulatory mechanism of governance of capital markets was divided between those associated with stock exchanges, shares and bonds (the Securities and Exchange Commission) and those with commodities markets (Commodities Futures Trading Commission), including, as they developed, trading in derivative contracts based on stock market indexes and bond yields. Trading in options on individual company shares was divided between the two, but with no clear dividing line.

The reasons for these complexities lie in American history and specifically scepticism about any attempts to centralize power. The American states resisted early attempts to create a strong federal government. Except for a brief and contentious period in the early nineteenth century, the federal government operated without a central bank until after the First World War, and even then what came about was a *federal reserve system* made up of several regional banks and only a small coordinating Federal Reserve Board in the middle. Powers not explicitly given to the federal government in the US Constitution are, according to the Constitution, for the states to decide. These principles arose, after all, from a revolution that had to do with freedom from a distant and sometimes tyrannical ruler.

The complexity of these arrangements, which persisted until the subprime crisis in 2007 spilled over into a global banking crisis the next year, has had a profound impact. Banks could choose whether they wanted to be involved with state or federal bank inspectors, and then choose which states and whether federal agencies should do the supervision. While supervision of trading on stock and commodity markets was clear enough, it was not with respect to options trading. And the firms involved in any of these markets could easily be involved in all of them.

The complexity also had an impact on corporate governance. In essence, companies can choose in which state they will have their legal seat. This selection leads to competition between state governments about which would offer corporations the best terms. The companies do not have to re-base their operational headquarters in the state or even have significant operations in it for that state to become their legal seat. The law of the state with the legal seat, however, governs relationships between the company and its shareholders. About half of all companies with stock market listings in the US choose to have their legal seats in one state, Delaware, and many larger private companies choose to do the same. The reasons: Delaware has adopted provisions that give managements and boards of directors a wide degree of discretion over their decisions, shielding them from many possible lawsuits from shareholders. It has developed courts with great expertise in adjudicating such cases, meaning that lawsuits could be dealt with expeditiously, rather than dragging on while the judges had to refresh their minds on the intricacies of company law and all the precedents established in a case-law legal system.

Among the provisions in Delaware is one known as the *business judgement rule*, under which decisions by the board in the normal line of business may not be challenged by shareholders. Moreover, resolutions put to a vote of shareholders are, in the main, merely advisory. The board may, therefore, ignore the recommendations of a majority of shareholders without fear of reprisal. The only real right of shareholders is to elect the directors, but even that is less of a right than it seems at first glance. Delaware law, copied by most of the other states, allows companies to set up in such a way that shareholders may not vote against a candidate for director, they can only vote in favour or withhold their vote. The board also controls nominations to the board, so in the normal run it may never offer shareholders a choice of candidates. In the cradle of democracy, some more cynical observers have noted, elections to boards are run by the principles of dictatorship.

Not quite: shareholders are allowed to mount what is called a proxy battle, putting forward a new slate of directors and demanding an election. To do so, they have to communicate with all shareholders – not an easy task, even after the internet revolution – to convince them of the case and hope that a sufficient number will vote for the alternative slate. It is a costly and risky idea, unless those supporting the new group of directors already own a very large number of shares. And if they do, other shareholders could well doubt their intentions – the new boards may act as stewards only for the special interests that got them there, and not look after the interests of shareholders as a whole.

With little chance of controlling the board, shareholders see power gravitating to top management. The danger is this: a powerful chief executive will influence which candidates are put forward as directors, and they in turn influence the rest of the policies the board may adopt. It is perhaps not surprising under these circumstances that many CEOs can gain almost unfettered power. They become 'Chairman and CEO', setting the agenda for the board meeting that will then scrutinize the work of the CEO. By guiding the nominations process, the CEO identifies directors who will support his plans, select the auditors who will scrutinize his performance, and then decide how much the CEO should be paid for having done so.

The potential for the abuse of power by a powerful CEO is considerable, and it lay behind the great governance failures of WorldCom and several other US corporations. But it also lay behind some of the great successes of American capitalism. Throughout his two decades as Chairman and CEO of General Electric Co., Jack Welch was lionized for how he took one of the most successful companies in US history and made it even more successful, propelling it to an increase in market capitalization more than 30 times what it was when he took over. Bill Gates, founder of Microsoft, was Chairman and CEO for more than 20 years, during which it went from a completely new start-up to rivalling GE as the most valuable company in the world. If American corporate governance was so wrong, how could American corporations create so much wealth? A more sceptical reflection on Welch's performance comes from the economist Uwe Reinhardt. His comparison of GE with the index of all Nasdaq stocks (Reinhardt, 2009) throws doubt on the power of one person to create corporate value. But by showing that Jeffrey Immelt, Welch's successor as chairman and CEO, also managed to outperform Nasdaq, perhaps to a greater extent, provides evidence that the American system of a powerful chairman–CEO does immediately impede value creation.

Is a distant and sometimes tyrannical regulator going to know better how to operate these businesses? Are, for that matter, distant and often ill-informed shareholders going to do a better job of determining what's needed in the boardroom? Shareholders may lack 'voice', but with a large and liquid capital market they can at least exercise 'exit'.

United Kingdom

UK corporate governance does not follow the American model, despite sharing many economic and cultural traditions and having a large and liquid market in which companies can raise capital and in which investors can sell their shares when it suits them to do so. It does not follow the German approach, with its emphasis on workers' rights that also underpin the social democratic orientation of company law in much of the rest of continental Europe. Family ownership of companies gradually gave way to broad public ownership; not with the stampede – the thundering herd effect – that happened in America in the 1920s, but also avoiding the compromises on shareholder rights that accompanied Germany's *Mitbestimmung* and laws in many other countries giving workers substantial protections against corporate decisions that might affect their jobs.

Britain's long tradition of commodity trading and international banking markets gave it a springboard that created a capital market for corporations looking to push their horizons. Although its empire fell into decline after the First World War, the UK was home to rather large businesses that still needed to raise capital. The controlling families could not afford to supply the funds themselves, so they turned to capital markets. But unlike continental Europe, where families were reluctant to invite outsiders to share control, British families quietly relinquished control, selling shares rather than taking on debt or restraining their ambitions to match their fortunes. Yet they stayed to a large extent in control.

The economic historian Alfred Chandler claimed that this odd mixture – outside capital but inside control – is one of the reasons for Britain's decline as an industrial and commercial power early in the twentieth century. While the US worked under a form of 'competitive managerial capitalism' and Germany under 'cooperative managerial capitalism', British companies for a long while retained 'personal capitalism' as the mode of governing many of its largest enterprises. Even where entrepreneurs made the investments to compete, 'they recruited fewer salaried managers and placed a smaller number of them on the governing boards of their enterprises than American or German industrialists did' (Chandler, 1990, p. 286). As competition pressured them to consolidate, Britain's industrial families engaged in friendly mergers and outside shareholders – now increasingly coming from the growing ranks of financial institutions – acquiesced in the families' decisions over leadership. Class and an education at Oxford or Cambridge were sufficient proof of capability. With gentlemen-amateurs in charge, Britain's industrial base was sure to decline.

Julian Franks and his colleagues challenge some of Chandler's conclusions, though not the main thrust. Unlike companies in continental Europe, families in the UK relinquished control through ownership at quite an early stage, in that regard like the Americans. They often kept hold of the chairmanship or their board representation was disproportionate to their ownership. In continental Europe, by contrast, extensive family ownership persisted, but with managerial control delegated to professionals, as Chandler noted in the case of Germany. 'In Britain families exerted power without responsibility whereas in most countries they had responsibility with at least limited power' (Franks et al., 2004, p. 3).

What really made a difference to corporate governance in the UK was, however, the transition to widespread ownership of corporations by asset management firms: insurance companies, pension funds, and the unit trusts and investment trusts that provided individual investors with a way to diversify their portfolio through collective investing. These investors began to demand better performance. In the final quarter of the twentieth century, and with families no longer having strong voting power, the heirs to family fortunes found themselves pushed out through hostile takeover bids: a resurgence in the market for corporate control.

Some adopted the mantle of managerial capitalism (initially like the Cadbury chocolate company). Many succumbed to takeovers by foreign companies (like the confectionary firm Rowntree swallowed by Nestlé; now Cadbury by Kraft), or merged with rivals (Glaxo with Wellcome, then GlaxoWellcome with SmithKline Beecham). A few turned themselves into predators (like Hanson Group) with a sharp focus on the bottom line of financial performance. A few powerful founders remained in charge, exerting a strong influence on policy in their organizations. But these were new companies, and some, including Maxwell Communication and Polly Peck International, would come to ignominious ends. It was, in fact the failure of these two, together with the collapse of the Bank of Credit and Commerce International that would make Britain in some ways the centre of thinking about corporate governance (Wearing, 2005, gives an extensive account of each).

As a direct result of the frauds that led to the collapses of Polly Peck in 1990 and Robert Maxwell's two listed companies, Maxwell Communication and Mirror Group Newspapers, in 1991, Britain's accountancy profession had to act to restore its reputation. With the support of the London Stock Exchange and the Bank of England, they empanelled a committee to investigate what could be done. It was originally supposed to look at accounting issues alone, but under the leadership of Sir Adrian Cadbury – ironically, the scion of one of the surviving family-led businesses from the turn of the previous century – it changed direction, exploring the functioning of the board of directors as a whole. We will examine the origins of the Cadbury Code (1992) and its subsequent development in Chapter 6, but we will consider the main points briefly here to establish the contrast with corporate governance in other locations.

Britain has emerged with a system of corporate governance that relies, like America but unlike Germany, on a unitary board of directors, including both executive managers and outside or *non-executive* directors, whose overriding mandate is to look after the interests of shareholders. Unlike America, however, the balance between executive and non-executive directors is in general – by custom and practice, not law or regulation – more nearly even. Moreover, the Cadbury Code created a large and enduring difference with American corporate governance by demanding that no one individual should dominate the boardroom. While in the US it was and still is commonplace to have someone titled chairman and CEO, British companies come under sharp criticism from shareholders unless they separate the two roles and have a chairman who is independent of the management. Together with a stress on the independence of the non-executive directors, the Cadbury Code aimed to create a dynamic in the boardroom that can be at once both collegial and confrontational, making it a place of debate and decisiveness.

By contrast, Japanese boards typically function like committees, through consensus rather than leadership. US boards traditionally have a powerful chairman–CEO who also controls the nomination of outside directors, ensuring that his power remains largely unchallenged. German supervisory boards have no executive representation and therefore have much less influence over how policy is enacted in operations. Moreover, with half the supervisory board seats in the hands of the workforce, the management board has a strong incentive to allow as little as possible of important company business to reach the agenda of the supervisory board. Although so different in many ways in its history, structure and dynamics of corporate governance from other countries, Britain has also become a model of good governance. And it did so by having a few rotten apples threaten to spoil the barrel.

'The UK is a strange country,' Franks and his colleagues write. 'It does not have concentrated ownership; most countries do. It does not have pyramid structures; most countries do. Family ownership is of limited significance; in most countries it is extensive. There are few dual class shares; in many countries they are extensive. It has an active market in corporate control; elsewhere, it is largely non-existent' (Franks et al., 2004, p. 1). And yet it has come to be the model for so much of what has happened since.

Governance in other European countries

Before examining how the history and the emergence of these principles of corporate governance has turned into practice, it may be useful to consider what alternatives there are to the four approaches we have just explored, the models Franks et al.(2004) have listed.

Concentrated ownership and control   Belgium is perhaps the archetypal example. A small country, it has been home to some rather large enterprises in banking, chemicals, steel and other industries. But unlike Britain and America, its founding families never happily relinquished control. As a result, only a small proportion of the shares of most of Belgium's listed companies trade on the Brussels Bourse (now Euronext-Brussels), and raising funds through share issues for expansion is difficult. Institutional investors from abroad fear their interests, as minority shareholders, will be ignored in boards with a high proportion of directors named to their posts by the family. The main concern of outside investors – individual small shareholders as well as international institutions – becomes one of defending the rights of the minority when a takeover bid emerges or when the company might have business dealings with other companies in which the family has a stake.

A variation on this theme is the situation in which a company has a single large shareholder, perhaps a bank, insurance company or strategic partner. These used to be common in Germany, but as we have seen, competitive pressures and changes in law have already begun to make them less significant. Similar issues can arise where government is a major shareholder in a partly privatized corporation. The chance that corporate policy could be bent to serve the electoral needs of politicians is the subject of an extensive body of academic and practitioner analysis.

Dual-board structures   Corporations in some European countries like Italy and Spain have a unitary board, similar to those in the UK and US, but in others a two-tier board structure applies. A management board, in effect the most senior managers, reports to a supervisory board made up in part of outsiders. In Austria and Germany such dual boards are mandatory. German supervisory boards often have members affiliated with specific shareholders or with the company's main bank, alongside those who are members of the workforce (Dittmann et al., 2008; Fear, 1997). In Switzerland and the Netherlands such dual-board structures do not give direct voting power to employees, and they often become more deeply involved in business policy than in Germany. In still others like France, the choice of dual or unitary boards is left up to the choice of shareholders themselves, and some with hybrid dual boards have executives sitting on the supervisory board (Albert-Roulhac, 2009; Hopt & Leyens, 2004).

Dual boards can eliminate the role ambiguity we see in American and British directors: members of a Swiss *Verwaltungsrat* have no illusions that they are in charge of managing the day-to-day affairs of the company. Theirs is a role of monitoring and control. The chairman becomes a powerful conduit between the management and the monitors.

Pyramid ownership and control Italy is perhaps the strongest example of a place where pyramids dominate the landscape of public capital markets. Because many shareholders cannot or at least do not vote, a 30 per cent stake is often sufficient to ensure control. If an individual person can own 30 per cent of a company that owns 30 per cent of another company that owns 30 per cent of another, that person can in effect set policy for the wide bottom of a pyramid of holdings while having what we call a *beneficial interest* of just 2.7 per cent of the third company in the chain. Each layer of ownership in effect leverages the interest of the layer before. This practice is commonplace in Italy, even among some of the largest companies. It makes business highly personal, and makes outside shareholders – who are not party to the discussion that small but controlling shareholder might be having with management – very wary. The economic effect must, in the long term and in truly competitive markets for goods and services, make the company uncompetitive. But if markets can be protected – say, by applying political pressure – neo-classical economic theory suggests the system can run for a long time, ultimately damaging consumers.

News Corporation, the US-based company that Rupert Murdoch controls, has a pyramid structure in place to control the satellite television company, British Sky Broadcasting.

Dual-class shares Sweden is the archetypal use of dual classes of shares. We used to talk about Switzerland in this regard, but competitive world markets for Switzerland's large chemical, pharmaceutical, food, banking and insurance companies eventually led most of them to abandon the practice. The system involves giving some shareholders shares with greater voting rights than they have capital at risk. The Swiss used to do it to ensure that large Swiss companies remained under the control of Swiss citizens. It was a significant danger for a small but wealthy country with a long border with a large, powerful and often aggressive neighbour. But the economic arguments won out in Switzerland during the 1980s and 1990s, and one by one Swiss companies ended the practice of having some shares more equal than others.

Dual-class shares remain commonplace, though, in Sweden and are used in many other individual companies around the world. Sweden permits A and B shares. Both may represent the same nominal capital at risk, but A shares typically carry 10 times the voting power. As a result the holders of A shares – perhaps a family trust – control decision-making without exposing themselves to quite the same degree of potential loss. It may have a downside, too, by making it more difficult to find a buyer for the shares should the trust wish to sell. But these trusts – such as the Wallenberg family working through their listed company Investor AB – are usually very long-term investors and therefore less interested in having a liquid market for the shares. What they want is control.

Swedish companies, including those controlled by Investor AB, ought to suffer the same problem as ones held in pyramids: a long-term loss of competitiveness as capital-providers baulk at investing at favourable rates when they are systemically disadvantaged when it comes time to vote. But such is the trust in the fairness and stewardship of the Wallenbergs', Investor AB and similar owners that Swedish companies have managed to avoid much of the discount for poor governance that, say, Italian companies suffer. You may have noticed the Wallenbergs' partial ownership of Investor AB means that it combines a dual-class structure with a pyramid to leverage the family's power.

This is not peculiar to Swedish companies. When Google floated its shares in 2004, the founders set up a dual-class structure to allow them to retain control even while issuing new shares vastly in excess of the capital they themselves retained. The New York Times Company has had a similar structure for many years. Dow Jones & Co., publisher of the *Wall Street Journal* and the Dow Jones Industrial Average, also had disproportionate voting, justified – as by the *New York Times* – on the basis of preserving editorial integrity.

A variation of this theme emerged in 2001 when France introduced changes to company law to permit corporations to grant double voting rights to shareholders if they maintained their stake for at least two years. It was designed as a way of aligning voting, and as a result put pressure on management with the notion that corporations should pursue long-term value creation. Although this went against the wishes of many institutional investors and their assertion of equality for all shares, the French counter-argument held that all shareholders were treated equally. The double voting rights applying to the person, not to the shares, and were not transferable. Any shareholder could receive them – by holding the shares for at least two years. Whether this will achieve the desired aim is open to question. It could as easily protect management from pressure for needed changes by strengthening the power of insiders and complacent shareholders.

The European Union and corporate governance

Many institutional investors regard pyramids and unequal voting as a violation of the rights of owners of the other shares and sometimes lobby governments noisily about it. Twice in the early 2000s their complaints led the commission of the

European Union – in effect its executive branch – to set in motion attempts to overturn these practices in the interests of creating a free and transparent, pan-European marketplace for shares in public companies. First came the Takeover Directive, which finally passed in 2004 after 15 years of negotiation. A few years before, however, a fight over voting rights almost ended the chances of any legislation. The European Commission, the executive arm of the bloc, sought to set aside unequal voting rights and to limit the power of pyramids when a merger or a hostile takeover was on the table. First Germany objected to measures that would have reduced the power of large blockholders to forestall hostile takeovers. Though it lost the argument in a vote of ministers of member states, it mustered sufficient support in the European parliament to stop the directive becoming law. Then the Commission turned on unequal voting rights and pyramids. Once again, political opposition – not surprisingly from Italy and Sweden, assisted by Germany, which feared another attack on its system of corporate governance – wiped out any chance that the Takeover Directive would pass in that form.

A few years later, under internal markets commissioner Charles McCreevy, it tried again through an attempt to form a Shareholder Rights Directive. This legislation also sought to break down national laws that had the effect of preventing shareholders from exercising their votes. The 'rightness' of that cause was widely accepted, even in countries like France, which had rules to make cross-border voting very awkward. But opposition to 'one share, one vote' remained solid. And when a study, ordered by McCreevy and conducted by a distinguished panel of academics and practitioners (Caprasse et al., 2007), determined that dual-class shares did no long-term economic damage, the attempt to eliminate dual-class fizzled.

These efforts indicate just how difficult it can prove to overcome what Mark Roe, Jeffrey Gordon and others (Bebchuk & Roe, 1999; Gordon, 2004; Gordon & Roe, 2004; Roe, 2003; Schmidt & Spindler, 2004) have called path dependence. The legal, social and cultural influences over company law persist despite economic pressure from the integration of capital markets. In the European Union, where strong, new political impetus has developed to break down national differences, we still see a political reaction to preserve the privileges of those who have political power in corporations. Silvio Berlusconi, Italy's prime minister during much of the time the EU Commission was pressing for convergence, came to power in part through his ability to control a large commercial empire of newspapers, television stations and other industries. He achieved that by exploiting the power afforded through pyramid control. It was perhaps politically naïve to imagine that appointed officials in Brussels would easily manoeuvre him away from that position in a system in which national governments still have the ultimate say.

Corporate governance in emerging capital markets

If continental European corporate governance can differ so much from the practice in Britain or the United States, surely the practice must vary significantly in countries where capital markets have a much less well-established tradition? But many of the potential problems are the same, whether the company is based in Russia, China or other countries where a communist system has only relatively recently adopted the notion of capital markets at all, or in yet other countries with low levels of social trust, unstable currencies or weak enforcement of laws on private property. In many countries that have moved from centralized systems of control to more liberal capital markets, the state has nonetheless retained a strong interest and sometimes a controlling shareholding in enterprises privatized in the economic reforms. These privatizations often took the form of selling some of the shares to institutional investors from abroad and giving vouchers to citizens so they could participate in the proceeds of making private what had been state assets. The extent to which governments are involved in setting the policies of individual enterprises ought to challenge concepts of monitoring and control developed in countries like the US and UK, where shareholding has long been widely dispersed.

Emerging capital markets – in Asia, Latin America and elsewhere – have different legal and historical backgrounds to those of the former state-controlled economies. Much enterprise has been concentrated in private hands, either founding families or those who enjoyed patronage of the state in running corporations. But as they open to outside sources of capital, they meet similar concerns about whether the corporation's funds will be managed in the interest of shareholders or exploited for private gain by controlling owners.

Developing capital markets, therefore, see much pressure towards convergence in the practice of corporate governance, coming in large part from internationally active institutional investors, whose interests are often very similar whether they are based in Paris, Frankfurt, Edinburgh or Fort Lauderdale in Florida. Because they are often the dominant players in investment markets when companies in the emerging markets are moving from state ownership to private control, we can expect their influence to become apparent in the way corporate governance takes hold in emerging economies. We look briefly at corporate governance in the countries the investment bank Goldman Sachs once dubbed the BRICs: Brazil, Russia, India and China.

Brazil and Latin America   A longstanding joke in global economics had it that Brazil is a country of great potential – and always will be. As the twenty-first century dawned, however, it looked as though that potential might finally be realized. With vast mineral resources and agricultural capabilities together with an educational system able to produce a highly talented workforce, Brazil has long had the makings of a major economic power. But politics, patronage and corruption seemed always to derail progress towards development of a modern economy. The corporate landscape was dominated by large family-owned and operated businesses, but political and currency instability long limited their potential by limiting access to foreign capital. Moreover, a cumbersome legal system, with courts that often lacked judges qualified in company law, deterred outside investors who feared their rights might not be upheld.

Recognizing these issues, Brazil started to develop a culture of improved corporate governance. A Brazilian Institute of Corporate Governance was formed in 1995 and developed standards in line with those developing around the world (see Chapter 6). The stock exchange in Sao Paulo developed requirements for companies, some of which came close to the standards foreign investors had demanded, that called for greater board independence and protection for minorities (IIF, 2004). One example of the changes is in Companhia de Concessões Rodoviárias, a toll-road builder and operator. The founding shareholders – enterprises from different parts of the country that combined their regional operations to increase their power in negotiating with government agencies – knew they needed market credibility to attract new capital for the business. It was not to be an easy task in light of the shareholder structure, however. So the board hired the consultants McKinsey & Co. to develop an approach that would contain the effect of potential conflicts of interest affecting the founding shareholders and the new shareholders' rights (IFC, 2006, gives a fuller account).

In some ways the work of the Brazilian Institute has become a model for companies based in other countries around Latin America. Despite – or perhaps because – Brazil is so different from the rest of the region, its efforts demonstrated that working with international investors on corporate governance could bring tangible benefits. But that did not eliminate all the potential for difficulties. When AmBev, Brazil's and Latin America's biggest brewery, merged with the Belgian beer-making giant Interbrew in 2004, minority shareholders protested loudly about how the terms favoured the founding family. The completion of the creation of the merged InBev took considerable time and negotiation to resolve issues over minority shareholders' interests.

Russia and the former communist states   After the collapse of the Soviet Union in 1991 and following the disintegration of its hold over eastern and central European states in 1989, the legacy state-owned enterprises faced pressure to raise capital from private sources. Rapid privatization of industry resulted in powerful individuals seizing effective control of one industry after another. But they needed to raise new funds from investors to modernize factories and develop new resources and sought to invite investors as well as managerial expertise from abroad.

Russia presented something of a special case in corporate governance. Seventy years of state ownership of the means of production and indeed of almost everything else left a legal system that offered little protection of property rights. The rapid privatization of enterprises in the early years of the new regime took the form of key individuals acquiring large stakes by buying up the vouchers offered to individual citizens. In some cases spontaneous privatizations occurred, in which managers of factories simply sold off the enterprises or their assets. But the need to expand required outside capital, and capital providers sought assurances – in part through an emphasis on mechanisms of corporate governance – that their stakes in the newly privatized companies would not be abused.

Stanislav Shekshnia tells the story of a Russian company, Loser, which in the throes of post-Soviet opening to foreign capital brought in a western investor as 75 per cent shareholder with the balance held by Russians. The boardroom became a battleground until the investors individually sought to bypass the board and take their wishes directly to management. The company went through five CEOs in rapid succession (Shekshnia, 2004). In a study of Russian state-owned enterprises, Alexander Filatov and colleagues (2005) found ministries would override what should have been board decisions or go directly to managers to implement the ministry's policies.

Many of these enterprises, in Russia, other eastern European states and in the Balkan region of the former Yugoslav republics, took guidance from the World Bank and its International Finance Corporation affiliate, or from the Organisation for Economic Co-operation and Development (for examples, see IFC, 2007; OECD, 2003). That pressure from the outside did not address the problems of self-dealing, government intervention and the abuse of minority shareholders, but it did at least draw attention to the risks of investing in the region and led to greater transparency and accountability than might otherwise have been the case.

India   India may have inherited much of its political and legal structures from Britain, but not its mode of doing business. For many years after independence in 1947, the Indian authorities supported with law and regulation mechanisms to protect the country from what they thought might become economic colonization through the back door. Though enterprise flourished to an extent, it did so largely on the basis of a domestic market, shielded from outside competition, with foreign ownership either not allowed or restricted to minority stakes that limited investor rights. While strategic alliances developed in many industrial sectors, the country suffered from a lack of capital to build world-class production capabilities. The families that controlled heavy industries like the Tata and Reliance Groups did well, but economic development was otherwise discouraged in a society with strong central government and state control.

With the start of the new century, some of that changed. Whether it was the success of the information technology sector, as the spread of the internet created new opportunities, or the collapse of an ideology of central control, after the collapse of the Soviet Union and as the country faced an exodus of many of its brightest scientists and entrepreneurs, a change in attitude led to an opening to foreign sources of capital, including much portfolio investment – shareholdings by foreign investors – on top of direct investment in plant and equipment. But this opening brought with it what must now seem like familiar issues in corporate governance: the power of founding shareholders and the possibility they would abuse the perceived rights of the new minority shareholders. Here, unlike in Russia and to some extent Brazil, there was at least a strong legal tradition and considerable respect for property rights. But the property that seemed to attract the greatest rights was that of Indian citizens, not foreign investors. Here, too, much needed to be done to give comfort to the providers of new capital. The traditional links to Britain came into play, and the forms of corporate governance rapidly evolved into something like the ones the UK had developed, that we explore more fully in Chapter 6. It was not enough, however, to prevent at least one case of malfeasance of international proportions – something the authorities wished they had not allowed to be copied from the West. We learn more of that case – Satyam – in Chapter 8.

China   The issues in corporate governance in China come from a different direction altogether, but they have a common refrain: how to protect the interest of outside investors from the power exerted by a dominant force, in this case the state. China's opening to outside investment initially came mainly in the form of foreign direct investment, in which companies in other countries would establish joint ventures with Chinese enterprises – some in state ownership, others in private hands – to build manufacturing facilities to exploit China's vast pool of inexpensive labour to meet demand for low-cost goods in the west. But an indigenous capital market sprang up, and, coupled with well-established markets in Hong Kong, in Chinese control since 1997, made China a magnet for portfolio as well as direct investors. Chinese companies quickly adopted many of the formal elements that such investors expected to see in companies, which included appointing foreign, independent directors to represent outside shareholder interests.

Agenda point 8: A Chinese solution to an international problem?

The growth of the Chinese economy and its importance for enterprises around the world is hard to underestimate. But much about the operation of Chinese corporations – including their practices of corporate governance – is less than clear. So there's a worrying sense for foreign direct investors and foreign institutional investors that buy into Chinese stocks that something could go wrong while they weren't watching. The recruitment firm Heidrick & Struggles, working with researchers at Fudon University, has published a study of Chinese board practices

(Cont'd)

---

that showed how they vary from what we see in western countries. Among the findings:

Strong chairmen: Like Chinese society, patriarchy – especially in private enterprises – prevails: The tendency of a 'weak board and strong chairman' is common. Boards tend to be tight-knit groups, built on business or personal networks. Independent directors are mostly brought in to fulfil legal requirement and are limited to advisory roles.

Board evaluation: Only 50 per cent of boards are evaluated, and their power to influence interests of those outside the boardroom is limited.

Nominations: Boards in China have limited influence on CEO selection. A high proportion of chairmen are also the CEO of the company. And except in private enterprises, boards have little influence on daily operational matters.

Committee work: The study shows that 71 per cent of boards in China have at least one supervisory committee. Of these, few have committees overseeing risk management, budgeting and accounting.

The report concludes: 'as China works to improve its corporate governance, it will continue to be influenced – but not controlled – by international standards. History shows that no matter which steps China takes to improve corporate governance, whatever emerges will be a distinctly Chinese solution.' (*The Board Agenda*, 14 October 2007; http://www.edgevantage.co.uk/categories/article. asp?i=3790.)

But form does not in itself create function. With the state never far in the background, too, the question always looms about whether boards of Chinese companies can or will reflect the interests of owners if those interests those differ from other of the state and the communist party that runs it.

Effectiveness, globalization and convergence

In law and in practice, then, corporate governance varies from country to country and from one legal tradition to another. Set against this, however, has been the tendency – in markets for goods and services, for capital, and for top managers – for corporations to be competing in the same ways. A company like Allianz, for example, works in markets around the world, and even in its home market – Germany – the rules under which it operates, either for its insurance products or in its investment activities, are increasingly similar to those in other European countries, thanks to the European Union's efforts to harmonize markets in financial services. Moreover, Allianz's corporate clients are often themselves global enterprises, seeking global insurance coverage from a company – and a board – that understands international business. Even if its shares were not held increasingly by globally active institutional investors, it is easy to see why in the twenty-first century a company like Allianz might take advantage of the opportunity to make its corporate governance less tied to the historical arrangements at home of twentieth or even the nineteenth centuries.

Product markets have left many companies wanting to achieve or retain competitiveness by exploiting the benefits of low-wage economies to undertake work with a large component of manual labour. We see this in the development of China as a base for manufacturing for companies around the world, and in the development of companies in India as everyone's outsourcing partner for information technology and related services. Risk management as well as efforts to build the corporation's reputation lead companies to develop operations in other countries. Sometimes it is a way of balancing costs against the revenues from international activities; sometimes it serves mainly to raise the profile of the company in foreign markets.

Capital markets are becoming more deeply integrated. The UK and the US provide the home to or the brainpower behind much of the institutional investment that has become the driving force in equity markets around the world. Much of the financial surpluses of oil-producing countries or the fast-growing economies in Asia have been reinvested through internationally active investment management firms either with a base in Britain or the United States, or through local firms drawing on western expertise. The growth of hedge funds, too, has arisen from the same culture, even though the funds themselves may be domiciled in offshore tax havens. Moreover, fund management firms in other markets – Germany, France – have adopted an increasing number of techniques and personnel with experience of Anglo-American approaches to investment. Major banks in Italy moved their asset management operations to Ireland for a combination of tax advantages and proximity to the investment management skills and knowledge of the UK.

One result has been increasing pressure from these firms on the boards of the companies in which they invest, pressure for boards to put the interests of shareholders first so they adopt the structures and processes seen as best practice. They have not, by and large, demanded a single set of rules for corporate governance, a feat that would prove difficult if not impossible to achieve under the varied legal practices and customs in different countries. But in the gap between law and board practice, they have sought to rein in the discretion that boards had in the past, exercising their individual – and sometimes their collective – voice to influence board decisions or using the exit, and thus punishing corporations through making more difficult their task of raising capital at favourable rates.

Institutional investors are not enamoured of corporate governance regimes, like Germany's, that give large amounts of formal power to the workforce. They cannot do much about it, apart from investing less in Germany than its economy would justify. But they can and did lobby for the European legislation that allowed Allianz to reincorporate as a *Societas Europaea*, setting an example for others operating internationally and seeking to reduce the size of their board and diminish the strength of a block of votes from the workforce of one country. But they also have expressed preferences (see ICGN, 2005, for an example) that companies adopt many of the most important practices and structures recommended in what we have come to call the Combined Code on corporate governance in the UK, whose origin and provisions we discuss at length in Chapter 6.

Further readings

Aguilera, R. V. & Jackson, G. (2003). The Cross-national Diversity of Corporate Governance: Dimensions and Determinants. *Academy of Management Review, 28*(3), 447–65.

Buck, T. & Shahrim, A. (2005). The Translation of Corporate Governance Changes across National Cultures: The Case of Germany. *Journal of International Business Studies, 36*(1), 42–61.

Charkham, J. (2005). *Keeping Better Company: Corporate Governance Ten Years On*. Oxford: Oxford University Press.

Chizema, A. & Kim, J. (2010). Outside Directors on Korean Boards: Governance and Institutions. *Journal of Management Studies, 47*(1), 109–29.

Goergen, M., Manjon, M. C. & Renneboog, L. (2008). Is the German System of Corporate Governance Converging towards the Anglo-American Model? *Journal of Management and Governance, 12*(1), 37–71.

Gordon, J. N. & Roe, M. J. (eds) (2004). *Convergence and Persistence in Corporate Governance*. Cambridge: Cambridge University Press.

La Porta, R., Lopez-de-Silanes, F. & Shleifer, A. (1998). Corporate Ownership Around the World. National Bureau of Economic Research. Retrieved 15 Jan. 2009, from http://ssrn.com/paper=103130.

La Porta, R., Lopez-de-Silanes, F. & Shleifer, A. (2008). The Economic Consequences of Legal Origins. *Journal of Economic Literature, 46*(2), 285–332.

Roe, M. J. (2003). *Political Determinants of Corporate Governance: Political Context, Corporate Impact*. Oxford: Oxford University Press.

SIX

Codes of corporate governance

Case: Adrian Cadbury and the power of 'non-executives'

The collapse of Maxwell Communication and Mirror Group Newspapers in 1991 (Case: Robert Maxwell, in Chapter 2) was not exactly a straw, but it broke the camel's back in the world of corporate governance. Britain had by then suffered three important corporate failures in rapid succession. The fall of the Bank of Credit and Commerce International was not quite a 'British' corporate governance failure – the bank was headquartered in Luxembourg with its origins in Pakistan – but it reflected badly on how Britain and the Bank of England in particular looked after the interests of investors. Polly Peck International, however, was more straightforward: a Turkish Cypriot entrepreneur turned a defunct company with a London Stock Exchange listing into a giant textile and fresh food import and export concern, propelling it into the ranks of the top 100 listed companies. But when its chairman and chief executive Asil Nadir fled the country for exile in northern Cyprus just before fraud charges were laid against him, it was clear that UK registration and a London Stock Exchange listing were not sufficient to protect investors. So when Maxwell failed, British industry decided that it needed to act (Wearing, 2005, describes all three cases).

The accountancy profession was particularly stunned. The UK Financial Reporting Council, at the time the self-regulatory body of the profession, sought out Sir Adrian Cadbury, scion of the family of famous English chocolatiers, to lead an inquiry to determine what accountants and audit could do to prevent another disaster. But Cadbury and his panel of experts decided to interpret their brief more widely. What emerged after 18 months was a package of recommendations that had sweeping impact on corporate governance around the world. The Cadbury Code (1992), a voluntary code of conduct for the boards of listed companies, almost certainly prevented the government from having to impose in law mandatory measures with much less freedom of action. It preserved some semblance of the self-regulation on which the 'City', London's financial district, had long prided itself.

Sir Adrian was in many ways an ideal person for the job. He came from a long line of Quaker businessmen and entrepreneurs. The Quakers are a religious sect with a strong pacifist leaning and an even stronger stance on the responsibilities of the wealthy and their businesses to social welfare. They campaigned against slavery in the early part of the nineteenth century, and for smoke abatement from the factories that grew all through the Industrial Revolution. The Cadbury chocolate factory, built in the late nineteenth century in Bournville, near Birmingham in the English Midlands, included a new town for its factory workers, a model of social awareness providing schools, parks and comfortable, beautiful and affordable homes at a time when 'industry' was often synonymous with 'exploitation'. More than a hundred years later, this village still attracts tourists and town planners from around the world to learn lessons in architecture and social welfare.

Sir Adrian was, therefore, the acceptable face of capitalism, on top of being a man of intellect and integrity. His recommendations included none of the radical notions some on the political left-wing had called for. There would be no wholesale effort to give workers greater rights – as they enjoyed in many continental European countries – nor any seats on boards of directors, as the workforces in German companies had. There would be no explicit requirement that directors look after the welfare of employees, suppliers or customers, as the social responsibility lobby had sought. All these might have been included in a revision of company law that the Labour party had promised, were it to win the election taking place that year. Indeed, the collapse of the Maxwell companies after their all-powerful chairman-*cum*-CEO had raided the workers' pension funds, might have been enough to precipitate a Labour victory in the polls, if the problem of corporate governance had been allowed to fester. The Conservatives just barely managed to stay in power in 1992, and when Labour did win power five years later, it was a different Labour party, a New Labour party, and one rather more sympathetic to the interests of corporations and their shareholders.

Questions arising

The Cadbury Code seems in hindsight a modest 'revolution' in governance, a non-binding arrangement for larger listed companies only.

1 What alternatives might there have been to an industry code?
2 What difference might it have made that the backing came from the accounting profession and the stock exchange?
3 How might the voluntary nature have improved compliance?
4 How might the threat of delisting have affected the willingness of boards to comply?
5 How important was the fact that the code came in response to a 'home-grown' crisis?

Codes of corporate governance

The events that precipitated the Cadbury inquiry were perhaps particular to Britain, but they had ramifications across Europe and around the world: voluntary codes of conduct in some countries, codes backed by legal sanctions in others, and even – after the Enron and WorldCom debacles – highly prescriptive legislative and regulatory approaches in Canada and especially the United States (for an overview of codes in selected countries, see Table 1 below). In this chapter, we review how codes of conduct developed around Europe and then in Asia, Latin America and elsewhere, before coming to the United States and the famous – some would say infamous – case of the Sarbanes–Oxley Act. We start, though, in the place where it all got started: the UK.

UK governance after Cadbury

What the Cadbury Code recommended was instead only a rather modest set of changes in corporate practice. There should be no more all-powerful chairmen and chief executives, where one person held the reins of the company, himself enjoying unbridled power, In the words of the Cadbury Code:

> Given the importance and particular nature of the chairman's role, it should in principle be separate from that of the chief executive. If the two roles are combined in one person, it represents a considerable concentration of power. We recommend, therefore, that there should be a clearly accepted division of responsibilities at the head of a company, which will ensure a balance of power and authority, such that no one individual has unfettered powers of decision. (provision 4.9, Cadbury, 1992)

Non-executive directors, people who were not employed by the company but sat on boards, should be given more power. Moreover, those non-executives ought to demonstrate independence from management: they should not be bankers, lawyers or other business people with whom the company did business or close friends or relatives of the chief executive or other senior managers. A majority of the board ought to be such independent, non-executive directors. 'This means that apart from their directors' fees and shareholdings, they should be independent of management and free from any business or other relationship which could materially interfere with the exercise of their independent judgement' (provision 4.12, Cadbury, 1992). These two provisions lie at the heart of the 90-page document, which also considered how directors might be trained, how they might seek professional assistance independent of management's advisers, what committees they ought to empanel, and what the scope of their activities might be.

Also at the core was a phrase that would be repeated in corporate governance codes around the world: 'comply or explain'. This was, at its heart, a voluntary code. Cadbury did not tell directors how to run their companies. The

Table 1   Spread of codes of corporate governance (source: adapted from ECGI)

Year	Europe	Americas	Middle East, Africa, Asia-Pacific	Multi-lateral
1992	UK: Cadbury			
1993				
1994		Canada: Toronto Report	South Africa: King I	
1995	France: Vienot; UK: Greenbury Report		Australia: Bosch Report, AIMA	
1996				
1997	Netherlands: Peters Report	US: Business Roundtable	Australia; Japan	
1998	Belgium: Cardon Report; France; Germany: KonTraG; Spain; UK: Hampel Report		India; Thailand: SET	
1999	France: Vienot II; Greece; Ireland; Italy (Preda); Portugal; UK: Turnbull Report	Brazil; Mexico; US: CalPERS	Australia; South Korea; Thailand	ICGN; OECD
2000	Belgium: Directors' Charter; Denmark; Germany; Romania; UK: Combined Code		India: Birla; Indonesia; Malaysia; Philippines: ICD	
2001	Czech Republic; Denmark: Nørby; Germany: Baums; Greece; Malta; Portugal; Sweden	Canada: Saucier Report; Peru; US: NACD	China; Indonesia; Japan; Singapore	
2002	Austria; Cyprus; France; Germany: Cromme; Hungary; Italy; Poland; Russia; Slovakia; Switzerland; UK: Institutional Shareholders Committee	Brazil; Peru; US: American Law Institute, Council of Institutional Investors, Business Roundtable, NYSE, Sarbanes-Oxley Act	Australia: Horwath Report; Kenya; Pakistan; Philippines; South Africa: King II; Taiwan; Thailand	
2003	Cyprus; Denmark; Finland; France; Germany: Cromme; Lithuania; Macedonia; Netherlands Tabaksblatt; Portugal; Spain: Aldama; Sweden: NBK; Turkey; Ukraine; UK: Higgs; Combined Code; Smith (audit)	Canada; US: Breeden Report, NYSE final rules, Nasdaq listing rules	Australia; New Zealand	Latin America white paper

Table 1   (Cont'd)

Year	Europe	Americas	Middle East, Africa, Asia-Pacific	Multi-lateral
2004	Belgium: Lippens (large firms); Czech Republic; France; Iceland; Poland; Slovenia; Spain; Sweden	Argentina; Brazil; US: CFA code for asset managers	Bangladesh; China; Japan; New Zealand	OECD
2005	Austria; Belgium: Buysse (small firms); Denmark; Germany: Cromme; Iceland; Latvia; Malta; Norway; Slovenia; UK (internal control)		Singapore	ICGN; OECD (state-owned)
2006	Austria; Cyprus; Estonia; Finland Germany: Cromme; Italy; Luxembourg; Norway; Portugal; Spain; Switzerland (family firms); UK: Combined Code	Canada; Jamaica; Trinidad & Tobago	Egypt; Indonesia; Lebanon; Nigeria; Sri Lanka; Thailand	
2007	Austria; Bulgaria; Germany; Hungary; Moldova; Norway; Poland; Portugal; Slovenia; Sweden; UK (private equity)	Colombia	Australia; Kazakhstan; Malaysia; UAE	
2008	Denmark: main code & private equity; Finland; France; Germany; Hungary; Italy (for banks); Netherlands; Serbia; Slovakia; Sweden; Switzerland; UK: Combined Code	US: NACD	Tunisia	Santiago Principles (sovereign wealth)
2009	Austria; Croatia; Belgium Germany; Iceland Luxembourg; Montenegro; Netherlands (banks); Norway; Romania; Sweden; UK: Walker Review (financial institutions)	Colombia	India; South Africa: King III	ICGN; OECD review
2010	Portugal; UK: Combined Code revised and renamed; Stewardship Code			

government would not either. Instead, directors would tell their shareholders why they had chosen not to follow the Cadbury recommendations. That, too, was voluntary, but a company might lose its listing on the London Stock Exchange if it failed to do so. This was not, therefore, quite the same thing as the cosy, gentlemanly self-regulation the City of London was famous for. Nor was it quite what we have come to call 'name and shame'. It was still gentlemanly, but rather less cosy than the system that had seemed to tolerate such malfeasance in the recent past.

The codes, combined

In the spirit that you cannot have too much of a good thing, further codes of conduct emerged. Public outrage in Britain over the large salary paid to the chairman of a formerly nationalized utility company newly listed on the stock exchange led to a new inquiry, chaired by Sir Richard Greenbury, chairman of Marks & Spencer, everyone's friendliest store. Greenbury's panel refused to succumb to the clamour for formal constraints on the remuneration of directors and senior managers. Instead, it urged that companies disclose in the annual report details of how much key individuals earned, following a practice then required in the United States. But in Britain, it would follow the Cadbury model of comply-or-explain, enforced by the London Stock Exchange, with the threat of delisting should the board refuse to explain any non-compliance (Greenbury, 1995).

Two years later another panel of eminent men, led by Sir Ronald Hampel, chairman of Imperial Chemical Industries, convened to reconsider the findings of Cadbury and Greenbury. Published in January the next year, the Hampel Code (1998) decried the practice of 'box-ticking' – in which investors and other interested parties looked for compliance with best practice codes, instead of seeking to understand that explanations of non-compliance. That led them to explore the company's and the board's relationships with external parties, making a more than passing reference to stakeholder theory: 'A company must develop relationships relevant to its success,' they wrote. 'These will depend on the nature of the company's business; but they will include those with employees, customers, suppliers, credit providers, local communities and governments. It is management's responsibility to develop policies which address these matters between companies and their shareholders.' But the duties to shareholders – and the board's obligation to communicate with them – remained at the centre: 'It is management's responsibility to develop policies which address these matters; in doing so they must have regard to the overriding objective of preserving and enhancing the shareholders' investment over time' (provision 1.16, Hampel, 1998). Boards should be 'responsible <u>for relations</u> with stakeholders; but they are accountable to shareholders' (provision 1.17, Hampel, 1998).

The primacy of shareholder interest thus asserted, Hampel's report also called upon shareholders – and especially the institutional investors who control much of the capital in listed company – to be responsible owners in their steward-ship of the company. Investors should make 'considered use' of their votes at shareholder meetings; boards and institutional shareholders should be ready to 'enter a dialogue'. Hampel's report wanted small investors to be involved too, but acknowledged the impracticality of that apart from at the annual share-holders meeting. The emphasis again was on comply-or-explain.

The three reports were then brought together into what came to be called the Combined Code on Corporate Governance later that same year, with the notion that it would be reviewed periodically. In 1999, yet another report emerged: Sir Nigel Turnbull discussed internal controls, including risk man-agement and internal audit. His panel concluded that it would be difficult for companies to explain their risk positions in detail in public. What they recom-mended was that the board state annually whether it had considered matters of risk, and if not to explain why it had not.

The Higgs Review and the Combined Code, revisited

The next major change to thinking about corporate governance in the UK arose not from a British problem, but from across the Atlantic. The sudden demise of the gas and electricity trading company Enron in 2001 – followed shortly there-after by the collapse of the telecommunications company WorldCom – rocked confidence in American capital markets. Enron had been called the best com-pany in the world. When it imploded, a sorry tale emerged of collusion between management and the company's auditors, Arthur Andersen, to move risky busi-ness off the company's balance sheet in a way that hid but did not eliminate the risk. Meanwhile, the company had encouraged employees to invest their self-administered, 401-K pension savings in shares of the company itself, adding fuel to the already supercharged share price. When the company disintegrated, many in the workforce lost their pension benefits as well as their jobs (for details see Wearing, 2005).

The response in the United States was a piece of legislation that made the most sweeping changes in US company law and securities markets since the Great Depression in the 1930s, the so-called Sarbanes–Oxley Act (Library of Congress, 2002). We will discuss it in a later section of this chapter, but the events that triggered the act also led the governments of Britain and many other countries to look hard at their own practices.

In the UK, what came about was the Higgs Review, named for Sir Derek Higgs, its principal author. Unlike the Cadbury Code and its offspring, this report was instigated by government. Since coming to power in 1997, the Labour government had been struggling with how to rewrite company law. Should the Combined Code be made statutory? What of comply-or-explain? Should stakeholder interests be enshrined as duties of corporate directors? The issues raised were so fiercely contested that legislation kept being delayed. In response to the emergency across the Atlantic, another review of voluntary arrangements seemed the prudent thing to do. But the Higgs Review (2003) would need to be more forceful than what had gone before.

Higgs made his recommendations in January 2003, six months after the Sarbanes–Oxley Act passed in the US Congress. On the same day another report of the accounting and audit profession (Smith, 2003) was published, with a strong push from government. A third independent report (Tyson, 2003), pushed again by the UK Department of Trade and Industry, tried to address issues about widening the representation on boards of directors by including more women, minorities, academics and others who were knowledgeable and talented by did not belong to the old boys' network that dominated British boardrooms.

This heavier hand of government was evident, too, in the detail of the Higgs recommendations on board practice. Non-executives would be deemed to lose their independence if they served more than three three-year terms on the board. All members of audit committee should be independent non-executive directors. Remuneration committees should be at least three members, all independent non-executives. Nomination committees should be made up of a majority of independent directors – the chairman could sit on the committee but not chair it, even if he or she were clearly independent of management. Moreover, no one independent non-executive should sit on all three committees. That too might concentrate power too strongly in one person's hands. Boards should undergo an annual performance appraisal, conducted by independent outsiders and examining the board as a whole, all board committees and each board member individually. New board members should undergo a formal induction to the company and the board and undertake training as a director. And a retiring chief executive should leave the board entirely, and certainly not become its chairman. As before, the recommendations were voluntary: comply or explain, said Higgs.

Though the Higgs recommendations were incorporated into the Combined Code later that year, some of the provisions caused such consternation among company chairmen that the Financial Reporting Council called for an early review, and in 2006 a few of the provisions were diluted. The 2008 revision made no further changes on matters of great substance. By adopting the Higgs recommendations, however, UK companies perhaps spared themselves an even more legalistic response to the troubles at Enron, WorldCom and the other problems in those early years of the new century. When the company law reform eventually passed (UK Parliament, 2006), directors' primary duties remained to shareholders, and even they had little extra scope to sue directors for improper actions. Comply-or-explain remained the watchword of corporate governance in the UK. Like Cadbury, the main thrusts of the Higgs Review would be widely copied around the world.

In early 2009, with the global economy reeling under the weight of the banking crisis, the UK Financial Reporting Council, the watchdog of the accountancy profession and custodian of the Combined Code, decided to look again at the code to determine what if anything needed to be changed. Was there a general failure of the code? Did banking and financial services require a different type of corporate governance than ordinary companies, given their central role in the economy?

Beyond Higgs

The financial crisis of 2007–9 prompted a fresh review of the Combined Code and a special report looking into possible changes in corporate governance for financial institutions (Walker, 2009a, 2009b). The two-stage Walker Report argued that financial services played a special role in the economy and perhaps needed somewhat different treatment. Sir David Walker questioned the balance between independence and expertise in the boardroom. One of the problems in the financial crisis came from a lack of understanding by senior bankers of the risks associated with structured products using derivatives in complex combinations. One cost of having independent non-executives dominating boards would be even less expertise.

His first report, which like the final version did not crack down on remuneration policies, promptly met with criticism from one of the ministers in the UK Treasury Department, who suggested more radical steps might be needed, including much broader transparency about pay level – and not just of directors and senior managers. The minister – Paul Myners, who had a long career in investment management and as a company chairman before joining government – even suggesting copying the French idea of double voting (Peston, 2009).

A review of the Combined Code the same year (Financial Reporting Council, 2009) followed to some extent Walker's ideas that formal independence needed to be balanced with expertise, accepting at least implicity that the pendulum had swung too far. To increase board accountability, however, the new version in 2010, now called the UK Corporate Governance Code, urged the largest 350 companies to put all directors up for election every year. It also joined Walker's suggestion of a voluntary code of stewardship for investors, urging asset management firms, pension funds and insurers to take a more active interest in what happens inside the companies in which they invest.

Governance codes in Europe

The Cadbury Code itself sparked reflection on governance practices in other European countries, though it took the dot-com collapse and Enron to create a wave of interest in establishing firmer guidelines concerning monitoring and control. The European Union also has considered whether an overarching set of principles might be appropriate, but it backed away from the notion in view of opposition from member states, based on persisting structural differences in national law, custom and practice. The EU has, however, pursued a more general approach in seeking to eliminate barriers that have tended to prevent shareholders in one country from exercising their voting rights in another. The following discussion of the codes in several European countries seeks to show the similarities while highlighting differences as well.

France

In France, Cadbury's conclusions prompted the Vienot Code in France. Its first iteration came in 1995, three years after the Cadbury Code, and it acknowledged its heritage in the opening section. 'Privatization and the growing presence of non-resident investors on the Paris stock market has led to the rapid emergence of a new type of shareholder with little knowledge of the rules and practices applied by the boards of directors of listed companies in France,' it said in its introduction. 'Such shareholders have naturally sought clarification.' But it was more than a descriptive document, for the benefit of 'non-resident', that is, British institutional investors.

Backed by industry – the inquiry was launched by two lobbying organizations, the federation of employers CNPF and the association of private business AFEP – the Vienot report did not seek to overturn existing practice, but rather to explain and spread to other companies the practices it found of value. In contrast to Cadbury, Vienot I, as the 1995 code was known, defended the power concentrated in the hands of the chairman of the board, who was also, de facto, chief executive officer: 'Separation of authority is not a universal remedy,' it stated (Veniot, 1995, p. 10). But French law gives companies the option of choosing a single board combining executive and non-executive directors, or a two-tier board, like those in Germany. Companies wishing for a greater separation of powers could adopt the latter, Vienot suggested. The code was mindful of the risks of conflicts of interest, and urged boards – for the sake of their reputations with capital markets – to take steps to reinforce independence of judgement in the boardroom. It urged that the balance of directors in unitary boards not be in favour of executive directors. It also opposed inclusion of directors representing special interest groups, a practice that had been commonplace. In recognition of the issues faced by minority shareholders where a large, controlled owner dominates, Vienot urged appointment of several independent directors to provide a counterbalance to the controlling shareholder's voice on the board.

Subsequent revisions, taking into account changes in legal frameworks, brought recommendations further into line with the model established in the UK Combined Code. They highlighted the possibility of separating the role of chairman and CEO in companies with unitary boards, echoing the Cadbury Code, and urged that a majority of board members be independent non-executives. The 2003 versions expanded recommendations concerning board practices including definitions of independence and the need for formal evaluations of board performance, preferably by external consultants, and suggested that non-executive directors should meet periodically without the presence of executives, when they would evaluate the work of the chairman and CEO.

Germany

Board practices were already more heavily prescribed by law in Germany than in many other countries, but the wave of concern over corporate governance swept them along in the aftermath of the collapse of Enron and other companies in 2001 and 2002. The Cromme Commission, named for the supervisory board chairman of steelmaker Thyssen AG who headed the inquiry, came up with a new voluntary code that was, nonetheless, anchored in law. Like the UK Combined Code and the French codes, it too suggested that boards have the freedom not to comply with its recommendations. But companies were required by law to report publicly on their compliance and on the explanations they gave for any deviation from it. The Cromme Code was published in 2002 and then amended and strengthened just a few months later, in the immediate aftermath of the Higgs Review in the UK.

Analogously to Britain, the German code sought to increase the independence of supervisory boards by requiring that members of the audit committee should not be former members of the management of the company. It allowed the supervisory board chairman to be a member of the audit committee, though not lead it. It sought to limit the numbers of former management board members on the supervisory board to two. In contrast to the UK, it stipulated that the supervisory board chairman should chair committees that dealt with contracts with the management board members. Stirring the greatest controversy, it sought to prevent former management board members from becoming chairman of the supervisory board and asked for publication of executive pay on an individual basis. This final provision was the one that saw the greatest resistance from company boards (von Werder & Talaulicar, 2006, 2007, 2009).

Sweden

The Swedish code grew from developments in the UK in the early 1990s too, and was influenced by the Organisation for Economic Co-operation and Development and the European Union. The Swedish Companies Act and traditional Swedish corporate governance principles differ in several ways from the British and American approach as well, but it explicitly echoed Cadbury and the Combined Code in its adherence to the principle of comply-or-explain. In protecting disproportionate voting rights for certain classes of shareholders at many companies, Sweden does not enshrine equal treatment of all shareholders and the independence of directors in quite the same way as other codes. 'Swedish society takes a positive view of major shareholders taking particular responsibility for companies by using seats on boards of directors to actively influence governance,' the 2008 version of the code says. 'At the same time, major holdings in companies must not be misused to the detriment of the company or the other shareholders' (Swedish Corporate Governance Board, 2008, p. 10). Stock exchange rules mean that few listed companies have more than one executive on the board – usually the CEO – so the majority is made up of non-executives. But tied directors play an important role in representing the interests of holders of shares with multiple voting rights.

Committee processes give Swedish shareholders – and therefore the holders of multiple voting rights – more voice than in many other countries. Members of the nominations committee, for example, are appointed by shareholders directly, in the annual meeting, or specify how they should be selected. Separation of the chairman and CEO roles is not mandated in the code, but if the roles are combined the board should make a clear statement of the division of work, so as to point out that the CEO is subsidiary to the board. While the chairman may chair the remuneration committee, other committee members should be independent of management, if not entirely independent of important shareholders. Moreover, shareholders should be given the right to review all equity-related pay plans for senior management. The audit committee should be entirely independent of management, too. Annual board evaluations should take place, in line with the Higgs recommendations in the UK.

Belgium

Belgium represents something of a special case in corporate governance, not least because of the prominence of major shareholders – founding families, banks and key investors – in virtually all major companies. Other countries in Europe also have large blocks of shares in the hands of powerful owners, but in few places is it as universal as in Belgium. Moreover, in few places did the effort to account for their interests in the corporate governance code run into such opposition from international investors. When the Lippens Committee convened in 2004 to revamp three partial codes of conduct, it felt it needed to accommodate in formal structures the role of the chairman, most often a representative of the major shareholder.

Corporate governance in the United States

Scholars of US foreign policy often write about 'American exceptionalism'. The same could be said about corporate governance. The American system is highly legalistic, and discussions of corporate governance are full of compliance with the rules laid down by the US Securities and Exchange Commission and the threat of shareholder lawsuits. Far from the gentlemanly codes in the UK, and inspired in part by an accounting profession worried about it reputation, US corporate governance practice is widely described as being driven by lawyers looking to help their clients avoid fees, fines and possibly jail.

Historically, the practice of corporate governance was different, as we have seen, with early development of capital markets that favoured widely dispersed shareholdings, the persistence of a large retail market for shares long after the development of institutional investment practices, and an infrastructure – through disclosure regulations and the means of communicating information to the investing public – designed to protect investors to a far greater extent than in other capital markets. We revisit this subject at length in Chapter 12.

As we have seen in Chapter 5, these conditions led to a rather different way of organizing boards of directors and their relations with shareholders. Laws to protect corporate managements from the influences of noisy shareholders exercising their voice were matched by laws to give nosy shareholders the information they needed to exercise their right to exit in an intelligent way. This controlled stalemate persisted for a long time, even through the period of the corporate raiders in the 1980s who sought to shake up managements through proxy battles and greenmailing, as state laws allowed corporation to build defences in the form of poison pills or through statutes that made hostile takeover bids difficult to mount.

With the collapse of Enron, WorldCom and others in the early 2000s, however, the public mood changed. Enron's failure exposed not just a risk to shareholders but to employees, pensioners, suppliers, customers, and the company's counterparties among financial institutions in its extensive derivatives business. Followed promptly by WorldCom and others – and with its roots in the apparent willingness of staff from its audit firm, Arthur Andersen, to collude in the financial chicanery – Enron led to a widespread loss of public confidence in the American system of capitalism. The once imperious SEC became suddenly quite sheepish that it had not performed its duties very well. Perhaps the heavy handed interpretation of rules by the SEC staff, who trained in the main as lawyers, had inspired the lawyers working for corporations to look for defensible loopholes rather than complying with the spirit of the law.

Perhaps the strict, precise and detailed accounting standards, independently set but in many ways subject to SEC approval, were too strict, too precise and too detailed. In the view of many commentators, the unthinkable was about to happen. The US – through the SEC and the Financial Accounting Standards Board – was poised to admit that US capital markets had something to learn from the rest of the world. In a series of steps, the SEC and FASB set the US on a course that would see it adopt the main tenets of the newly promulgated International Financial Reporting Standards. The SEC, in a controversial series of votes, some of which would later be overturned, sought to give more power to shareholders, more along the lines of European practice. An official of the SEC and other regulatory and industry agencies began to speak aloud about the virtues of key aspects of corporate governance as developed in the UK Combined Code.

Most directly in response to the WorldCom case, New York State authorities asked Richard Breeden, a former chairman of the New York Stock Exchange, to make recommendations about corporate governance and financial markets. Called *Restoring Trust* (Breeden, 2003), the report's findings endorsed what was by now the dominant UK view that the role of chairman and chief executive should be separated. His was a nuanced view, citing advantages and disadvantages, and one worth considering in some detail (see Agenda point 9), as it highlights the issues that surround what was becoming a 'standard' view of corporate governance.

Agenda point 9: *Restoring Trust*

'In Europe and particularly the United Kingdom, a structure utilizing a "non-executive" Chairman of the Board and a separate CEO is commonly used. This structure is not a panacea for fixing all governance problems. Indeed, the old WorldCom was one of the few major US public companies that had separated the positions of Chairman and CEO, yet this structure did not prevent either the financial fraud or the gross abuses involving [Bernie] Ebbers' [the WorldCom CEO] compensation and loans. However, in the old WorldCom structure, the Chairman was essentially powerless. Enron also used a variant of this structure, while Tyco had a "lead director", in both cases to no avail.

'Separation of the offices of Chairman and CEO, like any structural reform, is dependent on other factors to make it most successful. A Chairman who is disengaged or overly deferential to the CEO may not only fail to provide board leadership, but this may also delay board action if other board members rely on a chairman who fails in the role. Also, this structure can create confusion and a corrosive effect on overall managerial leadership if the chairman is perceived to be a rival for internal power and does not strictly respect the "non-executive" nature of the role. A separate non-executive Chairman must be extremely cautious to avoid creating issues of divided loyalty or confusion as to the overall status of management.

'Despite these potential drawbacks, the "non-executive Chairman" structure offers considerable potential advantages when used properly. First, for a board with frequent meetings and active committees, the time commitment for coordinating activities of committee chairmen and individual board members can be very significant. Since most CEOs will not have the time to do this personally, board communications may be delegated to a General Counsel, Corporate Secretary or other member of management. This is undesirable, as board leadership then rests on a non-board member. Thus, creating a non-executive 'Chairman separate from the CEO will facilitate adequate time being devoted at a very high level to board interaction and communication. This should facilitate an active and involved board, which is essential to healthy governance.

'A second advantage of this structure is its superiority in creating checks and balances against excessive executive power. Boards will most often be strongly supportive of the CEO and management team, and there should not be any suggestion that conflict or contention is desirable. Nonetheless, the fact remains that CEOs and their management teams will be naturally defensive of their own policies and management decisions, sometimes even in the face of evidence that performance has been poor. On specific issues ranging from compensation to potential removal of a CEO or succession planning, a non-executive Chairman creates a greater likelihood that the board's discussions will happen earlier, and will be more candid and robust, than under a combined Chairman and CEO.

'The separation of Chairman and CEO roles can create strong benefits when the right two individuals serve in these respective roles and work together smoothly, but the structure can also become a disadvantage if disharmony results. The advantages and disadvantages of the two structures will be affected to some degree by the chemistry of the individuals and the dynamics of a particular board and its members.

'Recommendation 2.01. Non-Executive Chairman.

'Though there are pros and cons, overall the separation of the role of board leadership from management leadership seems desirable . . . ' (Excerpt from *Restoring Trust* (Breeden, 2003, pp. 70–2).

The thinking that went into Breeden's report helped to inform decisions by the New York Stock Exchange (2003) to modify its corporate governance guidelines to listed companies. NYSE did not demand a separation of roles of the CEO and Chair, but it did urge companies to appoint a lead independent director if they chose to allow one person to occupy both the chairmanship and chief executive posts. Moreover, NYSE followed Breeden's guidance to make board membership more openly independent of management and to put more power in the hands of these 'outside' directors through their committee structures, much as Cadbury had recommended in the UK in 1992, and Higgs had strengthened very early in 2003, several months before the Breeden report. The NYSE rules used language similar to the UK Combined Code in asking companies to explain why they had chosen not to follow some of its recommendations. The Nasdaq Stock Market, where many of America's technology companies were listed, also adopted similar ideas (Nasdaq, 2002, 2008).

While these changes took America down a route similar to the one Europe was following, the biggest change in corporate governance practice came not in codes of conduct, but in statute: the Sarbanes–Oxley Act (Library of Congress, 2002). Sarbox – one of several nicknames the act would attract – sought to assert federal law in areas that had previously been the preserve of the individual states. Its most important features required the chief executive officers and chief financial officers to certify personally the accuracy of their companies' financial statements, in both annual and quarterly statements to shareholders. If the information proved to be inaccurate, they face criminal sanctions, including prison, and not just action in the civil courts. Sarbox also created a new body called the Public Company Accounting Oversight Board, or PCAOB,[1] independent of but reporting to the SEC to monitor the accountancy profession, ending a century or more of self-regulation.

Sarbanes–Oxley also required, through a deceptively simple clause, that corporations pay much stricter attention to risk management. Section 404 demanded that a corporation's annual report '(1) state the responsibility of management for establishing and maintaining an adequate internal control structure and procedures for financial reporting; and (2) contain an assessment, as of the end of the most recent fiscal year of the issuer, of the effectiveness of the internal control structure and procedures of the issuer for financial reporting' (Library of Congress, 2002, p. 45). Auditors were required to 'attest to' management's statements. Moreover, Sarbox required that these provisions apply to all companies with securities – equities or bonds – listed on US exchanges. Auditors of such companies would need to register with the PCOAB and be subject to its oversight, irrespective of where they were based.

It is not surprising the Sarbanes–Oxley Act also came to be known as the 'law of unintended consequences' (Fletcher & Miles, 2004, p. 70), and not just Sarbox, SOX, SOx and some less gentle names. As a direct consequence of the law, corporate and investor organizations in Europe, backed quietly by their governments, successfully lobbied with the SEC to relax its stringent rules about how companies, once listed on a US exchange, could delist their shares or bonds and end their requirement to file financial statements with the SEC and comply with Sarbox. Several dozen companies from Europe promptly did so. Moreover, the law was widely thought to have led many companies in the emerging capital markets in China, Russia, central and eastern Europe and elsewhere to choose to raise funds in the London or Hong Kong markets, instead of listing on NYSE or Nasdaq.

Canada, with its close links to US capital markets, took steps that largely mirrored those south of the border. With the more general wave that swept around the world, it would modify its practices to come somewhat more into line with those following the broad outlines of the UK Combined Code.

Emerging economies and codes of corporate governance

This emergent codification of best practice was not limited to developed capital markets, either. Companies and stock exchanges that were developing in places like Romania, Serbia, Bosnia-Herzegovina, Albania, Kazakhstan and elsewhere joined established but small capital markets in Latin America, Asia and Africa in following advice coming from multilateral organizations including the Organisation for Economic Co-operation and Development and the World Bank about how best to attract funding from internationally active investors by demonstrating that the companies seeking foreign investment were ready to comply with internationally recognized norms of corporate governance.

OECD

From their first publication (1999) and subsequent revision (2004), the OECD Principles of Corporate Governance were intended as much for countries outside the organization's 30 large industrial economies as for those within it. The OECD, using the model of the UK Combined Code, laid out more general provisions than the UK's but with broad thematic similarities. It laid out the need for a framework in law to provide the basis for effective corporate governance, and detailed rights of shareholders and how they should be treated fairly. The principles took an open approach to the issues of stakeholder rights, saying they should be respected where established in law. Employee participation in corporate governance should be permitted to develop, the OECD said, when those mechanisms enhanced performance. While its steered clear of giving specific guidance on matters like the relationship between the chair and CEO or the structure of committees, the OECD principles set out the responsibilities of the board as those of reviewing and guiding strategy, monitoring the effectiveness of governance practices as well as the company's executives, and performing the functions of selecting management, setting their pay, nominating new board members and ensuring the independence of the audit. Boards should be able to exercise 'objective independent judgement', and to do so they should have access to 'accurate, relevant and timely information' (OECD, 2004, p. 25). The emphasis the OECD principle place on monitoring conflicts of interest is reinforced in the annotations to the principles with their concern for controlling related party transactions, in which the company does business with organizations closely tied to its management, directors or major shareholders.

World Bank and IFC

The World Bank and its affiliate the International Finance Corporation promote principles of corporate governance to the governments, stock exchanges and other bodies in developing countries around the world. Indeed, the close cooperation between them and the OECD has led countries emerging from communist rule as well as others in less developed parts of the world to establish institutes of directors, create local codes of conduct, and introduce rules of disclosure designed to offer transparency of corporate decisions and thus give outside investors the chance to make better informed decisions.

The IFC, which specializes in financing the development of private sector enterprises, advocates what it calls the 'irresistible case for corporate governance' in these terms: 'Good corporate governance will not just keep your companies out of trouble. Well-governed companies often draw huge investment premiums, get access to cheaper debt, and outperform their peers' (IFC, 2005, p. 1).

In 2007, for example, the IFC published a manual of corporate governance specifically tailored to the needs of Serbia (IFC, 2007), just a few years after the country was bombed by forces from the North Atlantic Treaty Organization in the final stages of the ethnic strife set off by the break-up of the old Yugoslavia. One of the steps seen as necessary to the integration of Serbia with the democracies of Europe was to create an active private sector economy. Following the path of the former Soviet bloc states, Serbia created a domestic capital market, privatized state enterprises, and invited foreign direct investment and portfolio investment to underpin economic development. Progress towards good corporate governance was viewed as a prerequisite for attracting foreign institutional investors to provide the capital necessary for the country's economy to move forward. The manual explains the basics of what a company is and does and speaks about shareholder meetings, the role of the board of directors, codes of ethics, board procedures, director duties, structures and processes. While tailored to the legal frameworks of the country, many of its provisions are drawn from blueprints developed in other settings.

Other advocates

These multilateral bodies are joined by a variety of private sector advocacy groups that have spread the doctrine of corporate governance to emerging economies. For example, the International Institute of Finance, a research group funded by major banks from around the world, created an equity market advisory group in 2001 to help companies in emerging economies to develop their share capital, rather than relying on bank debt. Its code of corporate governance (IIF, 2003) was developed explicitly following the principles of the UK Combined Code, UK audit committee guidance, the recommendations of the Higgs Review in the UK and the New York Stock Exchange guidelines on the role of non-executive directors.

Convergence in corporate governance codes

What the Cadbury Code set off was a collective reflection – among industry, the investment community and regulators – to find better recipes about how to run corporations. There are still substantial differences in the way corporate governance works in different countries. Even governments, stock exchanges and corporations in emerging markets face choices between differing systems as they emerge into the world of capital markets. The Serbian example cited above involved a decision to adopt, in the main, a two-tier board system modelled broadly on the German one, in recognition of the fact that enterprises passing into the private sector would need to retain legitimacy with the population as they undertook the necessary restructuring and the consequent job cuts that would entail.

But the two-tier system and a system under which large blockholders dominate decision-making are not favoured by internationally active, institutional investors. Still less do they like governments to have direct power over corporate affairs on top of the indirect power they exert through company law, regulation and, of course, taxation. The balance, though, has been to favour those investment institutions from abroad for the sake of raising the necessary capital to fund economic growth. So systems that differ widely from those in place in Britain and the United States are often discussed as transitional, helping companies and capital markets in those countries get used to the ideas and implications of a free market in corporate equity.

Among the developed economies, the power of these investors has been, if anything, even greater in setting the agenda for corporate governance. Increasingly, global markets for goods and services have meant that companies must also compete for the lowest cost of capital. If the great pools of savings represented by institutional investors can be tapped only by ceding greater power to these investors, then corporate governance will be under pressure to change to meet their wishes. We saw this in Belgium, when the code of corporate governance that emerged from the 2004 consultations differed in significant regards from the original draft. The drafters wanted to recognize the realities of investment patterns in the country, and allowed company chairmen, with their close links to dominant shareholders, a rather larger voice in the boardroom than the UK Combined Code did, especially following the Higgs Review of 2003. The code that emerged in Belgium limited the chairman's influence and gave more power and authority to independent non-executives.

Even in Germany, where law and custom enforce a vastly different approach to board structure and duties, the code of corporate governance made significant nods to Anglo-American practice and especially to the approach in the UK. The issues there focused on executive pay more than board structure, and what emerged was a policy on the disclosure of individual executives' earnings that many German executives had fiercely resisted. It was a provision that would be honoured perhaps more in the breach than the observance, as company after company invoked its comply-or-explain provisions not to give the details.

But German capital market practice had already begun to shift towards the Anglo-American ones as companies sought to gain competitive advantage through better access to capital. Following a tax change in the 1990s, German financial institutions moved to reduce or eliminate many of their large investments in manufacturing companies and to give up their seats on German corporate supervisory boards. This gave foreign investors greater comfort that the companies would be run more in the interest of all shareholders, rather than in the interests of the banks and insurance companies. In countries that followed that example, the share of foreign ownership of the equities of domestics business rose.

Capital markets – like markets for goods and services – have become increasingly global in character. In some countries, the World Bank funds early stage development and the IFC development of domestic capital markets. Members of private sector institutions like the IIF help develop those markets and build domestic pools of savings which join foreign pools of savings in pension funds, insurance companies and mutual funds who seek to achieve gains while diversifying their risk. Their interests begin to look more like each others' than they do the interests of any individual government or national system of corporate finance. The largest of these funds are in Britain and America, where the practice of active, liquid and powerful capital markets has the longest history. It is not surprising, then, to see similar institutional investors develop in countries like Germany, France, Japan, South Korea and elsewhere in the world, and then see them join together in bodies like the International Corporate Governance Network, a club of institutional investors, to demand roughly comparable systems of corporate governance around the world. Their agenda – of board independence, of constraints on the power of large shareholders, of mechanisms to maintain the voting rights of minority shareholders, of disclosure in sufficient detail that a distant shareholder, can monitor the business of 'one share, one vote' – looks similar even in countries with differing legal traditions and in differing levels of economic development.

The similarities of interest arise in part because the problems in corporate governance are similar. Agency problems, related to hiring self-serving managers who need monitoring, exist wherever there is a separation of ownership from control. They are complicated when one shareholder has the power to extract benefits from the corporation at the expense of other shareholders. Codes of corporate governance are meant to address these problems, to the benefit of shareholders. And some shareholders are more likely to benefit from these safeguards than others: the internationally active institutional shareholders which promote these codes.

Left unaddressed by the codes of corporate governance, though, is the other side of the board's agenda and in the eyes of some scholars and many practitioners the more important part: that of value creation. The codes in the main do not make recommendations about how to structure a board of directors so it is able to marshal the resources necessary to take best advantage of business opportunities. They describe the need for boards, populated with independent non-executive directors, to have control over audit and with it the corporation's finances. They emphasize the need for those non-executives to hold sway over the nomination of new directors, and with it the appointment of a new chief executive, a new finance director and the other new directors who might have close ties to the executives or ties to a dominant shareholder. They emphasize as well the need for non-executives to control the remuneration policy and the specific level of pay set for the most senior executives in the business. What they do not mention, except perhaps in passing, is the need for companies to create value, and with it any need for the board to be involved in setting and determining strategy.

These codes are backed by reporting obligations, forcing boards to account for their approach to corporate governance and especially any deviation they choose to make from the norm. These disclosure obligations force boards to report on their activities, giving the power of information to shareholders – and especially the large institutional investors who have an incentive to care and some degree of power either to provide capital or to harm the company's cost of capital by selling off their holdings. We will see in the next chapters how this general approach to corporate governance affects some of the key issues on the agenda of shareholders.

Notes

1 The use of the masculine is conscious here. Chief executives and indeed boards of directors were overwhelmingly male preserves at the time. Not surprisingly, therefore, abuses in corporate governance came overwhelmingly in companies where men were in charge.
2 The unwieldy acronym led many people to call it 'Peek-a-boo' instead.

Further readings

Aguilera, R. V. & Cuervo-Cazurra, A. (2009). Codes of Good Governance. *Corporate Governance: An International Review, 17*(3), 376–87.

ECGI (undated). Index of Codes. *European Corporate Governance Institute.* Retrieved 28 June 2008, from http://www.ecgi.org/codes/all_codes.php.

Enrione, A., Mazza, C. & Zerboni, F. (2006). Institutionalizing Codes of Governance. *American Behavioral Scientist, 49*(7), 961–73.

Hermes, N., Postma, T. J. B. M. & Zivkov, O. (2006). Corporate Governance Codes in the European Union: Are They Driven by External or Domestic Forces? *International Journal of Managerial Finance, 2*(4), 280–301.

Lane, C. (2003). Changes in Corporate Governance of German Corporations: Convergence to the Anglo-American Model? *Competition & Change, 7*(2/3), 79–100.

Seidl, D. (2007). Standard Setting and Following in Corporate Governance: An Observation-Theoretical Study of the Effectiveness of Governance Codes. *Organization, 14*(5), 705–27.

Seidl, D. & Sanderson, P. (2009). Applying 'Comply-or-Explain': Conformance with Codes of Corporate Governance in the UK and Germany. Retrieved 29 June 2009, from http://www.jbs.cam.ac.uk/news/events/governancesymposium/downloads/seidl.pdf.

Weil Gotshal & Manges. (2002). Comparative Study of Corporate Governance Codes Relevant to the European Union and Its Member States. Retrieved 28 June 2008, from http://ec.europa.eu/internal_market/company/docs/corpgov/corp-gov-codes-rpt-part1_en.pdf.

Zattoni, A. & Cuomo, F. (2008). Why Adopt Codes of Good Governance? A Comparison of Institutional and Efficiency Perspectives. *Corporate Governance: An International Review, 16*(1), 1–15.

PART 2

Issues on the board's agenda

In this section we explore in greater detail the issues that confront boards of directors as they seek to implement principles of corporate governance.

Issues within the board: What are the roles and responsibilities of the board? How is it organized?

Issues between boards and management: First and foremost are the questions arising from agency theory of how to address the possibility of self-dealing by senior managers and how companies have sought to use incentives through remuneration to keep managers' interest aligned with those of shareholders. We also consider how boards are involved in developing strategy and monitoring its progress.

Issues between boards and owners: The relationship between companies and shareholders takes us to consideration of shareholder rights in different countries and how, with the growth of global asset management firms, practice in investor relations has changed. We look at shareholder activism and how it has developed over time. We also revisit the issue of nominations of new directors, and mechanisms like poison pills and other anti-takeover devices that can entrench boards and managers while restricting the ability of shareholders to cash out of their investments.

Issues between owners: Shareholder interests have never been identical, although many discussions of corporate governance act as though they are. In this chapter we consider the range of different stances that shareholders may take and pay special attention to the role that newer forms of investors take – hedge funds, private equity firms and sovereign wealth funds – and consider their impact on the power balances that boards face.

Issues between the company and its publics: This chapter looks at growing calls for corporate social responsibility and how companies and their boards respond to them. Sustainability – once a part of the social responsibility debate – has taken on a life of its own with increasing awareness that political attention to climate change is likely to force changes to business policy as well.

SEVEN

Issues within the board

Case: Sparks at Marks & Spencer

Comply or Explain? Or was that: Comply or Complain? The board of the UK's iconic retailer Marks & Spencer spent most first half of 2008 in the corporate governance doghouse. It flouted the provisions of the UK Combined Code. The transgression was worse: it sinned against the Cadbury Code of 1992, which kicked off the global corporate governance movement. (See the discussion in Chapter 6 above.) Cadbury demanded the then unthinkable: that no one person should be both chairman and chief executive officer of a public company. It is now widely accepted as the most basic of governance norms in the UK and many places beyond. Even in America, home of the joint chairman–CEO, it is the preferred form in New York Stock Exchange corporate governance guidelines. The Cadbury Code – and the many worldwide that followed its lead – made its strictures optional, subject to a regime under which companies would have to explain why they had chosen not to comply. This time, M&S had gone too far.

The new chairman: Stuart Rose was brought into M&S as CEO in 2004, when the company was reeling. He warded off a hostile takeover bid, revitalized the product line, and launched a spectacular new advertising campaign that on its own boosted the share price by 9 per cent in just a few days. It was not a flash-in-the-pan, either. The changes stuck, the share price did well relative to the market as a whole, and M&S became a marketing case study – for the right reasons – again. But less than four years into the job, Rose wanted more. In early 2008, Terence Burns, the former civil servant who joined the M&S board in 2005 and has chaired it since 2006, wanted to retire. But rather than recruit a new chairman, the board decide to accede to Rose's wish be take on the chairmanship himself. A press release was drafted and sent out and no sooner had the email arrived with institutional investors but the clamouring for Combined Code compliance began.

Compliance or defiance? In a press statement on 10 March, Lord Burns wrote: 'My main tasks as Chairman have been to rebuild the Board and to put in place the right leadership for the future. Since Stuart returned to M&S, the Company has made substantial progress. It is my view and the unanimous view of the Independent Directors, that placing Stuart in this new role creates the right leadership structure for the Company. Stuart has the unique skills to continue the challenge of making M&S a world class retailer, and to develop the future leaders of the business.' It was not what those in the governance world considered an explanation, even if they were willing to consider this provision one that was still subject to comply-or-explain. Normally institutional investors take such matters quietly to the board for a discussion. Not this time. A noisy campaign, fronted by the fund managers at the insurance company Legal & General, developed through the press. On 3 April, the board, through Lord Burns, issued another, fuller statement, this time as a letter to shareholders. It put a time limit on the arrangement. After three years, the company would 'revert to conventional Chairman and Chief Executive roles' after Rose's retirement – or, as the statement curiously said, 'his departure'.

Why? The heart of any explanation has to answer that question. The Burns letter did not, except obliquely, after you read between the lines. The nomination committee wanted to prolong Rose's employment beyond the end of his current contract in to 2009 and discussed an appropriate time period for such an extension. The reason: to give the new crop of managers time to show their stuff, preparing for an orderly, internal succession. 'For this new structure to work optimally, the Board considered that it was important to give space for the senior management to develop in their roles over time. For this reason, the proposal for Stuart to take up the role of Executive Chairman forms an integral part of the overall Executive team,' Burns wrote. 'The option to confirm that Stuart was leaving in 2009 and that we were starting the process of finding a new Chief Executive was not considered an attractive alternative.' But an orderly succession in 2011 does not require that Rose becomes chairman in 2008. All it would take is for Rose to extend his contract as CEO and give his employees a little more breathing space, something any disciplined manager ought to be able to do.

Appeasement? The 3 April letter was meant to appease shareholders disgruntled to see the Combined Code ignored so publicly. Not only was this to be an interim measure, but Rose would not even take a pay increase despite the added responsibilities. The senior non-executive director would take the title of deputy chairman. Two new executive directors would join the board 'to balance responsibilities and allow Stuart to concentrate on the strategic growth areas of the business'. Another non-exec would be recruited, too, to keep the board balanced towards outsiders. And Rose would have to stand for re-election as a director every year, rather than just once every three – which would have meant, in this case, not at all. So who exactly was this package really meant to appease? Between the lines of the Burns letter it is plain to see: Stuart Rose himself, of course.

Power play? It is not greed. If Rose gets no more money, does he simply want the power? The proposed governance mechanisms, if they work, suggest that nothing much would change. But would they? Consider the alternative: recruit a new chairman and get Rose to extend his contract as CEO for another two years. How different is that from the arrangement laid out in the 3 April letter? Well, it is: Rose clearly must have resented that a new chairman might try to curb his exercise of power, challenge his way of doing business. Which is precisely what the Combined Code, and Cadbury, set out to achieve.

The case took such strong tones precisely because it was a challenge to the very principle on which governance reforms in the UK were based. If Rose and a quiescent M&S board got away with it, what would be left of the Combined Code's sway in the boardroom? The skirmishes continue.

- *Board independence?* The *Financial Times*, after what appears to have been a calculated leak, reported that Stuart Rose had personally invested money in a new venture of the internet entrepreneur Martha Lane-Fox, who had joined the M&S board in 2007. Was she still independent? The 3 April letter from Burns had claimed her to be.
- *Annual elections?* The letter offered to give shareholders the chance to decide each year whether Rose should continue. Why not make that rule apply to all board members? This suggestion from the Association of British Insurers met a cool response. 'We do not negotiate in public,' Rose was quoted as saying. He might have added: *We just wash our dirty linen there.*

It is worth recalling that M&S has a history of unorthodox corporate governance. Much of its recent, spotty history has seen a succession of boards short on independence and chairmen who played a particularly strong role in running the business. One of the more successful of them was Sir Richard Greenbury, who had chaired one in the succession of governance reviews in the 1990s. Greenbury told the online reporters at *The Times* at the time of the M&S decision that major institutional shareholders like Legal & General, a major insurance company, and the asset management firm Schroders had become 'little more than box tickers'. He added: 'The present situation reflects almost no credit on the City's institutional investors. Now that they have taken up such an entrenched position, there is a real danger this could turn from being a mess into being a crisis. The worrying thing is if Stuart says "I've had enough of this"' (Hawkes & Costello, 2008).

The 'mess' Greenbury spoke about was an economy slowing amid a gathering storm that would soon become a global economic crisis of uncommon proportions. Retailers like Marks & Spencer would face important decisions, and though the board could not have anticipated it at the time, competitors of M&S would soon be going into liquidation. The company needed the best brains it could find. Yet the Combined Code – and, as we have seen, best practice in much of the world – argued for M&S to find a new chairman and not simply give in to Rose's desire to take the title for himself.

Questions arising

M&S flouted the Combined Code in naming Stuart Rose executive chairman, de facto chair and CEO, upsetting institutional investors.

1 What does agency theory tell us about the risks of such a move?
2 What does resource dependency theory tell us about the value of such a move?
3 In what ways might stewardship theory explain the M&S board's decision?
4 Under what conditions should a company transgress the comply-or-explain conditions of the code?
5 How might tensions inside the board lead to better decisions?
6 How might tensions inside the board lead to worse ones?

Board structure and processes

Boards of directors have almost no defined role in the governance of corporations. Company law in most jurisdictions requires a company to have a board but gives it very little guidance about what it should do. That decision is left to shareholders, who approve the company's articles of association and the major decisions that arise from them. As a result boards have developed over time by copying what others seemed to do. In the early decades of the corporation, the board was the founder, his financiers and a few trusted allies. As the 'modern corporation' of Berle and Means (1932/1991) emerged with its distant and dispersed shareholders, boards in the US evolved into advisory bodies, giving friendly suggestions to the executives and providing a sounding board for corporate strategy. Boards of major corporations might include 20 or more people, including bankers and lawyers with whom the company did business, former politicians and regulators, even some academics. They were often hand-picked by the dual chairman and chief executive officer, a post that had become the norm in US practice. Famous personalities, Nobel Prize winners, even movie stars, were among the people sometimes disparagingly called the 'trophy directors' (Branson, 2006; Hamilton, 2000; Leblanc, 2004) a CEO might accumulate around him.

Boards in other countries were perhaps less willing or able to follow this approach, but with law giving boards great discretion about what the role of a director is, boards were free to set their own agenda, determine who should be on them, settle on a shape and composition, and decide what processes they should have. Codes of corporate governance and legal changes introduced in responses to recurrent crises were meant to restrict this freedom. As we have seen, directors serve two main purposes: they monitor the performance of management, and they provide access to scarce resources – the brake pedal and the accelerator. In doing so, they give the company legitimacy in the eyes of shareholders and the other publics the company faces. How can they achieve that? What other roles do they play?

Monitoring and control

In agency theory as well as in practice since the wave of concern over corporate governance has emerged, the board's main role is to keep the actions of managers aligned with the interests of shareholders. This role argues in favour of a board designed to challenge the executives and processes that will develop ways of keeping the executives on the selected path. This role is the main reason that institutional investors and the recommendations arising from agency theorists have pressed to have a separation of the roles of CEO and chairman. In the words of the UK Combined Code (Financial Reporting Council, 2008, p. 6): 'There should be a clear division of responsibilities at the head of the company between the running of the board and the executive responsibility for the running of the company's business. No one individual should have unfettered powers of decision.'

Other aspects of board design are often cited as helping to ensure the board is able to monitor and control the executives:

- *A majority of independent non-executive directors*: Some non-executives directors may not be independent because they have ties to a particular shareholder or have close associations with the company or with the chief executive. These ties can compromise their ability or willingness to be the shareholders' advocate in the boardroom. Various issues arise with this notion: What constitutes 'independence'? Codes speak of a need for directors to be independent of mind, but defining that has proved difficult. A director with close business ties to the company or to a particular shareholder might still exercise good judgement and independent thinking, while another with no ties might not have sufficiently forceful a personality to stand up to a powerful CEO. When might an independent director lose that status? In the UK, the Higgs Review (2003) suggested companies use nine years as a guideline, though later thinking (Financial Reporting Council, 2009; Walker, 2009a) questioned how important such formal independence was.
- *Board size*: Boards of even large corporations have ranged from the very small (say, three directors) to the very large (more than 25 was commonplace). The emerging consensus on corporate governance is that boards should be large enough to be able to challenge and even overrule a strong CEO, but small enough to ensure that the voices of individual independent non-executives do not get lost around a giant meeting table. Rules of thumb have emerged from the debate: fewer than six members might not be enough; greater than 15 might make discussion in the boardroom too fragmented. Either would enhance the power of the CEO, especially if he is also the board's chairman. Some early studies in the US, where large boards had been common, argued for boards of less than 10 (Jensen, 1993; Lipton & Lorsch, 1992).
- *Audit committees*: Much of the detailed work of monitoring and control arises in examining the company's finances to ensure that targets are being met and that the company has a good system of internal controls. One of the earliest 'remedies' for the issues in corporate governance was to suggest that boards create a committee that specializes in

examining these issues. The Cadbury recommendations in the UK, widely copied around the world, have been strengthened in the wake of recurrent problems. Arthur Andersen, the accountancy firm that was external auditor at Enron and WorldCom, earned more money from providing those clients services other than audit, with the danger that the 'independence' of their opinion was questionable. Post-Enron reforms have sought to make the audit committee responsible for the work of the auditor, not the finance director or even the board as a whole. Audit committees now are overwhelmingly populated only by independent non-executive directors, and the internal controlling function at companies increasingly reports to the audit committee, not the finance director. The danger with this practice is that the board as a whole may not take audit seriously. Moreover, with risk management rising up the agenda, the work of audit committees runs the risk of being too large for part-time directors.

- *No former CEO on the board*: Institutional investors have backed efforts to ensure that a CEO does not 'retire' to the chairmanship of the company she has led or even keep a seat on the board. The idea here is to create a structure that allows a new CEO to clean house, making changes in managerial practice without having to account to the person who put those practices in place. The danger is that in forcing a CEO to leave, the company is robbing itself of expertise and organizational wisdom. CEOs may have crucial links to customers, regulators and other parties of interest.

- *Remuneration committee*: Another innovation of the Cadbury Report was that boards create a committee to look specifically at how the CEO and other senior managers are paid. Setting the performance targets for the company may be the responsibility of the whole board, but the CEO should help to determine how much he will be paid for meeting them. With the Higgs Review, UK practice moved towards having remuneration committees entirely made up of independent non-executive directors. The danger with having executives involved in setting their own pay is so self-evident that there is little disagreement – at least in public – about the wisdom of this approach. But should a chairman be a member of the committee, in view of the close working relationship that he has with the CEO?

- *Nominations committee*: Another widely copied innovation of Cadbury was the recommendation that boards have a separate committee to search for new candidates for the board itself. That role includes the planning for who will succeed the incumbent CEO, perhaps the most important appointment a board can make. If having a former CEO on the board is an issue, then so too must be having the current CEO select his successor. Yet business continuity also has a value. Taking a long-term perspective on investments suggests that excluding the incumbent's view could lead to a loss of momentum. Following the Higgs Review, there was a move to exclude even independent chairmen from the nominations committee of UK boards. The reservations of chairmen were so strong that the issue provoked a hasty revision of the Combined Code in 2006.

- *Risk and the board*: Though it is often linked with the work of the audit committee, risk management has gained special attention in the debate over corporate governance. In the banking sector, the reasons for this attention are most obvious: banks are in the business of risk-taking. Most companies seek to mitigate risk by matching assets and liabilities, assessed by management accounting measures like the ratio of current assets and current liabilities or the debt-to-equity ratio. But banks deliberately borrow funds for the short term and lend it for the long term, building statistical models to help them predict the stability of their cash position. Indeed, the breakdown of these processes was a major reason behind the financial crisis of 2007–09. Risk-taking is inherent in all businesses, arguably at the core of strategy formation. Yet even the modest demand in the UK of the Turnbull

Review (1999) for an annual statement saying whether the board had considered risk unearthed acknowledgement by many companies that risk had not been an explicit item on the board's agenda. The Sarbanes–Oxley Act in the US made risk management inescapable for boards of companies listed in the US. One of the early questions boards had to ask themselves is whether risk management was an attempt to mitigate risk (that is, monitoring and control) or to determine just what the corporations appetite for risk should be (that is, setting direction).

The tensions on boards can be seen as arising from the interactions of the different actors: executive directors seeking to have their policies adopted, non-executives who view their role as checking the executives, and the chairman, at once arbiter of disputes and focus of the internal tensions (see Figure 3).

The demand for monitoring and control has led to a variety of other suggestions to strengthen board structure and processes. One option is for boards to create a separate committee dedicated to risk management, mentioned in the Smith Guidance (2003) as an alternative to risk oversight by audit committees. The 2009 Walker Review of UK banking governance recommended it for major financial institutions. Many codes of corporate governance now call

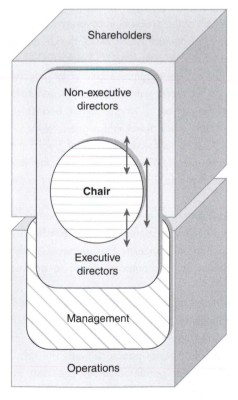

Figure 3 Issues within the board

for boards, individual directors, and all the board committees to undergo an annual performance appraisal, much like those that human resources departments conduct on ordinary employees. Such reviews would help to prevent a board from growing complacent. By keeping their own performance under review, this position suggests, non-executive directors and chairman will be more keenly aware of the need for them to be vigilant.

The danger in all the attention to monitoring and control is that the board will become too focused on one side of its role. The company will not go very far or get there very fast if the board spends all its time with its foot on the brake.

Agenda point 10: Women on the board

Resource provision is one of many arguments raised when critics of corporate governance raise the question about why so many boards of European and North American companies are 'stale, male and pale' (a phrase borrowed from Johnston & Phillips, 2005) – a response to the disproportionate number of middle-aged white men on corporate boards. Men occupy the boardroom because men occupy the senior managerial positions deemed to be prerequisite of board membership.

Many scholars, activists and policymakers wonder, though, whether the sameness of boards is not part of the problem in corporate governance. As part of the review of governance arrangement in 2002–03, the UK commissioned a study by Laura Tyson, a former economic adviser to US President Bill Clinton and then Dean of London Business School. Its recommendations for improving board diversity (Tyson, 2003) – not just for more women directors – generated a lot of headlines but several years later the number of women on UK boards was still small. And at one point, even as the number of directorships grew, fewer women held them: the few female directors took on a larger number of board mandates. In its tenth annual survey of board diversity (Sealy et al., 2008), the International Centre for Women Leaders at the Cranfield School of Management in the UK wrote of a 'lost decade'.

Having on the board a greater number of women, ethnic minorities, and even people without a long history of senior managerial roles is often cited as being valuable for voicing different concerns than those of traditional directors and reflecting the constituencies the company needs to address (Branson, 2006; Singh, 2007).

Women, it seems, make for better monitoring of management too. According to a study of US companies, they attend board meetings more regularly than men, and in so doing get men to attend more often. Women are more likely to join committees that monitor performance as well. The rub, this analysis found, was that boards with greater gender diversity presided over poorer financial performance (Adams & Ferreira, 2009).

Resource provision

The other role – the accelerator – involves the board helping to provide senior management with the resources it needs to make the business perform to the best of its ability. Here many of the admirable qualities needed for monitoring and control run the risk of being a drag on performance. Directors, and especially the outside non-executives on the board, provide a useful function by spanning the boundaries of the organization. Because they are directors, they can represent the company's interests in front of regulators and government bodies. Because they are outsiders too, they bring to the boardroom intimate knowledge of how other organizations solve problems, friendships with influential and knowledgeable people who might assist in developing the business, and experience of technologies or processes that the company might incorporate to increase revenue or reduce costs. If nothing else, they may bring a different perspective to the boardroom discussions, those of users of its goods and services, of the sorts of people the company might need to recruit in the future, or of the various publics the company depends upon for its legitimacy and the ones it may have to convince about its plans for expansion or indeed for contraction.

Boundary spanning is part of the justification that can be made even for trophy directors. A former legislator, public official or government minister may well have acquaintances in powerful positions and smooth the path of a planning application. They can lend credibility when the company decides to set up operations in a foreign country. Their presence on the board might even make a disgruntled business party think twice about bringing a lawsuit against the company. Having a famous musician on the board might bring an eccentric view to the boardroom and prevent discussion from slipping into what the psychologist Irving Janis (1972) famously called 'groupthink'.

Codes of conduct of corporate governance around the world say little about this aspect of the board. Some mention the need for good performance. Some refer to the role that boards play in setting strategy. Because the codes developed in response to the agency problem, the problem of self-serving managers whose power needs to the checked, the emphasis in corporate governance has fallen more on the side of balancing – offsetting – the power of the CEO. For that reason it is worthwhile examining in greater detail the types of decisions that boards have to make.

Board roles and responsibilities

The case of Marks & Spencer in 2008 shows some of the inner workings of a board brought to light through the notion that boards should explain when they fail to comply with a code of corporate governance. The incident at M&S involved the desire of an incumbent chairman to resign and the need in the face

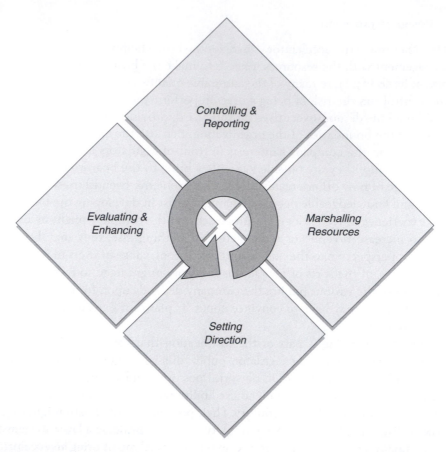

Figure 4   Board roles (Nordberg, 2007b, used with permission)

of a looming recession to retain a successful CEO. The inability of the board to have identified successors for either post meant it saw a need to set the norms of the code aside, at least for a while. The peculiar circumstances of this company, at this time, meant rewriting the rules. The case of Marks & Spencer also shows how boards can come into dispute with shareholders – or at least with certain types of shareholders – a theme we examine in Chapters 9 and 10.

A more detailed look at the roles and responsibilities of boards suggests they perform a wide-ranging set of tasks, with often overlapping and even conflicting aims and objectives, which is what makes the job of being a director so demanding (Nordberg, 2007b). Boards take on what can be described as four key roles, each couched in an active voice: setting direction, marshalling resources, controlling and reporting, and evaluating and enhancing (see Figure 4).

- *Setting direction*: The directors, quite naturally, direct. The degree to which a board of a large corporation can in fact direct day-to-day business is rather limited; that is, after all, the task of management. But boards decide on the strategic direction, committing the company to its targets and giving senior management its instructions. The responsibilities within this role include things like ordering strategic reviews, endorsing or refusing management's strategic plans, deciding on mergers, acquisitions, disposals of major assets or lines of business, raising capital or giving money back to shareholders. In practice, studies of the board's role in strategy have suggested this is often limited to advising the CEO and other senior managers, rather than forming strategy itself (McNulty & Pettigrew, 1999; Pugliese et al., 2009; Stiles, 2001; Stiles & Taylor, 2001). But it would be rare for any management team to undertake a major strategic move without getting board agreement first. Disagreements on strategy often lead to changes in the senior management team – or changes in the composition of the boards where the CEO is a dominating figure.

- *Marshalling resources*: Perhaps the most important resource in a corporation is its senior management team, followed closely by the appointment of other new members of the board and deciding which of its members ought to be asked to step down. But boards, having decided when to raise capital or give it back to shareholders, also agree the corporation's budget, usually on an annual basis but also more frequently, if unexpected events upset the plans. Resource marshalling can also be seen at work in directors' responsibility for setting the pay of senior executives: pay provides the incentive structure and perhaps with it the motivation that will keep management focused on achieving the company's aims.

- *Controlling and reporting*: This embraces the core function as seen from the agency perspective, but more: boards are accountable to shareholders, if in no other way than in signing off the financial statements for the year and submitting them to the rigour of an external audit. Stakeholder theorists argue that boards have a much greater scope of accountability, that boards are responsible for the company's performance in society and for its impact on the natural environment, themes we will return to in Chapter 11. Boards are also accountable to the company's creditors, whether they are the banks and financial institutions that provide short-term loans or the investors who hold the company's bonds or other instruments. It is this accountability that gives credit rating agencies their particular and controversial gatekeeping role (see Chapter 4). Many writers on corporate governance also see the board as the conscience of the company, responsible for its approach to ethics and for determination of specific business policies that limit the range of actions open to management.

- *Evaluating and enhancing*: At the end of the process, boards also take stock of what has happened and decide on actions to improve performance. This includes deciding mundane matters like whether executives should receive their bonuses for good performance, or more momentous ones about whether the company faces undue risks, or indeed whether it is not taking sufficient risks as a way of increasing the return. It evaluates whether external factors present new opportunities or risks that need to be fed into the board's next round of direction-setting.

Viewing the board's roles in this way gives a more nuanced and complex view than the simple division between monitoring and control on the one hand and resource provision on the other. This view can be represented as in Figure 5. This picture captures the board's accountability to a variety of constituencies, rather than just the responsibilities it bears internally to the company.

This also suggests a division of emphasis between roles in which executives on a unitary board take the leading role and those where the non-executives

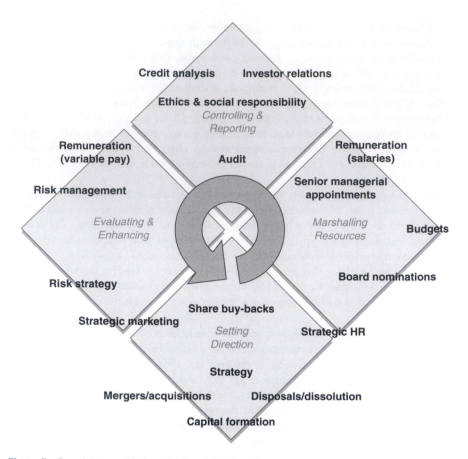

Figure 5   Board responsibilities (Nordberg, 2007b, used with permission)

naturally lead. Strategy originates mainly from the business and its managers, who are probably better placed to judge the marketplace and assess the operational capabilities that can be brought to bear. Evaluating performance, while in need of ratification from the non-executives, requires data and resources that lie more firmly in the hands of management. The company's risk appetite forms the basis of strategy and the lead lies perhaps more with the executives in boardroom. But decisions about budgets and who should be running the business as well as providing access to scarce external resources is more logically a role in which the outside directors would take the lead. Controlling and reporting, too, are areas in which the non-executives, and in particular those deemed independent of management, would in agency theory exercise control. Their role is to represent shareholders' interest in the board's decision-making. Stakeholder theorists count on them to keep management from running roughshod over the interest of employees, suppliers and customers.

These divisions of roles closely correspond to the practice of two-tier boards, and particularly in Germany, where the management board does most of the direction-setting and evaluation, while the supervisory board oversees finances and managerial appointments and bears the public accountability once management is formally relieved of its responsibility for the accounts at the annual meeting.

Unitary boards allow for a more nuanced division of tasks in the board, but the reforms of corporate governance introduced in various codes have tended to concentrate the approval processes and monitoring in the hands of non-executives, putting control of strategic direction and enhancement of processes more with the executives on the board. The balance is a theme we return to in Chapter 14. Meanwhile we will consider the substance of debates surrounding the marshalling of resources and the requirements of accountability that arise.

Further readings

Adams, R. B. & Ferreira, D. (2009). Women in the Boardroom and Their Impact on Governance and Performance. *Journal of Financial Economics, 94*(2), 291–309.

Finkelstein, S. & Mooney, A. C. (2003). Not the Usual Suspects: How to Use Board Process to Make Boards Better. *Academy of Management Executive, 17*(2), 101–13.

Gordon, J. N. (2007). The Rise of Independent Directors in the United States, 1950–2005: Of Shareholder Value and Stock Market Prices. *Stanford Law Review, 59*(6), 1465–1568.

Hambrick, D. C. & Jackson, E. M. (2000). Outside Directors with a Stake: The Linchpin in Improving Governance. *California Management Review, 42*(4), 108–27.

Higgs, D. (2003). Review of the Role and Effectiveness of Non-Executive Directors. Retrieved 15 Oct. 2006, from http://www.ecgi.org/codes/documents/higgsreport.pdf.

Ingley, C. B. & van der Walt, N. (2002). Board Dynamics and the Politics of Appraisal. *Corporate Governance: An International Review, 10*(3), 163–74.

Long, T. (2006). This Year's Model: Influences on Board and Director Evaluation. *Corporate Governance: An International Review, 14*(6), 547–57.

McNulty, T. & Pettigrew, A. (1996). The Contribution, Power and Influence of Part-time Board Members. *Corporate Governance, 4*(3), 160–79.

Minichilli, A., Gabrielsson, J. & Huse, M. (2007). Board Evaluations: Making a Fit between the Purpose and the System. *Corporate Governance: An International Review, 15*(4), 609–22.

Nordberg, D. (2007). Rebalancing the Board's Agenda. *Journal of General Management, 33*(2), 13–23.

Pearce, J. A., II, & Zahra, S. A. (1992). Board Composition from a Strategic Contingency Perspective. *Journal of Management Studies, 29*(4), 411–38.

Pettigrew, A. & McNulty, T. (1995). Power and Influence in and Around the Boardroom. *Human Relations, 48*(8), 845–73.

Pye, A. (2000). Changing Scenes In, From and Outside the Board Room: UK Corporate Governance in Practice from 1989 to 1999. *Corporate Governance: An International Review, 8*(4), 335.

Singh, V. (2007). Ethnic Diversity on Top Corporate Boards: A Resource Dependency Perspective. *International Journal of Human Resource Management, 18*(12), 2128–46.

Taylor, B., Dulewicz, V. & Gay, K. (2008). How Part-time Directors Create Exceptional Value: New Evidence from the Non-executive Director Awards. *Journal of General Management, 33*(4), 53–70.

Useem, M. & Zelleke, A. (2006). Oversight and Delegation in Corporate Governance: Deciding What the Board Should Decide. *Corporate Governance: An International Review, 14*(1), 2–12.

EIGHT

Issues between boards and management

Case: Satyam and the Golden Peacock

The name of the company is the Sanskrit word for truth. Would that it were true. Were it not for the Madoff scandal (Chapter 4), which hit at the same time, the convulsions at Satyam Computer Services in India during December 2008 and January 2009 would have caused Enron-esque anguish in corporate governance around the world. As it was, it still sent shudders through emerging capital markets and ought to be a salutary lesson for those who think family-run businesses are somehow necessarily better at monitoring and control than the 'modern corporation' with its widely dispersed ownership. We will probably never find all the pieces of the puzzle, not to mention a billion dollars, but the story that unfolded went something like this:

Once upon a time: Outsourcing IT has been the hottest business in this hottest of emerging markets. Indian companies have been climbing the ranks of world leadership ever since the spread of high-speed telecommunications lines to Bangalore, Mumbai and Chennai made the country the favoured destination. Satyam was not the first in the business, and it certainly was not the biggest. But it was a fast challenger, winning business that its bigger rivals would have embraced. Its shares traded in Mumbai, but it had grander ambitions. Its US client base provided a good excuse for a US listing, too: this company was listed on the New York Stock Exchange no less. In the year ending 31 March 2008 it acquired four companies, in Belgium, the US and the UK. Its revenues had pushed past $2 billion, and more than 20 per cent of that fell through to pretax profits. Its motto: 'A Commitment to Value Creation'. It seemed like a fairy tale, too good to be true.

Golden Peacock winner: Satyam was, if not a paragon of good corporate governance, a pretty good example for listed companies with a dominant shareholder. It had just won a Golden Peacock, an annual prize awarded by the World Council on Corporate Governance for quality in risk management and compliance. The Satyam board included nine people – not too large, and not too small. A clear majority of six were independent, non-executive directors. Nor were they lightweights: Prof. V. S. Raju had been director of the Indian Institute of Technology. He headed a board committee on investor grievances, as the board had anticipated that outside investors would want an extra watchdog in the boardroom. Prof. M. Rammohan Rao was the Dean of the Indian School of Business and had taught at the Stern School at New York University. He chaired the audit committee. Neither was a financial expert, but they were not unfamiliar with the field. And then there was Krishna G. Palepu, the Ross Graham Walker Professor at Harvard Business School. He taught on executive programmes aimed at members of corporate boards: 'Making Corporate Boards More Effective', 'Audit Committees in a New Era of Governance', and 'Compensation Committees: New Challenges, New Solutions'. His books include several editions of *Business Analysis and Valuation*. PricewaterhouseCoopers, the biggest of the Big Four global accountancy firms, was responsible for the audit.

The deal: On 16 December B. Ramalinga Raju, the major shareholder, founder and chairman, tried to push through two more acquisitions – this time of companies controlled by his family, where his sons led the management. It was a swaggering move: $1.6 billion – almost all the current assets on Satyam's books – for 51 per cent of Maytas Infrastructure and all of Maytas Properties. The latter was an unlisted company for which the only public information available was the size of its property holdings – measured in hectares, not rupees. Maytas, of course, is Satyam spelled backwards.

The World Bank: Just before taking its Christmas break, the World Bank Group in Washington struck Satyam off its register of suppliers for eight years. That more than confirmed the temporary suspension in had levelled against Satyam about 10 months before, concerned about improper payments to bank employees. Satyam urged the World Bank to withdraw its comments about the decision.

The resignation: On 25 December Dr. Mangalam Srinivasan, who had chaired the compensation committee, resigned from the board, ending a 17-year relationship. Her tenure was perhaps a sign that her independence might have been less than complete, at least according to the definition that the Higgs Review in the UK had thrust into corporate governance folklore in 2003. But her letter showed independence of mind: 'I am sending this letter,' she wrote to the chairman, 'to let you know that while I raised many of the issues related to the procedures and had expressed my reservations during the Satyam board deliberations, I had not cast a dissenting vote against the acquisition of Maytas, for which I take the moral responsibility. Under the circumstances, I am left with no other option but to resign effective immediately from the board, a privilege I had cherished.'

Other resignations: On 29 December three more independent directors resigned. M. Rammohan Rao, who had chaired the controversial 16 December board meetings where the Maytas acquisition was announced, joined Krishna Palepu and Vinod K. Dham in leaving the company.

The sell-off: Outside investors were getting a bit nervous, as you might expect. The share price was even weaker than the prevailing poor market sentiment around the world in these difficult weeks. But then one day, the selling pressure became intense as a very large block of shares hit the market. Perhaps some of the founders' stake had changed hands as collateral for a loan. The lender may have put it up for sale to cover the loan. The game was up.

Another, bigger resignation: On 7 January B. Ramalinga Raju, chairman and 'promoter' of the company, as Indian usage has it, announced that he was stepping down. It seems there was a hole – $1 billion – in the accounts. The reported 20+ per cent return on sales had really been only 3 per cent. Was the failed deal to buy the other Raju-controlled companies a last-ditch effort to plug the hole, as some of the early press reports said? Or was it instead to drain the remaining cash out of Satyam and into the family's bank accounts?

And where was the corporate governance?: The dust was still settling. The board had been reconstituted and urgent meetings had been underway to keep it afloat. A global recession did not help, of course, but Satyam would have been in trouble under any circumstances. This company had followed all the codes, indeed it exceeded governance standards as mandated in India, even sought to emulate standards in the UK and to meet the New York Stock Exchange's guidelines. The 'Shareholder Grievance Committee' – designed to anticipate concerns over related party dealing – now seemed a bad joke. If this was what boards do, then some people might well wonder: What are boards for?

Postscript: PwC's global CEO Samuel DiPiazza skipped the World Economic Forum's shindig in Davos, Switzerland, at the end of January. He was in India, dealing with the arrest of two PwC partners involved in the Satyam audit. KPMG and Deloitte had taken over audit duties.

A majority shareholding in Satyam was acquired by another Indian technology and consulting firm, Tech Mahindra. The rebranded Mahindra Satyam retained a listing on the New York Stock Exchange.

The World Council on Corporate Governance stripped Satyam of its Golden Peacock.

Questions arising

1 To what extent was the collapse of Satyam the result of poor board structure and processes? To what extent weak board diligence?
2 What role did the presence on the board of the founder-shareholder with a controlling interest play in the collapse?
3 How might the board's concentration on the success of the business have contributed to its fall?

4 What mechanisms might the board have developed to prevent abuse by a strong shareholder–manager?
5 How might having an outside, professional manager in charge of the business help? How might it hinder the success of the business?
6 Considering the agency issues with outside managers, how might the rewards – of managers and shareholder–managers – be structured to better effect?

The agency problem in action

In prescriptions of corporate governance arising from the agency perspective, the role of the board is to monitor the actions of management and keep them working in the interests of shareholders. Problems arise, so the theory tells us, from managers seeking to fulfil their own ambitions, but using the resources of the company to do it. If those aims involve leading the most profitable or productive company in the industry, or becoming famous for innovative and exciting new products, they may fit closely enough with the interests of shareholders not to be a problem. Indeed, it is probably fair to say that most investors want ambitious managers running the business they own. That is why they expect boards to hire the best chief executives and to pay them well. They want the CEO to feel as though she is the proprietor of the busi-ness – that it is *her* company, not just that she works there. They want her to develop a sense of leadership that brings the rest of the workforce to believe it is *their* company, too, so they will strive harder to do the best job.

First we look at what types of issues can arise when the interests of the managers do not coincide with those of shareholders. We explore the issue of executive pay to see how it developed from being a solution to the agency problems of self-dealing into becoming perhaps the biggest issue of all in cor-porate governance. We then consider the questions that arise when managers, left alone, pursue agendas that are rather different from 'just' being the most profitable or innovative. Monitoring of executive pay and performance is not the only issue that arises between boards and management.

Executive pay

This phrase has become almost a swear-word in the language of business jour-nalism, and often in academic writing as well. The issue of the highly paid chief executive, accountable to no one, had been a matter of concern for some years among those institutional investors who monitored corporate gover-nance. But it burst into public consciousness only with the global recession of 1990–1, when new corporate disclosure rules in the United States gave inves-tigators the information they needed to study what was actually happening. One of the early products of that research was a book that became a surprise bestseller around the world: Graef Crystal's *In Search of Excess*. The first edition had chapters headed 'On the Flying Trapeze', 'The Perk Barrel', and 'The Culprits'. Central to the book and the debate it provoked was the core of his complaint: a chapter more prosaically entitled 'High Pay, Low Performance'. The book went quickly into a second edition, in which CEOs were given a chance to respond, though little they said changed Crystal's mind. 'At a time when the American economy has shown itself to be all too fragile, every step to bring CEO pay into line with company performance is a step toward renewing American competitiveness,' he concluded (Crystal, 1992, p. 276). Crystal's methodologies have been challenged, and the data sources he and other analysts had available have been shown, if anything, to have understated the rewards top executives got.

The American practice of disclosing CEO pay has been copied in many countries around the world, though often on a voluntary, 'best practice' basis, rather than the mandatory publication in place in the US. The Greenbury Code (1995) in the UK followed the US line on disclosure, at least in outline. It emerged in response to a protest at the annual shareholders' meeting over the pay awarded to the head of the newly privatized utility company, British Gas. Protestors brought a pig to proceedings, and named it 'Cedric', after the chairman. The British press now writes regularly about 'fat cats', while Germans seem almost never to write about executive pay without the word *Skandal* nearby.

Nor have the years since Crystal's discoveries had much effect on what top executives get paid. If anything pay seems to have grown even more, whether measured in absolute terms, in relation to the economy as a whole, in relation to the average pay of the workforce or in terms of profitability of the enterprise. The American scholars Lucian Bebchuk and Jesse Fried called it 'pay without performance' (Bebchuk & Fried, 2004a). Some find good reason to pay executives well. They are, after all, in charge of large enterprises, and the contributions their leadership can bring is often substantial. The British pension fund manager Paul Lee of Hermes found the level of pay less of an issue than the mechanisms that tied large payments to contributions to shareholder value. Top managers in the United States were 'not badly paid but paid badly' (Lee, 2002, p. 69). Worse, their remuneration models were spreading around the world, he thought.

Boards of directors then face three dangers when settling on how much to pay the CEO. They can pay too much or pay too little. But they can also pay executives in the wrong way, in ways that encourage self-dealing and with it value destruction for shareholders, the company as a whole and perhaps even for the economy at large.

Paying too much

Paying too much is easy to detect after it is too late. When a company still has time to do something about it, the choices are very hard. One of the cases highlighted by Crystal is the pay award that Michael Eisner negotiated when he became CEO of Walt Disney Co. in 1984. Lionized at first, Eisner was then demonized in the press at the time when it became apparent he had earned well over $200 million during his first six years at Disney. Eisner was, as Crystal explained, on a high-risk, high-reward package. His base salary was low, and his bonus kicked in only once profits exceeded a high rate of return on equity. Stock options boosted his pay too, but most were options where the company's share price would have to rise substantially before Eisner would benefit at all. 'Compared to most other CEOs, Eisner plays the game fairly,' Crystal wrote (Crystal, 1992, p. 166).

Agenda point 11: Limits of power – Jack Welch and GE

Having an all-powerful CEO given wide discretion over how to run the business can be of tremendous value to shareholders – provided that individual acts as a steward and feels motivated to do a good job irrespective of what payment is on offer. Few investors begrudged Jack Welch the money he made while acting in unfettered oversight of the giant General Electric Co. of the United States during the more than 20 years he served as chairman and CEO.

They turned against him when, in divorce proceedings after his retirement, the world learned that the company would continue to fund his use of the corporate jet, company seats at major sporting events, restaurant bills and country club fees – and his use of an apartment in New York that would normally rent for $80,000 a month, all when he was no longer working for the company (for further details, see Fabrikant, 2002).

But then after 20 years in charge, with the stock price and the business in retreat, after failing to retain key executives, and following a disastrous attempt to bring in a successor, Eisner faced a revolt from two board directors. One was Roy Disney, nephew of the founder and himself a sizeable shareholder in the company. Eisner continued to earn large rewards. Board strife provoked an unwanted takeover bid. The Disney company resisted it and stayed independent. Michael Eisner found himself forced very reluctantly into retirement and branded one of the five worst CEOs in America by *Forbes* magazine.

When boards meet and when remuneration committees meet, the question of how much to pay the CEO is always near the top of the agenda. Even far from America, corporate directors, fund managers and others admit they fall victim to the 'Lake Wobegon Effect'. This mythical Minnesota town, invented by the humorist Garrison Keillor, is where 'all the women are strong, all the men are good-looking, and all the children are above average'. Every board, and every remuneration committee, wants to know that their CEO is above average, and they commission 'compensation consultants' to make sure their CEO is in the top quarter of everyone in the industry. The next year, every board and every remuneration committee does the same. Pay goes up and up (for a serious discussion of the effect, see Hayes & Schaefer, 2008).

While executives have benefited from the practice, which has become more embedded as disclosure regulations have made it easier to tell with certainty how much top executives earn, it is not clear that paying more automatically leads to better performance. Ever since Germany introduced a voluntary call for disclosure of the pay of named individuals as part of its corporate governance code, a sizeable proportion of companies have declined to go along (von Werder & Talaulicar, 2006, 2009). While that reluctance may have something to do with a culture of reticence about personal wealth or just a desire to keep what they see as private matters private, there may be other factors at work. German executives sometimes justify non-disclosure by saying that keeping pay details under wraps helps them to keep salaries, bonuses and other pay low.

Paying too little

Paying too little is easy to detect, again, after it is too late. Much as the board's role involves monitoring *and* resource provision, the task of setting executive pay involves a judgement about what is too little as well as too much. While boards need to be vigilant over excessive pay to prevent what economists call 'rent-seeking' by managers, they also must ensure they get the best executives they can. It is a judgement call, and not always an easy one to make.

One reason often cited for the great escalation in executive pay since the 1980s is that in a competitive market for top executive talent, candidates can demand high salaries, high performance-related pay and increasingly some form of incentive linked to the performance of the company's share price, even a direct stake in the business. If they do not get it, they will simply leave for somewhere else that is willing to pay. The resulting loss of executives can be devastating for a business.

Consider this: in many businesses – including capital intensive manufacturing companies – more of the value of the business, as measured by the value the shares trade at on the stock exchange, is made up of 'intangible' assets. That is, comparing market capitalization to the accounting 'book value' or net assets shows that investors believe that a business in more than plant and equipment it owns. For many, these tangible assets are insignificant. A software company, an investment bank, an advertising agency: each is far more dependent on the people who work there, rather than any physical objects the business owns. Many a top executive has said that the most important assets of the business walk out the door each evening. At the top of the employment hierarchy – and the top of the payscale – sits the CEO. Losing key people, particularly to a competitor, can deprive the company of valuable competitive knowledge and key relationships, with suppliers, regulators and customers.

But the market for top executive talent is not a particularly transparent one. Information asymmetries abound: corporations hire pay consultants to find out what the 'market rate' for top executives is. Executives being headhunted for top jobs sometimes do the same, much as movie stars and professional sportsmen hire agents to negotiate on their behalf.

In the US and countries that have followed its lead, while we know reasonably well what the top executives in a company earn, it is not always entirely clear. Bebchuk and Fried (2004b) analysed how the pension contributions companies made to top US executives amounted to a form of 'stealth' pay. Their work, together with lobbying from major institutional investors, led to even greater disclosure in the annual Compensation Discussion and Analysis that the US Securities and Exchange Commission requires from listed companies.

How to pay

The question is not just about the level of executive pay, but about its structure. Typical senior managers receive a base salary and then some sort of incentive to achieve more: a bonus, based on performance against targets, and often some form of equity-linked pay, tied to how well the share price develops. Get the incentives right, and top executives will do an extraordinary job for the company. Get them wrong, and the executives will have incentives to manipulate the system to their own benefit, and not shareholders', as agency theory warns. Alternatively, they might leave.

- *Salary*: Once the mainstay of top executive pay, this component has become in many ways just the starting point. In 1993, following Graef Crystal's disclosures about executive pay and Bill Clinton's presidential election victory, the US Congress passed a law it thought would force a greater link between pay and performance. Salary payments – those contracted and not linked to corporate performance – of above $1 million a year to any employee could not be deducted as an expense of doing business. The law had unintended consequences. Instead of taking salaries, executives demanded 'guaranteed' bonuses, 'deferred compensation', enhanced pensions, perquisites (or 'perks') like the use of corporate jets for vacations, and other non-salary items (for details, see Porter & Johnson, 1997).
- *Bonuses*: Based on some form of performance measure, bonuses can align an executive's incentive with the goals of the company. They are often, however, open to manipulation, especially by the chief executive and finance director, who are in a position to use their discretion allowed under accounting rules to report the sort of figures that will flatter their performance. Some companies targeted earnings-per-share, or EPS, a figure that is very sensitive to decisions about whether the company officially books its revenues or costs in a particular accounting period. In the long run, it does not matter. But in the short run it can matter – a lot. Other bonus plans try to use a variety measures to prevent abuse, but too complex a plan might prove not to be an incentive, and certain types of targets might not be all that much benefit to the business and its shareholders.

- *Stock options*: From the 1970s onwards stock options were used widely as a form of incentive pay. They seemed an ideal way to align the interest of managers with those of shareholders. The executive would be given the right to purchase shares, say at today's price. They could exercise that right at any time, say between three years and 10 years from the date of the grant. If the share price was higher than when the option was granted, the executive would sell the shares and make a profit, just as shareholders could. If the share price had not done well, the options would be worth nothing at all. What looked good on paper, though, did not always work out that way. Top executives were in a position to use the flexibility in accounting rules to engineer favourable news when their options could be exercised, moving earnings from one accounting period into another. When the share price had done badly, many companies felt obliged to 're-price' the options – lowering what is called the 'strike' price at which the executive would have to buy the shares – so as to prevent key executives from walking away from the company or joining a competitor. In the wake of the collapse of Enron, WorldCom and the dot-com era of the late 1990s, the authorities in the US found that many boards of directors at US companies had even 'backdated' options, declaring that the options had been granted several months before they actually had been, thus setting a lower 'strike' price than they were allowed to under law. The beneficiaries came to be called, with more than a hint of irony, 'Lucky CEOs and Lucky Directors' (Bebchuk et al., 2009). They could make their own luck. Shareholders paid the price, in terms of giving a greater share of the company to top managers than they had intended. Among the remedies enacted was a change in accounting rules – in both US generally accepted accounting principles and in the international financial reporting standards that apply in most of the rest of the world – to force companies to declare upfront a 'cost' for the options they granted, based on a notional value of what the executives had 'earned' from them, even if those earnings would only become real in three or more years. The use of stock options diminished as a result, though it has not entirely gone away, even for top executives.
- *Long-term equity incentives*: The dissatisfaction with stock options led some companies – often under pressure from governments or institutional investors – to adopt a different form of equity-based pay. Agency theory seemed to point to the value of giving top executives an incentive in line with shareholder interests, but stock options had proved flawed and open to manipulation. Long-term incentive plans, or LTIPs, came into use in the UK and elsewhere, giving cash incentives that paralleled share price movements over a long period. Other companies followed recommendations of some scholars and now use *restricted stock*, a grant of shares in the company, but with a proviso that they cannot be sold for several years, and sometimes until several years after the executive has left the company. These grants constrain the ability of the executive to manipulate the system in their favour. It remains to be seen, however, whether they provide a strong enough incentive to retain key executives when other companies provide packages that seem to promise larger, more certain – and faster – rewards.

These different approaches, together with the issue of how companies pay their non-executive directors, feature prominently on the agenda of remuneration committees. They are why the standard recommendations of many codes of corporate governance urge that only non-executives sit on the committee. The subject of executive pay remains a difficult, vexed question, with no obvious answers.

Self-interest beyond pay

Pay is not the only reason why top managers work, or why they choose to leave the company to work somewhere else. But like pay, this issue has two sides, one broadly welcomed, the other potentially dangerous, with little to help the would-be monitor know which is which. Self-interest can take the form using the freedom granted to an executive to achieve personal goals that are also good for the company, or it can appear as exploitation of the freedom to benefit at the company's – and shareholders' – expense. So the problem of how corporations deal with the risk of self-dealing by executives is particularly vexed.

By paying senior executives very well, boards and investors hope the executives will not feel the need for self-dealing – for stacking the deck in their own favour, using the company's resources to improve their own circumstances. Asking them to prove they have not is awkward, except in the most obvious of cases.

Stewardship and self-actualization

The best managers – those who can add the most value – are often willing to work, or leave to join another company, because they are granted the freedom to do what they want and achieve what they are capable of achieving, as the discussion of stewardship theory suggests (Davis et al., 1997; Donaldson & Davis, 1991). In the famous hierarchy of needs articulated by Abraham Maslow (Maslow, 1943, 1954), once the basic requirements of individuals have been fulfilled – for food, shelter, security and love – a higher set of needs come to the fore: esteem and self-actualization. Esteem arises from recognition by others, so a high-profile executive, known for his power over a large business, may well take a 'reward' of sorts from the admiration of others and the personal relationships it bring with it. Self-actualization is an even higher need, according to Maslow, involving personal fulfilment, achieved from a good job well done. Self-actualization may even require that the person is able to act on his or her own discretion, without reference to others, without having to justify decisions – without, in short, accountability.

The discretion afforded to senior managers is often considerable. Corporations keep a careful eye on the expenses that ordinary employees incur. They monitor the prices they pay suppliers and have escalation processes so disputes can be settled, if necessary, by someone more senior. But the more senior the employee and the larger the expense or contract involved, the shorter the escalation path becomes. By the time we reach the top of the corporation, who is there to challenge the CEO's expenses, the decisions on supply contracts reached by the chief financial officer? Boards of directors entrust these senior managers to run the business. That trust is important, for without it, few high-powered executives would want to stay with the company.

The types of people who lead corporations, that is, the types of people investors seem to want to lead them, are self-directed, decisive, with a great scope of knowledge and wide-ranging abilities. Because they are able to grasp complex situations and see solutions, they are often people who do not take direction happily – or kindly. Because these are talents widely in demand from other businesses, the individuals who possess them are likewise much in demand.

Donald Hambrick and Phyllis Mason (1984) began what has become an important body of study looking at the dynamics of what they called the 'upper echelons' of corporate management, and with it the study of managerial discretion. They suggested that top managers' own values inform the direction the company takes, and that the greater the discretion they have, the more the company will reflect their interests rather than just responding to the business environment in which they work. Decisions by the upper echelons are not, then, simply rational but rather rational in a way that is bounded by their experience and attitudes. Subsequent research suggested a variety of factors that influence that discretion (Finkelstein & Hambrick, 1996; Finkelstein et al., 2009; Finkelstein & Mooney, 2003; Hambrick & Abrahamson, 1995). Some industries – say, capital intensive ones like steel-making, rather than software – limit the ability of the manager to make a difference. Companies with powerful internal cultures will constrain managers too. But managers will also be constrained by their own attitudes. A CEO promoted from within the ranks of the company might be less ready to stamp his personality on the company than one recruited externally.

The degree of discretion afforded the executive is part of his calculus in accepting the job and how he performs in it. Well-paid senior executives have been known to quit lucrative and powerful positions for the sake of making their mark in fields they found new and exciting. Sometimes they succeed; sometimes not. In 1999, George Shaheen resigned from a prominent position as head of the distinguished consulting firm now known as Accenture to become CEO of Webvan, a start-up company with powerful backers that hoped to use the internet to revolutionize the way people received their groceries. It proved one of the most spectacular failures of the dot-com era. Shaheen joined no doubt in the hope of becoming fabulously wealthy when Webvan floated on the stock market. But it was probably also a decision based on his desire to demonstrate, to himself as well as others, that he could succeed in taking a business from something small to one that changed the way people live.

Self-serving executives, related party transactions

Granting an executive discretion can prove disastrous for reasons that arise from the agency problem. Whether it is a) the executive hired to run a business and then not held accountable by the board or anyone else, or b) the executive who may have founded the business or has a very large shareholding in it, the freedom from accountability they enjoy can be an invitation to use the company's resources as though they were their own. Preventing such problems often becomes the task of the board of directors, and of the non-executive directors in particular.

The cases of Satyam, which began this chapter, and Robert Maxwell (see Chapter 2) give differing examples of how an all-powerful CEO can wreak havoc on the companies they control. In Maxwell's case the boards apparently never sought or at least never succeeded in stopping Maxwell from using the companies' and even the pension funds' money to finance his ambition to become a powerful publisher and influential newspaper proprietor. In the case of Satyam, the board stepped in – albeit very late in the day – and the fraud came to light, though too late to protect the interests of the shareholders who had invested in this exciting new business.

Self-serving executives come on a smaller scale too. Managerial discretion can give executives the possibility of channelling business to companies that they, their relatives or their friends control. This, too, we see in Satyam, where the sons run the Maytas companies that do business with Satyam and which Satyam seeks to acquire, which would have had the effect of moving money from the listed company with public shareholders to the family.

The Italian dairy company Parmalat, whose failure in 2003 showed that continental Europe was not immune from the corporate governance disease that hit America in the previous two years, was run by its founder who regularly did business with companies owned by his children. Perhaps most spectacularly in recent history, Enron's struggle to prevent its own collapse meant that it did business with a series of companies set up by its own finance director, hoping that by putting the 'bad' business in what was in effect a 'shell' company with no substance, no one would notice just how 'bad' the business was (for further details of both cases, see Wearing, 2005).

For these reasons – and for the ethical issues they highlight – one of the issues between boards and management is how to monitor the practice known as *related-party transactions*. When a company does business with its own top managers – with the managers who decide whether to do the business – those individuals have a clear conflict of interest. Many employment contracts prevent members of the workforce from taking outside paid employment. Venture capital companies funding start-up companies require the entrepreneurs they back to sign quite onerous contracts that seek to prevent even ideas from escaping from the company into some new venture the entrepreneur might wish to start.

But senior managers of larger companies may well have the power to negotiate contracts that permit them to have outside activities, through which they can funnel dubious income. In countries with less well developed economies, stock markets and corporate governance practices, the area of related-party transactions is one the multilateral institutions like the OECD, the World Bank and International Finance Corp. take most seriously. They – along with internationally active institutional investors – look to boards of directors to establish special committees, made up entirely of independent, non-executive directors, to approve any contract of more than trivial sums of money made with an executive, his family or his friends.

Limits to board control of management

The case of Satyam demonstrates the risks that can arise when a company does business with parties closely related to those who have managerial power over the company's resources, and the discretion to use it. It might not have been quite so simple had B. Ramalinga Raju not also been the dominant shareholder and the architect of the company's early success. Here the board did constrain the manager, but not before the damage had been done.

The issues concerning executive pay, self-dealing and related-party transactions are those that figure prominently in agency theory and the solutions its proponents have advanced. Outside investors are wary of companies in which the founder or a major shareholder has direct managerial control. They often are willing to pay less to buy the shares in such a business than they would for another earning the same amount of money, in the same industry, but run by professional managers, unconnected with the controlling shareholder. That reluctance to fund the company means the company faces a higher cost of capital and therefore would – all things being equal – lose competitiveness over time.

Outside investors are often also wary of companies in which no one at all controls the CEO, even when there is no large shareholder or shareholding thought to be influencing the decisions. Institutional investors say – in a much-cited study by the consulting firm McKinsey & Co. – they will pay a premium price for shares of companies that follow good corporate governance practices (Newell & Wilson, 2002), giving well governed companies a lower cost of capital and greater competitiveness over time.

So it makes sense – commercial sense – to rein in the otherwise unfettered agent, a job that falls in the standard view of corporate governance to the independent non-executive directors and a watchful board of directors. The board, in this agency-based view of the corporation, is entrusted with working for shareholder value, as their agent overseeing the agents hired to run the business, the management. But what is shareholder value? What do shareholders value?

Further readings

Bebchuk, L. A. & Fried, J. M. (2003). Executive Compensation as an Agency Problem. *Journal of Economic Perspectives, 17*(3), 71–92.

Bebchuk, L. A. & Fried, J. M. (2004). *Pay without Performance: The Unfulfilled Promise of Executive Compensation.* Cambridge, MA: Harvard University Press.

Blair, M. M. & Stout, L. A. (1999). A Team Production Theory of Corporate Law. *Virginia Law Review, 85*(2), 247–328.

Finkelstein, S. & Boyd, B. K. (1998). How Much Does the CEO Matter? The Role of Managerial Discretion in the Setting of CEO Compensation. *Academy of Management Journal, 41*(2), 179–99.

Hallock, K. F. (1997). Reciprocally Interlocking Boards of Directors and Executive Compensation. *Journal of Financial & Quantitative Analysis, 32*(3), 331–44.

Lee, P. (2002). Not Badly Paid But Paid Badly. *Corporate Governance: An International Review, 10*(2), 69–75.

NINE

Issues between boards and owners

Case: Hermes, CalPERS and Investor

The overriding objective of a company should be to optimise over time the returns to its shareholders. To achieve this objective, the board should develop and implement a strategy for the company which improves shareholder value in the long term. Where other considerations affect the overriding objective, they should be clearly stated and disclosed.

Running a company in the long-term interests of its shareholders requires managing successful and productive relationships with the company's stakeholders, such as employees, suppliers and customers, and where appropriate taking their interests into account. Moreover, the company should behave ethically and have regard for the environment and society as a whole. However, given a company's overriding objective, the board is and should ultimately be accountable to its shareholders. (Corporate Governance Principles, Hermes, 2006, p. 3)

* * *

Beginning in 1993, CalPERS turned its focus toward companies considered by virtually every measure to be 'poor' financial performers. By centering its attention and resources in this way, CalPERS could demonstrate very specific and tangible results to those who questioned the value of corporate governance.

What have we learned over the years? We have learned that (a) company managers want to perform well, in both an absolute sense and as compared to their peers; (b) company managers want to adopt long-term strategies and visions, but often do not feel that their shareowners are patient enough; and (c) all companies – whether governed under a structure of full accountability or not – will inevitably experience both ascents and descents along the path of profitability.

We have also learned, and firmly embrace the belief that good corporate governance – that is, accountable corporate governance – means the difference between wallowing for long periods in the depths of the performance cycle, and responding quickly to correct the corporate course. (Global Corporate Governance Principles, CalPERS, 2009, p. 7)

* * *

Drive value in companies

Our work with the companies aims to make them best-in-class and thereby create value. We achieve this by having a strategic influence built on a significant ownership position. We take an active role in the Board to drive and follow up on value creation plans that focus on operational excellence, growth, capital structure and industrial structure . . .

Active ownership

We develop value creation plans for all holdings. These plans take an owner's perspective in identifying measures that can generate the most incremental value going forward.

The value creation plans are developed by our business teams. The plans are presented and discussed with our board representatives for each company. We extensively monitor the companies on an ongoing basis and benchmark their performance in relation to the plan and in comparison to competitors. The long-term goal is that the companies will be best-in-class and generate returns that exceed our return requirement. The value creation plans target four main areas: operational excellence, growth, capital structure and industrial structure. (Investor AB, 2009, pp. 7–8)

These three statements reflect the policies of asset management firms in three different countries. All three invest globally, though with the allocation of assets heavily weighted to their home countries and regions: Hermes in the UK, CalPERS in the US, and Investor AB in Sweden and other Nordic countries. Each is a very sizeable firm: In 2009 Hermes managed about $100 billion in assets, either owned directly or what it terms 'in stewardship', that is, on behalf of other firms. Although it is one of the largest pension funds in Europe, managing the retirement savings of BT, the former British Telecommunications, and the Royal Mail, Hermes is dwarfed by CalPERS, the California Public Employees' Retirement System, which had more than $700 billion in assets. Investor AB, a firm that looks after the finances of Sweden's wealthiest family, as well as outside investors, is tiny in comparison, with just $15 billion in assets in 2009. But it invests more selectively than the others, and when it does, it packs a big punch.

- *Hermes*: Its size and the number of people in the pension plan mean it almost has to invest in the entire UK stock market. It was formed in 1983 to manage the pensions as BT headed out of state ownership and towards privatization. Early on in its history, Hermes recognized that the only way it could improve the performance of its fund was to improve the performance of the companies in it. It simply could not afford not to engage actively with the companies in which it invested. 'Exit' was not an option, so exercising 'voice', it believed, was essential. Having put in place the mechanisms to do it, Hermes discovered it could make money another way: by taking very large stakes in poorly performing companies, agitating with the board for changes in strategy, key personnel, or both, and then selling out and moving on. A detailed study of its trading records showed this approach could generate returns roughly equal to the best performing hedge funds of the time (Becht et al., 2009). Though it shares with many UK asset managers a desire to operate in a 'gentlemanly' way, behind the scenes, it has learned that sometimes a public stance can be beneficial. It learned the benefits of this approach from none other than CalPERS.

- *CalPERS*: Managing the retirement savings of more than a million state employees, CalPERS pioneered the 'Focus' approach that Hermes then copied. It operates in the much larger capital markets of the United States, however, and where the governance model of the all-powerful chairman–CEO is still prevalent, so CalPERS takes a rather noisier approach to its engagement. Campaigns are often conducted in public, with news media and other investment firms invited to join in the hunt. It, too, is thought to be a highly successful investment strategy (Anson et al., 2003; Barber, 2006).

- *Investor AB*: The Wallenberg family built steadily on the legacy of its forebear, André Oscar Wallenberg, who founded one of Sweden's major banks in the mid-nineteenth century. Careful investing made it a powerhouse of Swedish capital markets, and Sweden's opposition to European attempts to require one share, one vote is often said to have the Wallenberg influence behind it. The family's investment vehicle owns minority stakes with majority voting rights or, if not, considerable influence over some of the biggest companies in the country and global leaders in their industries: ABB, a Swiss-Swedish power equipment giant, Astra-Zeneca, a Swedish-British pharmaceutical company, the industrial equipment manufacturer Atlas Copco, household appliance-maker Electrolux, the aircraft manufacturer Saab, as well as the bank where it all began, SEB. It does not just hold investments, it sells them too: Nasdaq bought OMX, the company behind the Stockholm and other stock exchanges; Volkswagen bought Investor's stake in the truck-maker Scania. When it invests Investor AB takes a big stake and one or more seats on the board. This is no 'distant' investor, as imagined in the 'modern corporation' that Berle and Means (1932/1991) had in mind, but instead a model of engagement that Oscar Wallenberg would recognize.

Postscript: Changes in senior personnel and strategy at Hermes in 2007 deprived it of some of its governance muscle. During his 18 months as chief executive of Hermes, Mark Anson, a former chief investment officer of CalPERS, oversaw the migration of most of the index-tracking funds for the BT pension scheme to another, lower-cost fund manager. As a result Hermes activism suffered from no longer having the voting power of the BTPS shareholders at its disposal. It then lost support from other pension funds, including CalPERS, which withdrew money from Hermes, forcing the firm into losses. In early 2010, however, it set off on a new strategy (Burgess, 2009). Governance pays, perhaps, but it is not a foregone conclusion.

Questions arising

Imagine yourself on the board of a public company, when you become aware that one of these investment firms has acquired a large stake in your company.

1 Do you welcome the attention of a powerful investor, one likely to attract others to follow suit, thus making it easier and less costly for you to raise capital, and make your business more competitive?

2 Do you worry that a group of interfering financiers who have never run a business, let alone one like yours, are going to start telling you what to do?
3 Or do you just worry they might soon tell you that *you* are not going to be doing it anymore?

Shareholder value

A humorous and yet penetrating look at Wall Street first published at the end of the Great Depression questioned whether investors were getting a good deal from the stockbrokers and investment banks who took their money and sold them shares. A visitor to New York's financial district is shown the harbour, where the bankers keep their boats moored. 'Where are the customers' yachts?' he wondered (Schwed, 1940/1995). After the stagflation of the 1970s, investors were asking a similar question, but this time about the management of the companies in which they invested, but it was not taken as a laughing matter. A rather duller phrase became the watchword – shareholder value – that nonetheless swept the world. Put those two words into an English-to-German translation tool and guess what pops out: 'Der Shareholder Value.'

It is a concept often associated with Jack Welch, the legendary chairman and CEO of General Electric during the 1980s, 1990s and into the new century. The US scholar Alfred Rappaport (1986) provided the intellectual muscle to back it up. Shareholder value is defined in a number of ways, all of them rough financial equivalents of each other. It is something thought of as the net present value of future cash flows, an accurate concept but one that is difficult to measure. Moreover, it treats shareholders as though they will own the business forever, which is not the case for public companies listed on a stock exchange, where real investors sell as well as buy shares. It is more, however, than mere profits, which is a technical accounting concept, subject to manipulation by managers. As a result, theorists of shareholder value have focused on a concept that investors can measure and use to assess the performance of management, and is entirely objective. It is sometimes called *total shareholder return* and is equal to the sum of dividends paid plus the change in the market capitalization of the business. The first part captures the traditional return to shareholders, a share of the surplus the business has created in a given time period. The second part of that equation puts the focus firmly on how well the share price performs. The investor can hold management to account for it over whatever time horizon best suits the investor. The focus on shareholder value is, therefore, a tool to keep management on its toes. It is another mechanism to solve the agency problem in corporate governance.

Shareholder value is also often thought to be to blame for the increasing short-term focus of corporate managements (Hendry et al., 2007; Tonello, 2006). In early 2009, Welch would renounce the term, at least in part: 'On the face of it, shareholder value is the dumbest idea in the world,' he told an interviewer. 'Shareholder value is a result, not a strategy . . . your main con-stituencies are your employees, your customers and your products' (Guerrera, 2009). Shareholder value is, therefore, a concept appropriately associated with institutional investors, who now dominate global investment.

Rise of institutional investment

The contemporary world of investment is very different from both the entre-preneur–financier model of the nineteenth century and the widely dispersed small shareholders that Berle and Means (1932/1991) saw in the modern cor-poration. In many companies, particularly outside the Anglo-American orbit, a single large shareholder dominates. But macro-economic pressures – including the growth of global capital markets – have begun to make investment practices increasingly similar around the world. Demographic pressures – in particular, increasing longevity resulting in ageing populations in the western world, Japan and China – have created an imperative to create vehicles for pension savings, pushing the world towards a new style of investment.

In the US, the most prominent type are called mutual funds. They began just before the Crash of 1929, and a similar trend emerged a few years later in the UK, when the first unit trusts were launched. Both gave small investors the chance to spread their risk across a wide range of investments by pooling their funds with those of other investors. An asset manager collected the funds and became the shareholder in a variety of corporations. After the Second World War, unit trusts and investment trusts, a different legal form of collec-tive investment, quickly came to dominate the landscape in Britain, and small investors holding shares directly were pushed to the sidelines.

Two other types of institutional investors developed in parallel with the increasing post-war prosperity. First, insurance companies put their money into the stock markets, in particular from life insurance policies, which needed money invested for the long term. Second, pension funds also needed to fund long-term liabilities and so invested in the stock market, with its promise of greater financial gains than those from government bonds or other invest-ment tools. Pension funds might manage investments directly or channel them through specialized asset management firms. Insurance funds might take simi-lar approaches to spread their investments more widely. And with the growth of private pension plans the differences between pension savings and life insur-ance became blurred.

In Britain, what gradually emerged was an investment landscape in which more than three-quarters of the shares of companies listed on the stock exchange were held by institutional investors. In the United States, individual investors remained more active, directly buying shares in companies. That approach persisted in part because of greater entrepreneurship and new companies, and

Table 2   European share ownership (FESE & ESC, 2008)

Type of owner	Weighted average ownership 2005 (%)	Weighted average ownership 2007 (%)
Foreign investors	33	37
Individual shareholders/households	15	14
Private non-financial companies	16	17
Private financial enterprises: collective investment	24	22
Private financial enterprises: banks and others	7	5
Public sector	5	5

in part because of the promotion of employee stock option programmes starting in the 1970s that encouraged ordinary employees to buy a stake in the businesses in which they worked. But the force of institutional investment proved irresistible in the US as well. Having gradually reached about half of the ownership of US corporations by 2000, the trend accelerated and within a few years institutions would come to own more than 70 per cent (Gillan & Starks, 2007).

These institutional investors – including pension funds like Hermes and CalPERS and asset managers like Investor – grew in significance in other markets too. The 'universal' banks, which are common in continental Europe, sell their customers investments as well as normal banking services, so they developed in-house asset management capabilities and collective investment products to sell to the public. Ageing populations created pressure in other countries to follow the UK and US model of private pension provisions, too, and insurance funds grew with greater prosperity. What emerged was an industry that became in many ways pan-European even before the European Union took steps to reduce national barriers to cross-border trade in investments in the mid-2000s. By 2007, for example, 37 per cent of equities across European markets – not just the EU – were held by non-residents (see Table 2). Within that overall figure we find greater variation: while in Germany only 21.3 per cent of shares were held by foreign investors, next door in the Netherlands the figure was 71.0 per cent. The data, from the Federation of European Stock Exchanges and the Economic and Statistics Committee (FESE & ESC, 2008), do not attempt to break down foreign owners into subcategories, but it seems reasonable to assume that most cross-border investment will be institutional, rather than private households or public sector. The figures do not reflect government action in the banking crisis of 2008–9, which increased public sector involvement in equity markets, but governments that took banks partly into state ownership stated the intention of reversing the position in the future.

It is tempting to view the rise of institutional investors as a large and homogenous block with common interests. Although it is a fragmented industry, the large funds share certain characteristics: they sell investment services to others, who become the beneficiaries but are not directly the 'owners' of the company in which their funds are invested. The beneficiaries are less interested, therefore, in the success of the company than they are in the success of the asset management firm and its ability to invest skilfully, and at the lowest possible cost.

The competition between them leads naturally to different investment strategies. Some focus on keeping the cost of investment low. Index-tracking funds, for example, operate on the premise that it is very difficult for any individual manager to outperform the stock market on a consistent basis. Rather than try, they develop investment products that match the performance of an index – the FTSE 100 or FTSE All-Share in the UK, the DAX-30 in Germany, the CAC-40 in France, or the SSE in Shanghai. Called *passive* investors, they then trade (and only when necessary) by computer rather than by hiring fund managers to watch the market and individual company shares. They tend, therefore, to be long-term investors, and in trying to keep costs down many do not try to keep track of how well the companies are performing. Unlike, say, Hermes, they are often docile as well as passive.

Others differentiate their products using the opposite strategy, paying high fees to people to conduct research into companies and try to find those that will outperform. These *active* investors seek to make a profit by buying shares they consider undervalued and then selling them when the stock reaches a target price, and then use the money to repeat the process on another stock. Their horizon may be long-term, but it is probably shorter than an index-tracker. Rather than vote at shareholder meetings or agitate with management for better performance they will exercise what has come to be called the 'Wall Street Walk' (Admati & Pfleiderer, 2009) by selling their shares.

Hybrids have emerged, too. Tracker funds may concentrate on a narrow index, say technology stocks or those identified as 'ethical' companies. In so doing they can mimic the offering of an active manager that selects individual stocks within an industry. Moreover, active managers may seek to outperform an index, and so keep most of their funds invested in the same shares that are in the index, mimicking the behaviour of passive funds, with a slightly different balance of shares than those in the index.

None of this would be particularly interesting to the director of a corporation were it not for one thing: whichever asset management firms holds the shares in the company at any given time is the shareholder whose 'value' the director is seeking to develop. Whichever asset management firm holds the shares at the time of the annual meeting is the one that will vote on whether that director is re-elected to the board.

Shareholder activism

Shareholders get their say about the corporation's affairs by voting at a shareholders' meeting. In most countries, under normal circumstances, this is an annual event, though it can be more frequent if a company is involved in a major transaction that might change the nature of its business or if another company mounts a takeover bid.

In nineteenth-century capitalism, the major shareholders of a corporation were active. They had seats on the board. They knew directly what was happening. Even today, a large, controlling shareholder will often still have direct access to the board and management. But in the modern corporation along Anglo-American lines, the holdings of even large institutional investors are rarely large enough to justify taking a seat on the board. Moreover, they often did not want to. Being an insider and having privileged access to information makes it awkward – and in most countries illegal – to buy or sell shares based on such exclusive information. Institutional investors make money by buying and selling shares.

Poor performance can spur shareholders into action, however. In the 1930s, activism emerged among some US individual investors who had suffered in the Great Crash and decided to make noise about it. They came to be called 'gadflies' who pestered the directors at the annual meeting. This type of activism arose again in the 1960s, first in the form of individuals seeking higher dividends or questioning whether the board was really working in shareholders' interest.[1] With the Vietnam War came a new type of activism: individuals or groups that would buy shares in companies with connections to the military, so they could attend the annual meeting in protest over the company's involvement in the arms trade. The early moves towards so-called ethical investing arose then, too, in protest against business involvement with the apartheid regime in South Africa. Churches and other charities, which regularly invest their surplus funds, were behind some of the earliest research into issues of corporate governance, though with a rather different agenda in mind than shareholder value.

By the 1980s, however, it had taken another shape. Some institutional investors, including CalPERS and the members of the Washington-based Council of Institutional Investors, concluded that the only way to make their funds perform better was to make management of companies perform better. Their holdings were too widely spread and some too large to be sold easily on the market. Robert Monks, who managed a private fund, set up a research company called Institutional Investor Services in 1984 to help them keep track of corporate governance issues at the companies in which they invested. They used the information to lobby government as well as corporate boards for changes in policy to improve shareholder rights.

Shareholder rights and issues

What are shareholder rights? In the first instance, they are what corporate law prescribes, and it differs from country to country, but it usually involves the right to elect the directors of the corporation and to ask them questions about the business, at least once a year. While investors sometimes like to call themselves 'owners', it is ownership with remarkably few rights.

That shareholder activism as we now know it arose in America is not surprising. Shareholders of US companies have rather fewer rights than those in other countries, as we saw in Chapter 5. Practices vary from state to state, but with about half of all listed companies having their legal seat there, Delaware has in effect the biggest say. Why? Because its laws have traditionally been friendliest towards the managements and boards that decide where to incorporate. Shareholders have the right to elect directors, but with special provisos, which we will come to in the next section. They also have to right to agree on mergers or take-over bids, though the definition here can be complex and practice may vary.

In other countries, shareholders have far greater rights. Across Europe, for example, shareholder votes are binding on companies, unless specifically written as advisory. Practice suggests, however, that shareholders do not always vote, sometimes for reasons of apathy, other times because of legal obstacles that prevent them from voting. In 2006, France changed the rules that had, in effect, prevented most institutional investors from other countries voting their shares. European Union reforms have aimed at breaking down other barriers to cross-border voting, too. But even so, often only half the shares will be cast at company shareholder meetings.

Then there is the issue: who votes? The shareholder, yes, but there are complications. A hot topic for many years in the US is the rule that allowed stockbrokers to vote the shares they held on behalf of clients unless the clients themselves had done so directly. The large stockbrokers are also investment banks that sell corporate finance services to corporate managements. They have an incentive, therefore, to vote with management and not for any dissident motions. This practice has become less important as institutional investment levels have increased, but conflicts of interest make the practice of broker-voting controversial.

Around Europe voting practice varies and is even more complex, in part because many countries permit companies to issue bearer shares. Ownership of these instruments is not registered officially with the company. Whoever comes to the annual meeting in possession of the certificates is entitled to vote. The practice has various benefits to shareholders. Those held in tax havens, for example, may escape notice of home-country authorities. Bearer shares permitted some of Europe's Jews from having all their wealth confiscated by the Nazis. But this practice also creates conflicts of interests or incentives for apathy. The bearer certificates may be in a bank vault, for example. The bank physically holds them and can vote the shares as they choose, unless the client collects them to attend the shareholder meeting. Like the case of broker votes in the US, banks would normally be inclined to support management. The greater temptation, however, is not to vote.

In Britain, as in the US, all company shares are registered. Shares owned by private individuals are increasingly held in 'nominee' accounts, however. It has the effect of making the custodian of those accounts the official shareholder of record, even though it has no economic interest in the company. In the US, custodians are obliged to pass along to the beneficial owners any information, including the proxy voting materials, they receive from the companies. In other jurisdictions, the end-owners may never hear from the company – and the company may never hear from them.

One share, one vote

The practice that every share in a company is the same as every other is so commonplace in the UK that even capital market professionals can be forgiven for thinking that this is a natural right. It is known as 'one share, one vote', echoing the nineteenth-century democratic ideal of 'one man, one vote' (now 'one person, one vote', of course). Indeed, UK-based asset management firms, insurance companies and pension funds regularly campaign to extend the practice around the world.

This is not, however, anything like a global norm. As we have seen, Investor AB uses Sweden's longstanding practice of giving some shareholders votes vastly disproportionate to the capital they have at risk. For many years Switzerland had two classes of shares, one which could only be held by Swiss citizens or Swiss domiciled companies, a practice the companies gave up themselves when it proved an impediment to raising new equity capital at favourable rates. German law gives the holder of more than 25 per cent of a company's shares veto power over many corporate decisions.

Efforts by institutional investors to implement a one share, one vote regime in the European Union have repeatedly faltered. The European Commission pressed hard for a Europe-wide rule that all shares should have votes equal to the percentage of capital they represent. The campaign ended after a study it commissioned (Caprasse et al., 2007) showed no harm and even some benefits from unequal voting rights.

The United States – so often seen as the other half of Anglo-American corporate governance – shows quite a different picture from the UK. Multiple classes of shares are not at all unusual. When the founders of Google took the company public in 2004, for example, they retained a large majority of the votes while selling off most of the company shares by using dual-class shares. Their shares carry 10 times the votes of ordinary ones. The case demonstrates that one share, one vote is not all that strong a principle for institutional investors. They will ignore unequal rights if the investment proposition is strong enough.

Director nominations

Shareholders elect the directors who will guide the corporation. That does not mean, however, they can *select* them, a source of contention between institutional investors and corporate boards, especially in the United States.

Boards, not shareholders, control the process of nominating new directors. The reforms introduced in the UK Combined Code and copied elsewhere have wrested control over nominations away from the CEO and concentrated the power with non-executives. But that does not give shareholders a direct say in nominations.

Shareholders of US companies do not even have the right *not* to elect directors. Practice varies state to state, and individual companies are free to adopt different rules. But in general, companies allow shareholders only to vote in favour of a director, not against. With what is called plurality voting, the director receiving any votes at all in an uncontested election will win as long as no other candidate for that post gets more votes. Almost all elections of directors are uncontested. In practice, therefore, the only way to defeat a director is to mount a 'proxy challenge', in which a shareholder solicits votes from other shareholders for another candidate. A costly and time-consuming process, it comes into play only when the company faces a hostile takeover bid.

Since the mid-2000s institutional investors have lobbied with the US Securities and Exchange Commission for a rule that would permit them, under certain circumstances, to nominate directors directly, on the same ballot paper as the board's own candidates. Initially passed by the SEC and then overturned by a court, the shareholder access rule resurfaced under the new Obama administration in 2009.

That US effort, though, raised some problematic issues for institutional investors themselves. Which shareholders should be allowed to nominate a director? Could someone with one share nominate himself? Might the board be hijacked by a clever band of one-issue candidates, seeking to have the company close down an operation they did not like or keep an uneconomic one open that they did like? This is not so far-fetched a concern. Protest votes are common and some have great traction, as a campaign against Chase Manhattan Bank's interests in South Africa in the 1970s showed. Trade unions have tried to gain representation on company boards as a way of preventing plant closures.

One solution is to limit such a right of nomination to only those shareholders with at least, say, 5 per cent of the company's shares, and perhaps only when they have held those shares for at least two years, showing they are not fly-by-night investors out to damage the company. These are positions that found resonance among many of the institutional investors that wanted to hold boards more accountable to shareholder value and to find solutions to the agency problem. But it they were adopted, what happens to the principle of one share, one vote?

Staggered boards – continuity or control?

For shareholders to oust a board of directors can be difficult if, as in many countries, directors are engaged for terms of several years and those terms do not coincide. These staggered election dates result in what American corporate governance calls classified boards. If directors stand only every three years, it will take two years to gain a majority of directors and three to turn over the entire board. Staggered boards have the advantage of giving continuity and long-term strategic development of the company. But they bring the disadvantage of giving power to the incumbents when shareholders are unhappy with the way the company is headed.

In Europe, shareholders seem more at ease about the idea, where three-year terms and staggered elections are common. In response to the financial crisis, however, the Walker Review (2009a, 2009b) in the UK urged that chairmen of banking and other financial firms stand every year, and committee chairmen stand again at the next shareholders' meeting if shareholders disapproved of their committee work. The 2010 code went further, seeking annual elections of all directors for the largest companies.

Say on pay

In 2002, the UK government gave shareholders a legal right to have an advisory vote on remuneration policy. It did not empower shareholders to vote directly on what level of payment the board and senior management should get, just on the way the board discussed how it had reached its conclusions. But it offered shareholders an extra lever, an additional way to get boards to pay attention to their interests, to what shareholders consider of value.

The UK move was copied in other European countries and outside Europe as well. Many UK-based institutional investors also have substantial investments in the United States. Many US-based institutional investors – including some of the world's largest: Fidelity, Brandes and Capital – have major operations in Europe, too, and through them ideas can travel quickly from one financial centre to another. A shareholder vote on remuneration policy, as the measure is known in Britain, became a snappy and memorable expression when it crossed the Atlantic: Say on Pay. Activist shareholders pressed the case for a say on pay with the SEC in Washington, with the state authorities, in particular in Delaware, and with individual company boards.

Agenda point 12: Care in activism

The Association of British Insurers explicitly rejected the idea of regulators limiting the pay of bankers (ABI, 2009), despite widespread public dissatisfaction with remuneration policies and despite the losses the insurance companies had faced on their own assets during the banking crisis. It praised the Financial Services Authority for not yielding to public clamour for a cap on earning.

'The FSA has stuck to its principle of linking remuneration to risk, while making the Code less prescriptive and narrowing the scope of the organisations covered,'

---

it said. 'We agree with the FSA that the focus should be on the structure of remuneration, not the size of the package, which companies must be able to determine based on their need to compete.

'And as shareholders, we support the proposal that bonus pools should be formed only after taking into account the cost of capital, adjusted for risk.'

Insurance companies are, of course, not just shareholders. They are also financial services firms, asset managers, in some cases with banking subsidiaries. Limits on executive pay might fall too close to home.

Remuneration is probably the single most fiercely fought, most debated issue in corporate governance, as we discussed in Chapter 8. Executive pay is therefore not just an issue between boards and management but between boards and owners, many of whom feel that boards have been lax or even complicit in the escalation of pay to senior managers and chief executives in particular. But it is also a topic that is vexed. Few institutional investors claim they know better than boards how much to pay a chief executive. That is, most argue, rightly a commercial decision for boards to make. By concentrating on process and policy issues, however, the movement for a say on pay has emphasized shareholders' determination that monitoring and control is firmly on the board's agenda.

Poison pills and anti-takeover devices

Shareholder activism since the 1970s has another root that is deeply important to institutional investors. The ultimate sanction against poorly performing management is that the company will be taken over. The aims of institutional shareholders differ from those of the companies they invest in. They seek to make money from investments, not to help the companies they invest in to sell more products and services. As a result, they want to be able to exit from their positions when it suits them, and on the best possible terms.

To do so, these investors have agitated, since the 1980s especially, for companies to dismantle any mechanisms that might constrain what is called the market for corporate control. Putting obstacles in the way of a potential bidder means that the investor might never hear that another company would be interesting in making an acquisition. A bid might go ahead anyway, but at a lower price. Anti-takeover devices take a variety of shapes and forms, many with colourful names. Golden parachutes give top executives, and even non-executive directors, a big payoff if the company they lead is taken over and they lose their jobs. These do not necessarily stop a takeover bid, but they mean that shareholders get less of a premium for their shares because money goes instead to the departing managers.

The PacMan defence was popular for a while: the company that found itself under attack from a hostile bidder would make a counterattack, bidding for its own bidder. Shareholders soon revolted against them and the practice has become less common in recent years. Other defences involve issuing new equity to existing shareholders only to make the cost of the acquisition higher, selling subsidiaries, or giving key executives very long contracts and extra share options.

Agenda point 13: Salutary lessons from the market for corporate control

Self-serving managers can construct defences against a takeover bid. Some work, but others fail. Barclays, the UK-based international banking group, agreed to buy its Dutch rival ABN Amro in 2007, a friendly takeover in which much of ABN's management would be kept on. During the discussion, Barclays negotiated a clause to repel any potential hostile bid. If another suitor emerged ABN would continue, as planned, to sell its Chicago-based subsidiary La Salle to Bank of America.

La Salle's assets, a retail banking network, were especially prized by Barclays' would-be rival for ABN, the Royal Bank of Scotland, which joined with Fortis of Belgium and Santander of Spain to mount a counterbid. Barclays thought that creating a 'poison pill' might deter the RBS consortium from making a counterbid. It failed. The consortium outbid Barclays for ABN Amro even though Bank of America would get La Salle. But ABN Amro shareholders were unhappy that the chances of an even higher bid for the company had been thwarted.

Two years later, Fortis had collapsed and RBS was teetering on the edge, having overstretched themselves in buying ABN. It was rescued from insolvency when the UK government took a 70 per cent stake in the business. Barclays, the loser in the contest for ABN, was the winner of the bigger competitive contest.

The principle remains the same. Institutional investors in general want to achieve the highest possible price for the shares they own. One way to do that is to sell the business to another company that considers the business worth more than current management and the current board is able to deliver. It is the same argument that most institutional investors have against disproportionate voting rights, and against companies that have a single large shareholder which might not wish to sell to the highest bidder, or might try to engineer its own exit on terms favourable to it but not available to the smaller shareholders with less inside information and less ability to influence corporate policy.

Whose value?

Institutional investors have been fairly aggressive since the 1980s in asserting shareholder rights and lobbying for more. Some of the most aggressive – as the cases of Hermes, CalPERs and Investor show – are those which have determined that the scale of their business means that 'exit' is not always an alternative to 'voice'. Their voice has been particularly important in development of the UK Combined Code and other similar measures around the world. Through the International Corporate Governance Network, they have spread a view of shareholder rights and a mode of corporate governance to emerging capital markets as well. The driving forces behind this movement have been traditional asset managers who take an active approach to engagement with companies. Some are passive investors that seek through improving corporate governance practices to improve the performance of the companies in which they invest. Others are active investors, who will buy and sell shares to achieve an extra margin and use shareholder activism – their engagement with companies and boards – to help them achieve the gains. The largest institutions can be very large indeed, but most try to limit their exposure to any particular company's risk by limiting their investments to a few percentage points of the equity. But others, like Investor AB, take major stakes and then demand more than just a dialogue about the business.

Concerns about corporate governance have led to discussions about not just the rights of shareholders, but also their responsibilities, and in particular the responsibilities of these institutional investors. Their own governance has been thrown into question: To what extent do asset managers put the interests of their clients first? How does that work in a business in which managers are paid mainly on the level of assets they manage, rather than how those assets perform? How well equipped are pension funds to look after the interest of their beneficiaries, especially in systems where the corporations that fund employee pensions can control the processes that trustees use? These issues are now recognized within the fund management industry (Cadbury & Millstein, 2005), and reflected in the 'shareholder responsibilities' section in various codes of conduct. The governance of asset management itself is perhaps a special case of the broader corporate governance debate.

This discussion has focused on the role these institutional investors play in capital markets and how that affects the work of the corporation's board. It takes one view of shareholder value – or better put, one general view of the way companies create value for one class of shareholder. We have considered, however, an example of how different shareholders can have differing views of the same decision: the family shareholder versus the distant institution. There are others: the employee shareholder might want to preserve his job rather than give the distant institution a chance to earn a bigger capital gain. Even distant institutions can oppose others: A trade union pension fund that thinks its beneficiaries would be better off if the company preserved jobs at home rather than reducing costs by outsourcing to a country with low-wage labour. A traditional fund manager, however, might value more the boost to profitability, a higher distribution through dividends and the chance to invest that money back home – even in the same town – in a new business promising jobs for the future.

The traditional institutional investor has become an integral part of the corporate governance debate, but it is in some ways in decline. Traditional insurance, pension and mutual funds remain, but they make up a decreasing proportion of the assets under management. By contrast, new types of investment vehicles or new, supercharged versions of businesses that have existed for a while have grown in importance, changing the character of shareholding around the world: hedge funds, private equity funds, sovereign wealth funds. Their methods of investing and purpose in investing can at times be qualitatively and quantitatively different from even the most active and activist of old-style shareholders, as we explore in Chapter 10.

Boards can find themselves puzzled, therefore, about just what constitutes shareholder value, if shareholders have different values.

Note

1 Be careful not to confuse shareholder activism with shareholders who are active investors. The same shareholder can be both, but the former refers to engagement in debate with the company over policy, the latter to whether they trade their shares actively in an effort to maximize their gain.

Further readings

Admati, A. R. & Pfleiderer, P. (2009). The 'Wall Street Walk' and Shareholder Activism: Exit as a Form of Voice. *Review of Financial Studies, 22*(7), 2645–85.

Aguilera, R. V., & Cuervo-Cazurra, A. (2004). Codes of Good Governance Worldwide: What is the Trigger? *Organization Studies, 25*(3), 415–43.

Becht, M., Franks, J., Mayer, C. & Rossi, S. (2009). Returns to Shareholder Activism: Evidence from a Clinical Study of the Hermes UK Focus Fund. *Review of Financial Studies, 22*(8), 3093–129.

Coffee, J. C., Jr. (1991). Liquidity versus Control: The Institutional Investor as Corporate Monitor. *Columbia Law Review, 91*(6), 1277–368.

Daily, C. M., Dalton, D. R. & Rajagopalan, N. (2003). Governance through Ownership: Centuries of Practice, Decades of Research. *Academy of Management Journal, 46*(2), 151–8.

Davis, S. M., Lukomnik, J. & Pitt-Watson, D. (2009). Active Shareowner Stewardship: A New Paradigm for Capitalism. *Rotman International Journal of Pension Management, 2*(2), 10–17.

Gillan, S. & Starks, L. (2007). The Evolution of Shareholder Activism in the United States. *Journal of Applied Corporate Finance, 19*(1), 55–73.

Hendry, J., Sanderson, P., Barker, R. & Roberts, J. (2007). Responsible Ownership, Shareholder Value and the New Shareholder Activism. *Competition & Change, 11*(3), 223–40.

Lysandrou, P. & Stoyanova, D. (2007). The Anachronism of the Voice–Exit Paradigm: Institutional Investors and Corporate Governance in the UK. *Corporate Governance: An International Review, 15*(6), 1070–8.

Monks, R. A. G. (2009). The Return of the Shareholder. Retrieved 13 April 2009, from http://www.ragm.com/ReturnShareholderMonks.pdf.

Picou, A. & Rubach, M. J. (2006). Does Good Governance Matter to Institutional Investors? Evidence from the Enactment of Corporate Governance Guidelines. *Journal of Business Ethics, 65*(1), 1–55.

Wymeersch, E. (2007). Shareholders in Action. Retrieved 25 Aug. 2007, from http://ssrn.com/paper=965661.

TEN

Issues between owners

In this chapter we consider two cases that raise similar issues in quite different circumstances.

Case: All in the family – VW, Porsche and Lower Saxony

By the middle of 2008, the big institutional investors had grown uneasy about their investments in the German carmaker Volkswagen AG. Owning the shares had become too political. More than 30 per cent of the shares were held by Porsche Automobil Holding SE. VW's supervisory board chairman, Ferdinand Piëch, was a member of the family that controls Porsche, which had become something of a corporate governance pariah, having refused to accept the unofficial norm of quarterly financial reporting in Germany. It had also irritated the country's Social Democrats by dropping the *Aktiengesellschaft* legal form in favour of the new European Union *Societas Europeas* form, which would allow it to reduce representation of German workers on the Porsche supervisory board. Moreover, Piëch had ousted the VW chief executive in 2006 and then entered a court battle with the company's second largest shareholder.

The state of Lower Saxony in Germany not only held more than 20 per cent in the company. It benefited from a special law giving it veto power over important managerial and board decisions, a statute recently reinforced by the German parliament after the European Court of Justice ruled parts of the old law illegal. The European Commission had said that the new version of what German news media like to call the 'VW law' was illegal, and Porsche agreed. But attempts at the VW's annual meeting by other shareholders – including activist institutional investors – to seek to challenge Porsche's creeping control of its rival carmaker fell on deaf ears (Milne, 2005, 2006; Milne et al., 2008).

Others characterized the manoeuvrings as a conflict of personalities between rival branches of the Porsche dynasty: Piëch at VW and his cousin Wolfgang Porsche, chairman of the company his (and Piëch's) grandfather had founded (Betts, 2009).

Within a few months, Porsche used a derivative instrument known as a contract for difference to acquire an economic interest equivalent to about 75 per cent of the stock of VW. Because it had not bought the shares themselves, it was able under German law to keep that fact secret. Speculators, including hedge funds, had expected a fall in the price of VW and sold short, selling shares they did not in fact own, a common if controversial practice in equity capital markets. Soon they faced a mad scramble to cover their positions. VW shares soared by 400 per cent, making it briefly the most valuable company in the world. Newspaper reporters began to liken Porsche itself to a giant hedge fund with a small carmaker attached (Schäfer & Mackintosh, 2009).

Within a few more months, Porsche was struggling with the debt levels it had accumulated to buy its stake in VW and all the derivative contracts. Piëch at VW would win this round. Instead of Porsche buying VW, VW would buy Porsche, bringing its greater capital to help reduce Porsche's debt, but with Porsche's shareholders still in majority control of the larger VW. Moreover, Wolfgang Wiedeking, once thought to be the best paid executive in Europe, was ousted as Porsche CEO, albeit with a €50 million severance package. The Middle Eastern emirate of Qatar, a country rich in natural gas, would become a major shareholder, too. And the German state of Lower Saxony retained its special blocking minority stake (Schäfer, 2009). No one asked the other shareholders for their opinions.

Questions arising

The battle between VW and Porsche has broader relevance than just how German law applied at the time.

1 Why should dominant shareholders have special rights?
2 What is fair and unfair about the veto power of government as a shareholder in an otherwise private enterprise?
3 What are the obligations and rights of share ownership?
4 Do they apply equally to all – long-term investors as well as short-term traders?
5 Equity derivatives give some parties an economic interest without shareholding. What are their rights and obligations to the company? To other investors?
6 What are the rights and obligations of investors who hold shares simply to back a short-sale?

Case: Locusts, eating – Deutsche Börse meets the 'Children'

Perhaps the most celebrated case in the brief history of hedge fund activism was the move by a fund with the cuddly name The Children's Investment

Fund, or TCI, which rocked the tradition-bound world of German equities. When Deutsche Börse, the German stock exchange company, tried to take over the London Stock Exchange in 2004, TCI sensed an opportunity to prevent the merger and generate a higher share price for Deutsche Börse.

The shares of the company making the bid often fall during or after a takeover, reflecting the premium paid for the acquired company. In cases of contested takeovers, the premium is likely to be even higher. TCI sensed that if it could thwart the merger, Deutsche Börse's share price would increase. It acquired a substantial stake and agitated for a change in direction through contesting the re-election of directors at the exchange company's 2005 annual meeting. The move attracted other hedge funds to follow suit, and soon a substantial minority and perhaps even a majority of shares in this most German of institutions was in the hands of foreigners, mainly UK- and US-based hedge funds.

The tactic succeeded to a greater extent than almost anyone had imagined possible. Deutsche Börse not only abandoned its bid, it dismissed the chairman of its supervisory board as well as its chief executive and chief financial officer (Nordberg, 2005). Germany's vice chancellor then famously warned about 'locusts' invading the capital markets (Bovensiepen & Blechschmidt, 2005), and a new term – hedge-fund activism – entered the corporate governance lexicon (Achleitner & Kaserer, 2005).

TCI's intervention in the case of Deutsche Börse was in the spirit of much of the activism of corporate raiders in the 1980s and 1990s, using leverage to invest heavily in a company and then using its voting power and an appeal to reason to persuade other investors to join it in seeking a change in strategic direction. We may never be able to tell whether it ultimately created value, as so many other changes in the company and its competitive landscape have ensued. TCI attracted support from other, traditional, long-term investors more associated with 'walking' than activism, suggesting that its interest was not what we might call *perverse*. But its chosen approach – to get its slate of directors elected, rather than the one proposed by the company – shows it engaged in a play for power with the board and management of Deutsche Börse and with the government and their trade union allies that rose up to defend the status quo.

(Both cases are exerpted from Nordberg, 2010a, with permission of the publisher, John Wiley & Sons Inc.)

Questions arising

Deutsche Börse was a German institution, but it ran into trouble with its largely foreign institutional investors, led by hedge funds.

1 What is the basis for the differences in view between different shareholders?
2 How might hedge funds differ in orientation from more conventional shareholders?
3 Through what mechanisms and processes might shareholder rights become the basis for power over corporate affairs?

4   When facing a decision over strategic allocation of resources, how should management and the board take shareholder interests into account?

5   Does it matter whether today's shareholders might not be there tomorrow?

Shareholder activism as politics

So far we have considered shareholder activism as a question of rights. Might it also be a question of wrongs?

Whichever way we look at it, one thing is clear: shareholders do not always share the same interests. Advocates of a shareholder-value-based approach to corporate governance often assume that the formula for that value suffices: dividends, plus capital gains, discounted by the time-value of money equals shareholder value created. When it comes to managing the business to deliver that, directors become aware of how different some shareholders are from others.

Value chain for shareholders

The equity capital in a corporation arises from a number of different starting points, taking a number of different paths.

Private individuals may invest directly in the stock. They may be ordinary members of the public, but some may have another connection to the company, say as employees. Those private individuals may be more interested in dividend income than capital gains, or vice versa. Employee shareholders may be willing to sacrifice both for the sake of keeping their jobs. Private individuals may also choose to invest via collective investments like mutual funds, in which case a money manager acts as intermediary – as agent to the end-investor, creating another layer of agency problems. Private individuals also save for the future through **pension funds**, either by direct, defined contributions or through employer-supported pension plans that promise to pay a proportion of final salaries or perhaps of average salaries earned during employment. Pension plan trustees act as agent for the saver, and while some invest directly, others employ specialist **asset management firms**. Private individuals may also take out insurance policies, perhaps life insurance but also casualty plans, and premiums they pay to insurance companies find their way in part to equity markets through **insurance funds**. Here the private individual is a contractual beneficiary of the insurance company, but the insurer is the principal of the investment. The insurance company may have an agency relationship as well with pension funds, as insurance funds often manage the assets of the pensions industry.

Corporations sometimes might make purely financial investments in other corporations, not expecting a strategic relationship. But such investments could also be strategic – the basis for a long-term partnership, or the outcome of a cash injection to facilitate research and development. Corporations also occasionally invest in other corporations as a 'spoiler' or something like 'shark repellent':

knowing that one company is already a big investor in the takeover target might deter another from bidding.

Private equity funds are special cases of corporate investors. These companies may work for wealthy individuals or for asset management companies seeking to diversify their investments. They may even be listed on a stock exchange themselves. They typically invest in a public company for the sake of taking it off the stock exchange, restructuring its operations and then perhaps selling it on to another company in the same industry, or even floating it on the stock market again.

Sovereign wealth funds grew out of the rise in the surplus income that some commodity-rich countries developed, money in excess of what they could spend on economic development. Funds like the Abu Dhabi Investment Authority or the Kuwait Investment Authority placed their national oil wealth in large investments in individual companies as well as spreading other funds widely in the stock market. The Norwegian government uses its oil surpluses to fund a generous state pension plan for all its citizens. More recently China's trade surpluses with the United States and other countries have led to creation of state enterprises to invest in equity markets abroad. Traditionally they have acted just as any other asset management firm; indeed, they have employed people with experience in insurance or mutual funds to operate the business. As government-owned entities, however, there is always a possibility their investments abroad could be directed for foreign policy rather than purely financial aims.

Hedge funds have grown rapidly in recent years. Initially they catered mainly to very rich private investors – high net-worth or even 'ultra' high net-worth individuals, a category of investors that now play a big role in world finance (for an overview, see Capgemini & Merrill Lynch, 2009). From movie stars to professional athletes to entrepreneurs and investment bankers themselves, these individuals routed money into hedge funds as their wealth started to escalate during the 1990s. Like traditional fund managers, they pool the money of other investors to achieve economies of scale. But unlike traditional funds, they often borrow substantial sums from banks to create greater leverage in their portfolio, increasing the scope for return. That would normally increase the risk of failure as well, but hedge funds use derivative instruments to hedge those risks (hence the name). The category includes funds with a wide variety of different investment styles. Some invest only for a few minutes, even a few seconds, taking advantage of brief price anomalies. Others may take large positions in a company's equity – as TCI did with Deutsche Börse – and use their shareholding to seek to influence corporate policy. So successful have many of these funds become that traditional asset management have come to invest in them too, seeking to boost their own performance by investing in these turbo-charged investment vehicles. Hedge funds suffered in the financial crisis of 2007–09 along with all other forms of investment, proving that hedging does not offer foolproof protection.

Dimensions of shareholder interests

Investors who buy shares in companies might be expected to share similar desires for good financial performance from the company. But it is not that easy. Investor interests vary over three dimensions – attitude, engagement and horizon – that can influence how they view value (for a fuller discussion of this section, see Nordberg, 2009b).

First, consider their **attitude** towards a stock. Investors may be inclined at any given time to buy the shares, sell, or hold them, or in the parlance of financial markets *accumulate, reduce* or *maintain*. Someone buying wants (temporarily) the lowest possible value for the stock, someone selling wants the highest. Stock exchanges grew up to provide a market mechanism to settle on the right price. But inside the boardroom of the company in which they have invested, such differences in attitude can occasionally affect policy. Take the example of a company that only recently joined the stock market through an *initial public offering* of stock. Perhaps it developed its business with the help of a venture capitalist, an investor who specializes in start-up businesses, or some other type of private equity fund. Those investors will want to exit from their positions to take up another, and so want management to take actions that will boost the share price in the near term. The traditional asset management firm that bought its shares during the IPO will probably be more interested in seeing the company achieve long-term, sustainable growth. So then, faced with a decision to invest heavily in research and development or to emphasize sales while preserving cash, which way does the board decide? How can the board be guided by shareholder value when the values of shareholders differ so radically?

Second, shareholders differ according to their **engagement** with the companies in which they invest. Some take an *activist* stance, choosing to influence corporate boards and management through direct conversations. Others are *walkers*, more inclined to sell their positions if they do not like corporate policy than to seek to change it. A third possible approach is being *docile*, the situation that many investors adopt when they wish to forgo the cost of monitoring corporate performance. It is particularly in evidence with index-tracking funds that seek to compete on having the lowest possible cost.

The third dimension on which investors can differ is their investment **horizon**. Some funds are in general inclined to invest for the long term, whatever attitude they might have towards an individual stock at the moment. They expect managements in general to act, therefore, in the long-term interests of the business, corresponding with the investor's long-term orientation. Others trade frequently and are more interested, therefore, in seeing better performance over the *short term*. Such active traders often stress the need for corporate managements to meet quarterly earnings targets. While sometimes associated with hedge funds, this type of approach is widespread among actively managed traditional funds, where the speed at which funds turn over their portfolio can be quite short. By one calculation, actively managed funds in the US have

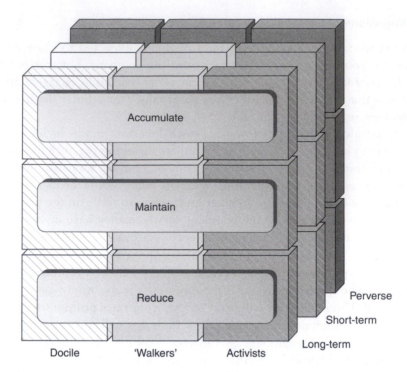

Figure 6 Shareholder stance

been selling the equivalent of their entire holdings every 11 months in the early 2000s, compared with seven or eight years during the 1950s and 1960s (Montier, 2007). John Bogle, who founded the mutual fund group Vanguard in the US, once said: 'We are no longer an *own*-a-stock industry. We are a *rent*-a-stock industry' (Bogle, 2003). A third type of horizon is one we might call *perverse*, in which the economic interest of the investor is opposite from what you would expect from their share ownership position, most often related to stock lending and short-selling.

The three dimensions are summarized in Figure 6, suggesting how widely the economic basis of shareholder interests might vary over corporate decisions. We shall examine a *perverse* horizon in greater detail because it can lead to strange decisions and because it has become increasingly important in capital markets and the public policy debate.

Stock lending, short-selling

Stock lending and short-selling are often linked but they do not have to be to create perverse situations in corporate governance. For many years institutional investors have borrowed and lent shares to each other. The process takes the form of a repurchase contract, in which one investor sells the shares while agreeing simultaneously to buy them back at a future time and a specified price. The reasons for doing it may vary. Perhaps one fund is designed for tax reasons to want to emphasize capital gains rather than dividend income. It might lend stock to another investor over the period during which the dividend is paid, earning a bit of money in the meantime on the difference between the price at which it sells and the price at which it buys the stock back. The counterparty may be interested in receiving dividends or in balancing its portfolio ahead of a valuation date, or have other reasons for wishing to borrow. The impact, however, is that for a period of time the economic interest in the development of the corporation's business becomes separated from the ownership of the shares. The lender has a long-term interest in the business, even though it is no longer the share*holder*.

Agenda point 14: The 'naked' short

You could be forgiven for thinking that if someone had his shorts on, he couldn't possibly be naked. But like the emperor's new clothes, life in financial markets isn't always what you imagined. Naked short-selling, another colourful phrase from the world of investment, involves the situation in which a trader sells stock in a company that he doesn't own. In 'normal' short-selling, the trader borrows shares on a repurchase agreement, allowing him to deliver real shares against his sale, and then buying them back at a future date and hopefully at a lower price. The 'naked short' doesn't bother with the cost of borrowing shares: he just sells.

It works well if the trader is expecting to buy the shares back the same day, thus closing his position before the trades go into settlement at the end of day. It helps liquidity by providing counterparties for normal buy-orders that might not otherwise have found a willing seller. But sometimes these positions aren't closed immediately, a trade doesn't complete and the market has an imbalance.

Unlike 'covered' short positions, naked short-selling shouldn't have an impact on the principles of corporate governance, as the seller never holds the shares in question. But aggressive naked shorting can depress the share price, causing the management, the board and other investors to question what is happening, even their strategic decisions. Combined with false rumour-mongering, it could damage the business.

With a naked short-sale at the time of a shareholders' meeting, there's a new 'owner' who thinks – quite legitimately – that he has the right vote. Indeed, the broker might well record the transaction as complete, and the non-holder of these phantom shares might well get proxy materials.

It's not surprising, therefore, that naked shorting comes under even closer regulatory scrutiny than the covered variety. (*The BoardAgenda*, 2 May 2005, http://www.edgevantage.co.uk/categories/article.asp?i=2455.)

This may not in practice have any impact on the company. Lenders and borrowers are often otherwise similar in their stances: for example, inclined to hold and docile in engagement. But in some circumstances it can, and with particularly perverse implications for corporate governance. Short-selling is a fairly common practice in developed capital markets, and with good reason. A short sale arises when a trader seeks to benefit from an expected fall in the share price. Perhaps he anticipates poor economic news or has reason to believe that management is taking the wrong direction. He sells the sales with the intention of buying them back at a lower price at sometime in the future. It is a speculative exercise, but so is holding shares in expectation of a rise in the price. Proponents of short-selling argue that allowing the practice helps buyers and sellers to agree on the 'right' price of the stock more easily. When most investors think a stock is going to rise in value, it helps to have a contrarian in the market willing to sell – it improves *liquidity*.

To deliver against the sale, the trader might borrow stock from another investor, promising to return it once he has closed his position. If this happens over the period in which the company is holding a shareholder meeting, corporate governance issues can arise. The short-seller is temporarily the holder of the shares, and therefore the one entitled to vote. But that trader's economic interest is in seeing the share price fall – and the further the better. In this way, the economic interest of the shareholder is strongly at variance with the economic interest of the business.

In a few exceptional cases, and mainly to do with smaller companies, traders have borrowed a majority of the stock in a company to sell them short. For the interim period, the wishes of the majority of the shareholders would be best served by closing the business down, not by trying to make it better. These have been extreme cases, of course, but they underscored the conceptual problem if in setting business policy boards rely on doing what is in the best interests of shareholders.

Agenda point 15: Mylan and 'empty voting'

An example of the governance problem in this type of perverse relationship is the case of the 2004 bid by Mylan Laboratories to acquire King Pharmaceutical in the US, which resulted in so-called 'empty voting'. The hedge fund Perry was a major shareholder of King and stood to benefit from the transaction. However, shareholders in Mylan needed to approve the transaction, and opposition to the deal arose from some larger ones, including the activist investor Carl Icahn. To push the deal through, Perry bought a stake in Mylan, simultaneously hedging the investment with equity swap with two investment banks; indeed, the swaps

---

> more than covered Perry's exposure. That gave Perry 9.9 per cent voting rights at a time when it had a net negative economic interest in Mylan (Hu & Black, 2006; Kahan & Rock, 2006).

For this reason, too, policymakers have always kept a close eye on capital market practices that can create perverse relationships between the interests of investors and the companies in which they invest. Short-selling is illegal in some markets and tightly regulated in others. In the wake of the collapse of Lehman Brothers in the autumn of 2008, governments and regulators around the world tightened up their constraints on short-selling in financial company stocks, wanting to avoid 'bear raids' aimed at driving down the value of the banks and insurance companies, which might threaten their solvency or make them vulnerable to exploitative takeovers.

Even in the United States, the authorities clamped down on short-selling when the crisis took hold in September 2008, only to reverse the decision three weeks later. Christopher Cox, who stepped down as chairman of the SEC a few months later, called it the worst decision of his tenure (Paley & Hilzenrath, 2008).

Issues with major shareholders

Having a big shareholder can bring benefits. Their interests are large enough that it pays for them to keep a close eye on management (Sabherwal & Smith, 2008). Indeed, their monitoring can be seen as a mechanism that allows other shareholders to become corporate governance 'free-riders', gaining the benefit of monitoring without bearing the costs.

There is a downside, however, as a large shareholder can influence business decisions in ways that drain funds away from the company, and therefore from other shareholders. This worry sits behind the concerns of so-called minority shareholders, especially in civil law countries including France and Belgium, where the courts have seen as legal a variety of devices sometimes called *tunnelling*. Simon Johnson and his colleagues (2000, p. 26) write: 'In civil-law countries, the expropriation of minority shareholders by the controlling shareholder in a transaction with a plausible business purpose is often seen as consistent with directors' duties, especially if the controlling shareholder is another firm in the group. Self-dealing transactions are assessed in light of their conformity with statutes, and not on the basis of their fairness to minorities.'

With the spread of Anglo-American equity market practices and the globalization of institutional investment, market pressure for greater shareholder

Table 3 Investor types

Fund type	Investment approach	Governance implications
Business angels	Seed funding for small ventures, often by successful business people taking a gamble on what they see as an interesting idea Takes large stake, alongside owner–manager Highly speculative, these might exit to a venture capital fund or later stage Horizon is long-term, perhaps for life of a small business	Investors often behind close scrutiny, board places, perhaps role in management Engagement probably activist
Venture capital	1st or 2nd stage funding for new ventures Takes large stake, alongside owner–manager Exit sought, probably to IPO or private equity Modelled on early capitalist financiers but often by aggregating investment of high-net-worth individuals or even large asset managers Horizon is long-term, with possible early exit	Investor seeks rigorous over sight of operations, board Highly interventionist seats Engagement highly activist
Traditional asset Managers	Invests in companies listed on stock exchange, also in bonds, real estate and other assets Risk diversification means stake in individual businesses kept at modest level Holds and trades shares Through aggregating large volumes of savings, these investors are together able to provide large amounts of capital May themselves be listed companies, private companies, attached to insurers or pension funds Most are long-only, i.e. not engaged in short-selling, many have statutes requiring them not to use leverage Horizon may be long or short, occasionally perverse through stock lending	Exercises governance through exit (sale on exchange) or voice (voting at shareholder meeting May demand briefings from management on other occasions Tend to be hands-off unless something is going wrong Engagement may be docile, activist or 'walker'
Private equity funds	Similar to VCs, but with even larger sums available May take a listed company off the stock market by buying all the shares and taking while the company out of the public eye for a while Aim is often to restructure the business with a view to selling it on, either into a trade buyer (as subsidiary of large company) or by relisting the stock at a future date Aggregate funds from private investors, traditional asset managers Often highly leveraged, using large-scale bank loans to boost returns	Like VCs, investor demands rigorous oversight at detailed operational level Control of board expected Engagement highly activist

Table 3 (Cont'd)

Fund type	Investment approach	Governance implications
	Horizon usually long-term, but may seek opportunistic early exit	
Hedge funds	A mixed category with differing investment approaches Aggregate funds from high-net-worth individuals, increasingly from traditional asset managers Almost always highly leveraged, often using derivative instruments to hedge downside risk Horizon can be very short term – many funds engage in intraday trading, buying and then selling the stock within minutes or even seconds Some funds take a long-term horizon (hedge fund activists), but trade opportunistically Position sizes may vary from the small to occasionally very large economic stakes in the target companies, through combinations of shares, options and other derivatives Horizon can also be perverse through short-selling, stock lending	Intraday traders will not have scope to engage in governance directly Danger that unfounded rumour mongering by traders could push shares up or down to meet trading objective of the fund Engagement of some, however, can be highly activist to meet a trading objective

protection has led to development of stock-market rules as well as changes in law to prevent such self-serving actions by major shareholders. Board-level review of related-party transactions, with independent directors in charge of the committees, is among the solutions used.

Power balances in corporate governance

The cases of Volkswagen/Porsche and Deutsche Börse show just how fiery the disagreements between shareholders can be, especially when some use financial derivatives and leverage to fan the flames. In the case of Volkswagen, the mixture of family tensions and government involvement in what was once viewed as a strategic industry would raise complex governance issues even without the addition of global investment, hedge funds and the use of derivatives by Porsche to exploit a loophole in German disclosure rules. Deutsche Börse might have gone ahead with its plans to acquire the London Stock Exchange in a traditional way had not the untraditional world of highly leveraged hedge funds intervened. These differences in views between shareholders mean that we can view corporate governance as a battle for power over the resources of the company. The different types of shareholders are summarized in Table 3.

The assertion of shareholder rights can be viewed as an attempt of one set of shareholders – those with a stance that is *maintain* in attitude, *activist* in engagement and *long-term* in horizon – to gain power not only over management but over shareholders who are short-term in horizon and seeking to boost the share price as quickly as possible, or those who are usually long-term on horizon but at the moment inclined to sell that stock at the moment.

What we see developing is, therefore, the potential for various coalitions of interests among shareholders that would normally take different stances towards a company in which they invest. Traditional asset managers will tend to work on a long-term horizon, even if they may be inclined to turn over their portfolios quickly, because they need to stay invested and across a wide range of stocks to reduce the risk of the portfolio as a whole. It is not surprising, therefore, to find common ground between them over the broad purpose of the corporation: the creation of shareholder value. Some Marxists scholars go so far as to say their common interests unite in such a way as to seek to turn their investments into commodities (a standardized flow of dividends and capital gains) to make the fund managers' own products (mutual funds) more reliable, irrespective of the best outcome for the individual business in their portfolios (Lysandrou & Stoyanova, 2007).

Though they once dominated the investment landscape – especially in the UK – their influence is now waning. The rise in institutional investment in equities in the US as well as the UK, for example, has been largely a result of the growth of hedge funds. Sovereign equity funds have grown in importance in all markets. Their contribution to the rescue of the global banking system in 2008 was important, if perhaps eclipsed by the later intervention of national governments to stabilize the banking system. Insurance funds and pension funds together once held the majority of equity of UK listed companies. In 2009 it was little more than a quarter.

The interests of hedge fund investors can often align with those of traditional asset managers, especially when the hedge funds take long positions and then hold them, seeking changes in corporate management and direction. We saw this in the case of TCI and Deutsche Börse, in which an aggressive hedge fund managed to enlist support for its cause from traditional funds like the US-based fund management giant Fidelity. But they will diverge again when the hedge fund wishes to exit its position having achieved a change in policy and a capital gain to go with it, while traditional fund managers may want or even have to keep the stock in their portfolios.

But the interests can also diverge – and radically so – when short-selling comes into play or when the use of derivatives, including the so-called 'contracts for difference' we saw in the case of Porsche and VW, in which the economic interests of investors and their formal shareholdings can get out of line. These situations raise questions for boards of directors and policymakers alike. Whose 'voice' matters, when the investor has only temporarily 'exited' its position? Should company law allow short-sellers to vote the shares? If not, should the lenders retain that right even though it has elected to sell the stock, at least for the moment, for the sake of a short-term gain from the repurchase agreement? Are that investor's rights to be considered the same as those of another investor who has kept its shares and forgone the extra money from stock lending?

These questions give rise to further questions for boards to address. Should directors pay attention to traditional institutional investors just because they assert that they are share*owners* and not just share*holders*? Should their voice be listened to more than those of private individuals or employees, who might hold of the equity but whose interests could be quite different from those of traditional asset managers or hedge funds? Should boards heed the advice that comes via a sovereign wealth fund from a foreign government whose interests may be different from the government of the home country, which – as is often the case – is not a shareholder at all?

These unsettled questions over corporate direction arise from the simple fact that shareholders do not have entirely common interests. The shorthand that comes closest to uniting them may well be 'shareholder value', as defined by the net present value of future dividends and capital gains. But even that equation leaves an open question over the horizon of the investment. Even long-term investors sell shorts sometimes, and another investor will have purchased them. That question of time, more so than the issues surrounding short-selling and the perverse horizon, is the issue that boards of directors face in seeking to advance towards the goal of creating shareholder value.

From the investors' point of view, leaving the horizon too long increases the risk identified in the agency problem: the problem that an unmonitored agent will engage in self-dealing at the principal's expense. Setting the horizon too short can lead to underinvestment, insufficient risk-taking, and the worry that the manager who sees herself as a steward of the business will be frustrated and leave.

The ambiguity about shareholder value goes back to the heart of the problem about corporate governance: What is the company for?

Further readings

Admati, A. R. & Pfleiderer, P. (2009). The 'Wall Street Walk' and Shareholder Activism: Exit as a Form of Voice. *Review of Financial Studies, 22*(7), 2645–85.

Anabtawi, I. & Stout, L. A. (2008). Fiduciary Duties for Activist Shareholders. Retrieved 29 Feb. 2008, from http://ssrn.com/paper=1089606.

Brav, A., Jiang, W., Thomas, R. S. & Partnoy, F. (2006). Hedge Fund Activism, Corporate Governance, and Firm Performance. Retrieved 8 Feb. 2009, from http://ssrn.com/paper=948907.

Bris, A., Goetzmann, W. N. & Zhu, N. (2007). Efficiency and the Bear: Short Sales and Markets Around the World. *The Journal of Finance, 62*(3), 1029–79.

Clifford, C. P. (2008). Value Creation or Destruction? Hedge Funds as Shareholder Activists. *Journal of Corporate Finance, 14*(4), 323–36.

Enriques, L. (2009). Regulators' Response to the Current Crisis and the Upcoming Reregulation of Financial Markets: One Reluctant Regulator's View. *University of Pennsylvania Journal of International Economic Law, 30*(4), 1147–55.

Greenwood, R. & Schor, M. (2007). Hedge Fund Investor Activism and Takeovers. *Harvard Business School Research Paper 08-004*. Retrieved 24 June 2009, from http://www.hbs.edu/research/pdf/08-004.pdf.

Hu, H. T. & Black, B. S. (2006). Empty Voting and Hidden (Morphable) Ownership: Taxonomy, Implications, and Reforms. *The Business Lawyer, 61*(3), 1011–70.

Klein, A. & Zur, E. (2006). Entrepreneurial Shareholder Activism: Hedge Funds and Other Private Investors. *NYU Law and Economics Research Paper No. 06/41.* Retrieved 8 Feb. 2009, from http://ssrn.com/paper=913362.

Nordberg, D. (2010). The Politics of Shareholder Activism. In H. K. Baker & R. Anderson (eds), *Corporate Governance A Synthesis of Theory, Research and Practice*. New York: John Wiley & Sons.

Park, D. J. & Tonello, M. (2009). The Role of the Board in Turbulent Times: Avoiding Shareholder Activism. *The Conference Board Executive Action Series, No. 300.* Retrieved 26 April 2009, from http://ssrn.com/paper=1390340.

Tonello, M. (2008). Report of the Conference Board Research Working Group on Hedge Fund Activism: Findings and Recommendations for Corporations and Investors. Retrieved 30 September 2008, from http://ssrn.com/paper=1107027.

ELEVEN

Issues between the company and its publics

In this chapter we explore two linked episodes in the history of one company, BP, showing the issues that can arise with constituencies outside the orbit of the management, the board and the owners.

Case: BP – beyond petroleum?

In July 2000, the formerly state-owned British Petroleum celebrated its own version of the millennium. It unveiled a new logo and a new slogan that would come to adorn its automotive service stations around the world, crown its letterhead and livery, and invade the consciousness and, it hoped, consciences of its workforce. Its image was a stylized sunburst and sunflower combined, in a variety of shades of green. BP now had a new purpose and a new meaning: Beyond Petroleum.

The groundwork had been laid a few years before. John Browne – Sir John, as he then was – used a speech at Stanford University in California to discuss in some depth the issues that had been worrying him for some time. When he took over as CEO in 1995, the company was only part of the way through an effort to revive its fortunes. Browne's early actions included the acquisition of Amoco, the former American Oil Company based in Chicago that had its roots in the Standard Oil Company trust controlled by the legendary John D. Rockefeller. British Petroleum became BP Amoco, but not for long. Browne then championed two further acquisitions, the American company Arco and the UK-based Burmah Castrol. BP now ranked alongside Exxon in the US and the Royal Dutch/Shell group as a new category of company: the 'super-majors'. Skilful integration of the businesses gave BP new economies of scale and levels of profitability that allowed it to justify the investments to shareholders, and give Browne's business judgement greater credibility.

But Browne was concerned about what he saw in the operating environment of the oil company. First, some oil industry economists had begun to talk about 'Peak Oil', the idea that petroleum production was about to reach the highest levels it could. Discovery of new oil fields had fallen behind the rate of consumption. With emerging markets and especially China increasing demand for oil, bottlenecks would arise, prices would soar again, but this time not because of action by governments in the Middle East and other oil-rich regions holding back supplies, but instead because oil supplies would have entered a long-term decline.

Second, climate change had started to appear as a concern not just among earth scientists, but increasing among economists as well. With profitability secure for now, Browne began to consider what an oil company could do to reduce the world's reliance on its products. Yes, there was a lot of 'noise' in the data on climate change, making predictions fraught with error and forecasts burdened with doubt. 'But it would be unwise and potentially dangerous to ignore the mounting concern,' he told the Stanford audience in May 1997. 'The time to consider the policy dimensions of climate change is not when the link between greenhouse gases and climate change is conclusively proven but when the possibility cannot be discounted and is taken seriously by the society of which we are part. We in BP have reached that point. It is an important moment for us. A moment when analysis demonstrates the need for action and solutions' (Browne, 1997).

An environmentalist in the oil industry? Oil is of necessity a dirty business. Attempts to develop new oil fields in many parts of the world lead to protests about environmental degradation. Oil spills – an inevitability that oil companies nonetheless try to avoid – still happen, sometimes due to negligence on the part of individuals, sometimes because policy decisions create a tradeoff between profitability and environmental protection.

Over the last century, inventive scientists have found ways to use the waste material left behind after the production of gasoline and heating oil to make plastics, paints and pharmaceuticals, fibres for use in clothing, resins for binding construction materials together and solvents to release the bonds. The world economy and modern life itself are so deeply rooted in the stuff that it is difficult to imagine living in a world 'beyond petroleum'.

Browne's speech and the actions that followed created a somewhat unlikely hero in the environmental movement. Browne did not just talk about climate change. The change of logo and slogan was backed by an investment programme in wind, biofuels and other renewable energy sources that would open options for the company to create – he reckoned – sustainable profits in an environmentally more sustainable way.

BP beat Browne's targets to reduce CO_2 emissions from its own operations. But as Browne and his key advisers pointed out, the CO_2 from operations was tiny compared with the CO_2 from the products it sold. BP's 2003 Sustainability Report contained a powerful graphic illustrating how of the 24 billion tonnes of greenhouse gas emitted annually, 1.3 billion came from the use of BP's products, 5 per cent of world emissions. Just 83 million tonnes of greenhouse gas emissions resulted from BP's own operations. So BP also invested in technologies that would make its gasoline burn better, giving more power per unit of fuel.

Especially compared with its great rival, now known as Exxon-Mobil following more industry consolidation, BP was the green giant of the energy industry. Exxon executives argued that the stock market is a place for investors to diversify their risk and place bets on the future. Oil companies should try to be good at oil, not waste shareholder funds chasing uncertain business ideas they did not know well how to exploit. Shareholders could invest in alternative energy companies if they wanted to pursue such strategies. It was an approach also backed by theory that had developed in the field of financial economics.

BP's image soared, while Exxon became a pariah in much public opinion. And Browne, now ennobled with a seat in the British House of Lords, became the embodiment of the caring, intellectual businessman, a Renaissance man presiding over the rebirth of the oil industry and perhaps even of capitalism. BP was a caring company, a socially responsible company, one that cared about its workforce and their families as well as about the future of the planet. The rebranding is reported to have cost $200 million. This was good for public relations too, but those close to Browne and many of the senior management of BP said it was much more than just PR. This was heartfelt stuff, yes, but honed on the grindstone of serious economic argument and measured by the best financial analysis that oil could buy. Yes, it would cost BP – and BP investors – some of their cash-flow over several years. Some investments might never pay off. But anyone who had explored for oil – and Browne had been in charge of exploration before becoming CEO – knows that taking big risks is what the oil industry is all about.

Questions arising

1 What is the responsibility of a company for the environmental impact of its operations? What about for its products?
2 How far – if at all – beyond the obligations specified in law do the responsibilities of the company and the board go?
3 What roles – for good and ill – do actions undertaken for the sake of a corporation's image and reputation play in a board's decisions?
4 Where the interests of the shareholders and the opportunities arising from socially responsible actions coincide that choice is clear. But in whose interests does a board decide when the costs of social responsibility exceed the financial benefits?

Case: BP – backing petroleum?

On 23 March 2005 a fire broke out at BP's refinery at Texas City, Texas, and burned for days. The death toll reached 15. Four days later, Lord Browne arrived with aides to inspect the damage and see the families of the victims. It seemed a respectful gesture, until the investigations started. In the public hearings and court cases that followed, what emerged was a picture of local managers who had scrimped on maintenance work so they could meet the profit targets set by headquarters.

The accident made people who had supported Browne and BP for their social responsibility take a harder look at the company and its activities. Why was BP lobbying to block legislation in the US Congress to limit greenhouse gas emissions? Why had the State of California sued the company from $319 million for violating emissions standards? And why, in 2003, had a major asset management firm in London dropped BP from its portfolio of 'ethical' investments? Rob Lake, who headed corporate governance at Henderson Global Investors, told a newspaper at the time: 'We have been talking to BP about this for seven or eight months but we have come to the conclusion that we are unable to invest in the company for these ethical funds' (Gumbel & Woolf, 2003).

Perhaps most damning was an email message produced in court three years later, sent by John Manzoni, head of BP's refining and marketing. He wrote: 'I arrived in Texas City at 3 am along with Lord Browne. And we spent a day there at the cost of a precious day of my leave' (McNulty, 2006).

Browne stepped down as CEO a year ahead of his planned retirement date, in May 2007, after repeated battles in the boardroom had led to repeated newspaper headlines about tension between him and the chairman, Peter Sutherland, a pugnacious Irish former politician and head of an intergovernmental organization. It was not a fight about environmental policy or Texas City, though it was about the direction of the business and its senior management. Tony Hayward, a youthful, almost boyish BP senior manager, won the promotion to CEO and worked with Browne for a thorough handover, and to ensure the continuity needed in a long-term business like oil.

But things change. In April 2009, Vivienne Cox, head of the new alternative energy division of BP, told a student blogging for the *New York Times* that her new position was not a demotion, even though she had lost responsibility for some more conventional parts of the business. 'To be successful,' she said, 'alternative energy has to be different from mainstream BP. It needs to be more like a venture capital company than a traditional gas and oil company.' This new division was in danger of being overwhelmed by the company's established governance, financial frameworks and other factors, 'so I had to push all of those away', Cox said. 'Tension certainly exists,' she acknowledged. 'Every dollar that we spend on renewable energy, for some people, that's a dollar we can't spend on their business' (Marlow, 2009).

Two months later, the *Financial Times* reported: 'Vivienne Cox, 49, the chief executive of alternative energy and BP's most senior woman executive, resigned. She previously ran the larger gas, power and renewables segment, which was broken up in the restructuring launched by Tony Hayward, the chief executive who took over two years ago' (Crooks, 2009).

A month later, announcing lower profits as a slump in global oil markets hurt earnings, Tony Hayward told reporters BP was not moving back to petroleum. 'We established the alternative energy business in 2005 with the purpose to explore options, which we did,' he said. 'It was now right to look at the array of options before us, and to step back and say "What can make commercial returns? What could be material to BP? And, frankly, what would have some synergies with the existing business?" It is a perfectly reasonable way of proceeding' (Teather, 2009).

In October of that year, the US Occupational Safety and Health Administration fined BP $87.4 million for what it called 'systemic safety problems' at Texas City. It was a record penalty issued by the agency, more than four times the size of its previous largest. That was a $21 million fine – also against BP – for the original Texas City fire (McNulty, 2009).

Questions arising

1 Some companies – including oil and gas corporations like BP – require formal licences from governments to conduct much of their business. To what extent does any business require, in effect, a broader 'social licence to operate'? How might it arise?
2 Corporations must abide by the law where they operate, but they also face pressure to operate globally at the legal standards that apply in the country in which they are based. To what extent should boards consider also the standards beyond those prescribed by law? How might that affect the legitimacy of corporations?
3 What notice should boards give to non-governmental organizations, lobbying groups and other activists?
4 What role might investors play in influencing both the strategic and compliance aspects of the corporation's activities in society?

Responsibilities of the corporation

The view has been gaining widespread acceptance that corporate officials and labor leaders have a 'social responsibility' that goes beyond serving the interest of their stockholders or their members. This view shows a fundamental misconception of the character and nature of a free economy. In such an economy, there is one and only one social responsibility of business – to use its resources and engage in activities designed to increase its profits so long as it stays within the rules of the game, which is to say, engages in free and open competition without deception or fraud. Similarly, the 'social responsibility' of labor leaders is to serve the interests of the members of their unions. It is the responsibility of the rest of us to establish a framework of law such that an individual in pursuing his own interest is, to quote Adam Smith again, 'led by an invisible hand to promote an end which was no part of his intention' . . . (Friedman, 1962/2002)

At the heart of this quotation is a phrase that has resonated in the long-simmering debate over the purpose of the corporation and the duties of directors: 'there is one and only one social responsibility of business . . . to increase its profits'. Indeed, the notion gained broad notoriety when it formed the title of an article that appeared several years later in the *New York Times Magazine* (Friedman, 1970). With it, the economist Milton Friedman became either hero or villain to those on either side of a debate that pits advocates of a stakeholder approach to corporate governance against adherents to the notion of shareholder value.

Read in its entirety, the quotation draws a line between what we have in Chapter 3 called the 'hard' and 'soft' versions of stakeholder theory. Friedman appreciates the view that business people do not have to be cruel to workers and should not seek to find ways around the law. His argument implies, rather, that business people should use whatever freedom the law allows to reward workers, help customers and look after the best interests of suppliers *provided these activities are instrumental in increasing profits.* His view, often viewed as counter to an 'ethical' stance of business, is not unethical or even amoral – it just takes a decidedly utilitarian view of the ethical demands on corporate directors, valuing outcomes more than duties (for further discussion of ethics and boards, see Bowie, 1999; Nordberg, 2008a, 2010b; Roberts, 2005; Zetzsche, 2007).

Friedman is often read as promoting the role of markets over the state. Implicit in his approach is the view that corporate governance in the broadest sense – embracing markets, law and regulation as a constraint on the freedom of companies to act – is a contest of political forces, a battle of wills in society to set and amend the 'rules of the game' and determine how to use the resources of the company. That struggle is evident in the growing public debate, the resulting changes in law, and the shifts in consumer attitudes, which themselves affect corporate behaviour concerning the topics we know as corporate social responsibility and sustainability, the issues that BP has been so central in confronting. It forms part of what we have called the new corporate governance agenda.

Corporate social responsibility

A growing chorus of opinion – among lobbying organizations, politicians, academics and also some shareholders – now argues that corporations have obligations to society that go beyond making profits (within the rules of the game) and paying dividends that can be reinvested in an even better economy and with it an even better society. Sometimes this notion comes with the label of *corporate citizenship*, other times just *corporate responsibility*. Most often it is known as *corporate social responsibility*, a phrase used widely enough that the initials CSR by themselves have achieved wide recognition.

Licence to operate

CSR grows out of the notion that a corporation exists within a society. Without society it could not function: it would not have customers, and therefore would not have a business. Nor would it have suppliers or employees to make the products and services it sells. Perhaps more importantly, the corporation would not have the legal and regulatory frameworks that governments and courts provide, giving assurance of property rights.

Corporations have even broader reasons to live up to obligations to society, this view of corporate purpose holds. Corporations depend upon the social 'commons' – the air and water resources; the beauty of the landscapes in which they operate; the sightlines their corporate headquarters buildings obscure; the road, rail and air transport resources they require to ship their goods and move their people about. This dependency places upon the corporation a responsibility to take care of the commons, not just to exploit it as though it were the corporation's own property.

In a narrow, *contractual* view of the corporation, these ideas appear to be vague notions, without clear definition and open to interpretation. How, then, can a corporation – a mere 'legal person' – decide on a course of action? Even boards of directors, the real persons charged with responsibility for the corporation, have difficulty grasping the complexity of setting direction, marshalling resources, monitoring and controlling their use and evaluating performance. How can they know how to choose between alternatives when the obligations are so difficult to quantify, so difficult to describe in the common language of business – the financial statement?

Stakeholder rights

Corporate social responsibility has its theoretical underpinnings in stakeholder theory, the argument that at the very least other stakeholders – suppliers, customers and employees – are owed something beyond what is specified in their contracts of engagement with the company. The employment side is particularly well documented in the literature of CSR. Workers get paid for their labour, but their also develop a psychological engagement with the company. They develop generic skills that could be used in employment with other corporations, of course, but they also develop company-specific knowledge and skills that are of less use and might have no value at all if the company closed or if they lost their jobs in an economic downturn. The more specific their skills, the greater danger they face. It is sometimes seen as a problem especially of the manual worker. Management, by contrast, is often thought of as a portable talent, one easily applied to a new situation.

The 'soft' view of stakeholder theory would see customers, suppliers and the workforce as instruments of profitability, and worthy of investment – through customer relationship management, supply chain management, training and personal development – because those investments have the potential to pay off by making the company more competitive: by lowering the cost of the next sale, by getting privileged access to innovations in raw materials and process technologies, through productivity gains in operations. These changes can be modelled, with greater or lesser precision, in the language of finance and built into the business models that boards approve, monitor and evaluate, as tools like the Balance Scorecard (Kaplan & Norton, 1992), ValueReporting (Eccles et al., 2001) and similar approaches suggest. Traditional financial accounting does not easily capture the value that people bring to the corporation, their 'human capital', the value of customer relationships or of supply chains (see Edmans, 2009).

The 'hard' view of stakeholder theory moves into the more complex – and for many business people and investors – the more problematic area of rights and obligations. It is an area sometimes discussed drawing on a metaphor from contract law. Corporations, this view holds, require a *licence to operate* from society as a whole, not just some formal licensing bureau in national or local government. Without such approval from society at large, the corporation lacks legitimacy (for differing views on how to apply this, see Graafland, 2002; Hampson, 2007; Porter & Kramer, 2006). This is a social contract, rather than a legal agreement, an implied claim on the corporation, rather than one to which its directors and officers have explicitly agreed. Others take a view from a moral rather than contractual standpoint and a normative not descriptive approach, in arguing for stakeholder rights as *a priori* claims on the resources of the corporation for fair treatment and a say over how the company operates (Evan & Freeman, 1993). Many business people find this pill hard to swallow: the word 'social' in CSR rings of 'socialism' and collective rather than individual rights. It is not surprising, therefore, than many corporations have moved to talking instead about 'corporate responsibility', leaving the 'S' in CSR behind.

CSR as politics

Irrespective of the view of stakeholder rights and its role in corporate governance, one thing is clear: from a *political* view of the corporation, CSR is something on the board's agenda. In the Netherlands, for example, corporate law imposes on directors a duty towards stakeholders. Trade unions in Germany fight every attempt to dilute their legal claim to representation on the supervisory boards of corporations. Across Europe, few politicians hoping for a place in government would argue to dilute the rights associated with employees' tenure in employment even in the face of repeated economic analysis suggesting that rigidity in employment law weakens innovation and economic growth. Joseph Schumpeter's notion of creative destruction (1942/1976) is fine, as long as someone else, in some other country, is the one whose job is creatively destroyed.

The UK has long adhered to neo-classical economics and market-based solutions to economic problems. It nonetheless gave directors a duty to 'have regard to' the interests of 'employees . . . suppliers, customers and others' as well as the 'impact of the business on the community and the environment' in the reform of company law (UK Parliament, 2006, p. 79) that finally passed after eight years of debate under a Labour government.

While the principles underpinning the notion of a social licence to operate may be in dispute, that licence can manifest itself directly in the business. In the face of pressure for lobbying organizations and occasional consumer backlashes, many corporations have begun to track and publish data about their efforts in social responsibility. Some impose standards on suppliers: that they too conform with the company's own policies on human rights, fairness to employees and ethical principles – or risk losing the business. As such, CSR becomes less an instrument of strategy or even an ethical constraint. Instead it is a feature of risk and reputation management.

CSR as opportunity

An alternative approach casts corporate social responsibility not as an obligation – that is, a cost of doing business – but rather as corporate social *opportunity* (Grayson & Hodges, 2004; see also Porter & Kramer, 2006). In this view, constraints on corporate behaviour deemed socially desirable, whether in law and regulation or through pressure from non-governmental organizations or by consumer boycotts, can become spurs to innovation. New products and services emerge from the cauldron of debate over ethics and purpose, conferring competitive advantage upon the inventors and their investors. This is the win-win view of CSR, and it has achieved its greatest influence in the debate over environmental issues.

Sustainability

The term *sustainability* is sometimes thought of as a new, business-friendly way of talking about corporate social responsibility (for an example, see Grayson et al., 2008). Where talk of employee rights might alienate some, few business people are in a position to deny the need to address the issue of climate change. The ecological transformation caused by rising levels of greenhouse gases in the atmosphere is not without controversy, but no one can deny that the political temperature has already risen in ways that no board of directors can afford to ignore.

The discussion of sustainability arose from the same core concerns as CSR: how do corporations balance the competing demands of *profitability* for shareholders, social justice for the *people* with which they work and the environmental consequences for the *planet*? Sometimes called the Three-P approach, it recasts the obligations that resonate through the CSR debate in terms of the resilience of the business for the long term. Using the terminology of sustainability, corporations and boards face increased demands to consider how the business can produce profits that can be sustained over years, through a business that has sustained relationships with customers, suppliers and workers, in a way that allows the environment to be sustained in a suitable condition. Add to that equation the suggestion that climate change might change the final phrase to 'in a state fit for human habitation' and you have a more powerful call on marshalling the resources of the corporation for your goal.

Agenda point 16: Carbon disclosure – the next standard?

Companies don't yet face mandatory disclosure requirements for environmental issues, but it can't be that far down the road. One sign of that came with proposals from a body called the Climate Disclosure Standards Board (CDSB) on what information directors should include on climate change in their companies' annual reports. As part of the run-up to the climate summit in Copenhagen at the end of 2009, CDSB released a global framework to clarify which climate change data should be reported and provide a set of guidelines designed to streamline disclosure procedures. It outlines four reporting templates:

Strategy: A climate change strategic analysis, giving management's view of the company's strategy, and in particular the drivers of operational performance, customers, brands and innovation.
Regulatory risks: Regulatory risks from climate change, which pose short-term risks to companies and affect decisions about long-term investments.
Physical risks: Physical risks from climate change, including exposure to extreme events such as intense storms and hurricane activity, or from more subtle changes such as shifts in species distribution and increased night-time temperatures. 'A qualitative overview of your company's current and potential material exposure to direct and indirect physical risks due to climate change is therefore a potentially important aspect of disclosure,' it said.
Greenhouse gas emissions: As far as possible, CDSB wants companies to use emissions data calculated and reported for purposes other than mainstream financial reporting to minimize duplication of work.

CDSB, an entity formed by the World Economic Forum and with close links to the UK-based Carbon Disclosure Project, drew up the framework using financial and business reporting principles. (*The BoardAgenda*, 15 June 2009; http://www.edgevantage.co.uk/categories/article.asp?i=4670.)

Balancing the competing claims on the company's resources lies at the heart of the job of directors. But in this case, there is an added complication. The long time scales involved in climate change mean that the economic logic requires a leap of faith. We see this in the logic employed by Nicholas Stern in a review of the economic consequences of climate change and climate policy (Stern, 2006). Although written for the UK government, it attracted interest from governments around the world – and criticisms from many fellow economists for the assumptions he made (see especially Nordhaus, 2007).

Stern started with the same techniques that corporations use in judging the financial soundness of possible investments: a view of the benefits the investment brings over time, compared with its costs. In the logic of finance and economics, the value of future benefits and costs are worth less than ones that arise now. Investment involves current costs for future benefits, so you discount the future benefits by some kind of interest rate reflecting what you might have earned investing in something else. Stern chose a discount rate of near-zero, arguing that it was unethical to discount the value of benefits for future generations. The choice of discount rate was decisive in determining his view that sustainability was affordable.

The debate over accounting for environmental damage takes a tone similar to the issues over CSR. As proponents of corporate social responsibility argue that financial data in corporations failed to capture the human capital in the business, many scholars and lobbyists alike say that accounting standards treat the environment as an off-balance-sheet item, much as traditional micro-economics treats it as an 'externality' – something outside the system, and therefore not relevant to decisions (Bebbington et al., 2001).

Whatever the view of the science or economics of climate change, the politics of it ensure that sustainability will be on the board's agenda, not least through growing expectations that corporations will report on what they are doing.

Triple bottom line

Explicit in the discussion of CSR and sustainability is the concept that came to be called the *triple bottom line*. The phrase was coined by John Elkington, the founder of a think-tank called SustainAbility, which focused mainly on environmental affairs but takes a broader view. Its clients were major corporations seeking advice on how to balance the competing demands on resources. In his book *Cannibals with Forks* (Elkington, 1999), he argued that companies needed to account for their activities not just by using profit – the 'bottom line' in accounting parlance – but with a triple bottom line, measuring their social and environmental performance as well. The expression caught on, sometimes in the guise of Profit–People–Planet, and sometimes with variations: ESG (for environmental, social and governance reporting) or SEE (for social, environmental and economic impact).

Parallel to these concerns, the reporting standards have developed, in a few cases (e.g. South Africa) required by law, not just custom and practice. Many corporations have signed up to use the reporting standards for environmental and social impact developed by the Global Reporting Initiative, now in its third iteration (GRI, 2006). The project began as an initiative of the United Nations Environmental Programme and gathered support from a wide variety of companies and industry organizations.

Many were looking for some sort of standard, a template of what is important and how the data should be collected. Even determining what is and is not appropriate data can be difficult. By comparison, financial accounting looks like a law of nature, even with all its vagaries and room for interpretation. The reason for reporting about these matters resides in increasing the accountability that corporations show towards their publics. One of the most important publics for this information is none other than the investment community.

SRI funds

Asset management firms have for many years catered to the interests of what we now call socially responsible investors. In the 1960s and early 1970s, for example, some churches and other charities with a pacifist orientation chose to invest their endowments in ways that avoided buying shares in companies involving in defence industries or otherwise serving military interests. Others sought to avoid tobacco companies or companies with extensive dealings with governments like the apartheid regime in South Africa. Asset managers would undertake *negative screening* by applying a filter to the investor's portfolio to exclude such stocks. It was always a small part of the business, but large enough to spawn supporting services, including research into 'ethical investments'. The logic was this: an investor boycott would dampen the share price, raising the company's cost of capital, and in the long run making it less competitive, putting pressure on management to change policy.

Over the years, negative screening was joined by *positive screening*, the attempt to identify companies that engaged in what such investors considered desirable activities. Positive screening helped to create a market for the shares in Body Shop International, for example, which became a public company in 1984 holding out the commitment – its differentiating factor – that it did not test its cosmetics on animals. The logic was this: some investors would be willing to pay a premium for shares, creating an incentive for companies to adopt business practices that were more environmentally or socially friendly, stimulating new business models and innovations. Social responsibility had become social opportunity.

These remained quite niche product offerings for fund management firms. SRI funds account for little more than a few percentage points of assets under management. As the debate over climate change grew more intense, however, the picture began to change to some extent. The companies that create stock market indices, including Dow Jones and FTSE International, developed products that allowed institutional investors to benchmark their performance, as they had done for years with their mainstream portfolios against the Dow Jones Industrial Average, the FTSE 100 and other measures. Index-tracking funds followed suit, offering retail and institutional investors a low-cost way of placing money in companies that might benefit disproportionately from growing demand for green product or growing governmental subsidies for new technologies.

With climate change have come new imperatives that have the potential of making at least environmental concerns an important element of investment decision-making. Climate change presents operational risks for almost every company, if not in the next few years, then sometime thereafter. More immediately, it creates the potential that business models will need to adjust to new regulatory and legislative requirements that governments seem likely to impose, whatever the board collectively or directors individually think about the science and economics of climate change. Investors will want to assess that impact on all the companies in their portfolios, if not now then soon.

Even SRI has been undergoing a rethink, though. The asset management company Henderson, a major player in the field, changed its way of talking about the business: Out went 'socially responsible investment'. In came 'sustainable, responsible investing'.

Divided duties?

BP has not been alone in the extractive industries of mining, oil and gas in wrestling with the dilemmas thrown up in satisfying the legitimate aims of the widely differing publics it serves. When investments that meet the interests of a range of stakeholders also show the promise of future profitability, then enlightening value maximization may well equal enlightened stakeholder value, as Michael Jensen (2001) has suggested.

Assessing the impact of this type of investment on corporate behaviour involves the same difficulties as tracking investors' impact on broader issues in corporate governance. With so many items on the board's agenda, it is difficult to tell which ones are having an effect.

Advocates of a strong form of stakeholder theory impose on corporations a series of demands that require the allocation of corporate resources to things other than, as Milton Friedman said, 'to engage in activities designed to increase its profits so long as it stays within the rules of the game'. They win support from those who argue that the accounting system undercounts the value that employees, suppliers and customers bring to the future profitability of the enterprise because their value is not easily translated into dollars and cents, into the balance sheets, profit-and-loss accounts and cash-flow statements that form the basis of the analysis on which investment is based.

Some companies include as assets the brands they control, an asset at least as intangible as 'human capital' or 'customer equity'. International financial reporting standards require companies to capitalize – to show as assets – the intangibles acquired when taking over another company that does not have them on its books. Doing the same for the 'people' element of the triple bottom line is difficult, though many scholars, accountants, corporations and standard-setters are hard at work to develop such metrics.

Climate change and other environmental impacts remain off the balance sheet as well, but with perhaps even more emphasis on working out how to change the 'externalities' that the economists discuss within the orbit of a broader notion of accounting and with it accountability. Getting some way of seeing their impact on the value of the business is becoming important for investors, not just environmentalists, lobbying organizations and other outsiders to the corporation.

Further readings

Agle, B. R., Mitchell, R. K. & Sonnenfeld, J. A. (1999). Who Matters to CEOs? An Investigation of Stakeholder Attributes and Salience, Corporate Performance, and CEO Values. *Academy of Management Journal, 42*(5), 507–25.

Bebbington, J., Gray, R., Hibbitt, C. & Kirk, E. (2001). Full Cost Accounting: An Agenda for Action. *Association of Chartered Certified Accountants*. Retrieved 24 December 2008, from http://www.accaglobal.com/pubs/publicinterest/activities/research/research_archive/acca_rr73_001.pdf.

Benn, S. & Dunphy, D. (eds) (2007). *Corporate Governance and Sustainability: Challenges for Theory and Practice*. London: Routledge.

Freeman, R. E. (1984). *Strategic Management: A Stakeholder Approach*. Boston: Pitman Publishing.

Friedman, M. (1962/2002). *Capitalism and Freedom* (40th anniversary edn). Chicago, IL: University of Chicago Press.

Friedman, M. (1970, Sept. 13). The Social Responsibility of Business is to Increase its Profits. *The New York Times Magazine,* 122–6.

Hillenbrand, C. & Money, K. (2007). Corporate Responsibility and Corporate Reputation: Two Separate Concepts or Two Sides of the Same Coin? *Corporate Reputation Review, 10*(4), 261–77.

Jensen, M. C. (2001). Value Maximization, Stakeholder Theory, and the Corporate Objective Function. *Journal of Applied Corporate Finance, 14*(3), 8–21.

Krosinsky, C. & Robins, N. (eds) (2008). *Sustainable Investing: The Art of Long-Term Performance*. London: Earthscan.

Porter, M. E. & van der Linde, C. (1995). Toward a New Conception of the Environment–Competitiveness Relationship. *Journal of Economic Perspectives, 9*(4), 97–118.

Schaltegger, S., Bennett, M. & Burritt, R. (eds) (2006). *Sustainability Accounting and Reporting*. Dordrecht: Springer.

PART 3

Reporting, rebalancing and the future

In this final section, we consider three themes that help to summarize the disparate roles and pressure that boards face.

Transparency – the universal antiseptic: As we have seen, the wide range of issues that arise in managing a corporation suggest that setting rules for everything is problematic and perhaps counterproductive. The alternative used in many countries – combined with a *caveat emptor* warning to investors, customers, suppliers, employees and other publics – is that corporations should talk about what they do.

Governance beyond corporations: Charitable organizations, government agencies, hospitals, schools, clubs and associations are all governed in some way. To what extent can the lesson in *corporate* governance help them?

An unsettled and unsettling future? In this chapter, we revisit the theme of the accelerator and brake pedal. To what extent has concern about corporate governance prevented companies and their boards from creating value? We conclude with a brief discussion of a nagging worry in the debate about corporate governance: How valuable is this? While the principles of corporate governance may contribute to better corporate performance and even more responsible corporations, something different may be needed to prevent the recurrent crises that have sparked concern about the subject.

TWELVE

Transparency – the universal antiseptic

For this chapter, we consider two companies where malfeasance was masked by the manipulation of accounting rules, making the case for transparency, but also demonstrating its limits.

Case: Polly Peck and the comparisons

In early September 1990, Polly Peck International reported pretax profits of £110.5 million for the six months to 30 June, a rise of 71 per cent from the level a year earlier. The company had a value of more than £1 billion on the London Stock Exchange. By 25 October, it was placed into administration – bankrupt for all intents. An analysis by the accountants Coopers & Lybrand showed that liquidating the company would yield a net deficit for shareholders of £384 million.

The stock market had sensed something was wrong, even if traders did not know what. In August the company had been valued at almost £1.8 billion, and Asil Nadir, the chairman and CEO who had masterminded its climb into the top flight of UK companies, the FTSE 100, had made an approach to other shareholders to take the company private, buying all the shares he did not own and delisting it from the stock exchange. He had then decided against the move.

Nadir's career was stunning. A Turkish Cypriot, he moved to the UK aged 18, and after inconclusive studies in Turkey joined a family textiles business, which prospered. He caught the bug of mergers and acquisitions, and soon a financial company he controlled bought Polly Peck, which grew into textiles and fresh fruit, and then water bottling. As the company grew, so did his ambitions. In 1986, Polly Peck gained a listing in the US, and with it even greater credibility. Polly Peck borrowed in Swiss francs, a strong currency where low interest rates applied, to fund projects in Turkey, with an unstable currency and high interest rates. On paper it looked a good bet, provided the Turkish lira did not fall too much against the Swiss franc. In 1989, Nadir pushed through the acquisition of the Del Monte brand of fresh and preserved fruits, based in the US and with extensive operations in Latin America. Then he bought a 51 per cent stake in a Japanese electronics company.

Between early September and late October, trading had been suspended on the exchange. The UK Serious Fraud Office had raided the offices of a financial services company with links to Nadir. It was the beginning of what would turn out to be the deepest recession in decades in the country. But that was not the cause of the crash. Polly Peck's balance sheet showed the company had a lot of cash – £405 million, according to the accounts from 30 June. But £300 million of it was in banks in northern Cyprus, Nadir's home country, or Turkey, and could not be remitted to the UK. Other funds were committed to new but unspecified ventures. Yet the accounts for the prior year had received a clean bill of health from the auditors, and even the final interim accounts released in September made the company seem healthy. There was, however, a telltale sign of the trouble to come. Buried in the accounts, a footnoted entry compared one line of the current year data with information from a different period than that used for all the other items. That line, with its footnote, was meant to 'disclose' (or was it 'conceal') some very sizeable foreign exchange losses. Why had nobody outside the company noticed? (For further background, see Gallagher et al., 1996; Smith, 1992.)

Case: WorldCom and the accountants

In 2004, Scott Sullivan pleaded guilty to fraud, conspiracy and making false statements. As chief financial officer of WorldCom, he was most directly involved in preparation of the accounts of what was once the biggest telecommunications company in the world, until it became the biggest accounting scandal. Bernie Ebbers, his boss, went to trial instead of pleading guilty on those charges. He might have been CEO of WorldCom, but that did not mean he knew much about accounting or about the accounts that WorldCom had published under his signature. The jury did not believe him; he was sentenced to 25 years in prison. Aged 63, Ebbers appeared likely to spend the rest of his life behind bars. WorldCom had grown from a tiny company to take over some of the biggest names in the industry, including MCI, second only to AT&T in the US long-distance market, and several of the largest companies involved in the booming internet access business. At the end of 2001 it was one of the largest businesses in the United States, by market capitalization. In June 2002 it filed for bankruptcy protection. Something close to $11 billion had to be written off the books. Its accountants had billed as capital expenditure items that should have been accounted as costs. As a result, stated assets on the balance were inflated, and profits too. Accounting rules give the profession discretion in how to treat a lot of expenses, including when some items can be capitalized rather than expensed. Through his guilty plea, CFO Scott Sullivan had agreed, in effect, that discretion had not been the best part of his valour.

Over the next few years, as the story unfolded, the courts learned that Ebbers had bought a yacht and a ranch in the Canadian province of British Columbia. He had a 65 per cent stake in a company that owned $400 million of timberland in the American South. Most of the money to fund these purchases had come from loans WorldCom made to Ebbers and agreed by the board whose members Ebbers had been instrumental in selecting (Wearing, 2005, gives much of the story).

With Ebbers ousted, new management in place and the WorldCom name dropped in favour of MCI, the company emerged from bankruptcy in 2004. In the meantime, the US Congress had passed the Sarbanes–Oxley Act – in a rush, just a month after the bankruptcy filing. Its provisions included a new government agency, the Public Company Accounting Oversight Board, to examine the books of the bookkeepers, to regulate the accounting and audit firms, in America and abroad, of any company that had any securities trading on US markets. PCAOB, which came to be known as 'Peekaboo' in Washington, and the Securities and Exchange Commission, to which it was accountable, then pushed the accounting profession into radical transformations in approach. They set the US on a course that was simply unthinkable before the WorldCom collapse: making US accounting standards merge with international ones, and in the meantime allowing US companies not to use US standards.

Postscript: Ebbers and his rivals often had close dealings with leading investment analysts on Wall Street covering the telecommunications industry. At Salomon Brothers, the investment bank owned by Citigroup, Jack Grubman wrote an email to a friend saying he had managed to get his children into a highly sought-after nursery school in New York City, with the help of his boss, Citigroup's chairman and CEO Sandy Weill. Citigroup made a donation of $1 million to the charity that ran the school. Grubman changed his view on AT&T stock. AT&T subsequently placed a large issue of stock through Citigroup. Perhaps there was no connection (Morgenson & McGeehan, 2002).

Grubman's analyses of AT&T and WorldCom were part of a rash of rose-tinted views of dot-com and telecom stocks by Wall Street investment banks. The analysts were supposed to be advising institutional investors about which stocks to buy and which to ignore. But part of the personal income came from helping their banks sell services – like issuing new stock, which the bank would sell for a fee – to the companies whose accounts they analysed. Together with evidence that some clients got preferred access to juicy deals and preferred exits from ones that were going bad, conflicts of interest were rife. Under investigation by the New York Attorney General and then the SEC, 10 investment banks agreed to pay in total $1.4 billion in fines and other charges, including $435 million to help independent analysts compete with the investment banks. The hope was that this new research would not be tainted as other's had been (SEC, 2003). The settlement ran from 2004 to 2009.

Questions arising

Both cases involve circumstances where the company's accountants, with or without the knowledge and assistance of the external auditors, bent the accounting rules to cover up a deteriorating financial position.

1 What roles do governments, the accounting and audit professions, and boards of directors have in setting the substance of what is – and is not – appropriate corporate financial reporting?
2 What is the value of using disclosure of behaviour as an alternative to regulating behaviour directly?
3 If financial disclosure has value, does something similar apply to disclosure of non-financial aspects of corporate performance? Consider especially: social and environmental issues, executive pay, operational matters, strategy, competition, and risk.
4 In what ways might disclosure be counterproductive?

Disclosure – good for markets

Disclosure is something like sunlight and fresh air. It either kills germs or lets us see where they might be lurking, so we can clean them up. It also prevents them from growing in the first place, because people are more careful about what they do in the first place when they know that everyone else can see. The famous American jurist Louis Brandeis once called sunlight one of the best of disinfectants (Brandeis, 1913–14).

In the early days of the corporation, entrepreneurs needing to raise capital found they had to relinquish something more than complete control of their companies. They had to give up their privacy too. The creation of stock markets, enabling business people to draw from a wider circle of investors than the large financiers, came at the price of publishing their financial records and submitting them to external examination, that is, to an audit (Micklethwait & Wooldridge, 2003).

It was a way of creating trust among potential investors to persuade them to support the company's ventures and believe that the money would be used wisely, and hold the board of the company accountable for their actions. As we saw in Chapter 5, the US political economist Francis Fukuyama (1995) argues that this element of trust, enabled in part by the willingness of entrepreneurs to forgo privacy, is what allowed the United States and Britain to develop advanced capital markets faster than other parts of the world. By comparison, what he calls low-trust societies – among them Asian countries where ethnic Chinese have a strong influence on business formation – companies tend to be smaller, family-based, where the familial ties provide the cohesion for a lack of social bonds. Funding of enterprises involves debt rather than equity. Continental Europe is marked by medium-trust countries: equity is used more than in Asia but less than in America or Britain, debt the reverse.

Fukuyama's observations have parallels in the cross-cultural analyses of the attitudes of business people conducted by Geert Hofstede (1980), which found that in some societies (the US, Britain, Scandinavia) business people were less concerned with hierarchies and more willing to deal with uncertainties, and developed market-oriented solutions. Asian countries (including Hong Kong, Singapore, Indonesia, Malaysia) were willing to deal with uncertainty. But to deal with a high level of 'power distance', they adopt family-based solutions that can often limit the potential of companies to grow.

In the intervening years, many countries around the world have adopted economic structures and regulations more like the Anglo-American model to facilitate development of a more dynamic private sector economy. But the success of those ventures depends on one thing above all: disclosure. Companies have to tell their shareholders what is happening to the business, how the money is being deployed, what results it is achieving, and what the prospects are for it to continue to perform in the future.

To support the trust that enables equity capital markets companies have faced mounting pressures for greater disclosures about their operations. With each wave of concern over corporate governance, the demands for disclosure have ratcheted upwards. They involve:

- *Financial reporting*: Publication of audited annual reports and more frequent interim reporting.
- *Operational reporting*: How the company is working on a more operational level, including major contracts won or lost, breakdown of financial statements by region or division.
- *Reporting on intangibles*: Reporting on aspects of the operations that do not show up directly in financial statements, including brand valuation, development of the workforce capabilities through training and other mechanisms, and other steps that might affect the company's intangible assets.
- *Governance reporting*: How the company is organized, how the board works, how much it pays its senior managers and directors, how it complies with governance codes or chooses not to.
- *Social and environmental reporting*: In parallel with the new corporate governance agenda, how the company works with its local community, its health and safety record, its philanthropy, and its environmental performance.
- *Risk reporting*: The company faces a variety of different risks, some of which are or can become material to the future of the business.

Agenda point 17: Disclosure – lessons from Switzerland

Public corporations in all capital markets face a requirement to publish annually a full account of their business, their annual report, with the auditor's judgement attached. As late as the mid-1980s, even as well-developed a market as Switzerland didn't require reporting more frequently than on an annual basis, not even for the largest companies quoted on the Zurich bourse. Moreover, they didn't have to issue the reports until more than 10 months after the end of the year. Few companies took advantage of the generosity of the authorities, publishing results reasonably soon after the end of the year, and after the end of the first six months of the year.

The longer the gap between transaction and disclosure, the greater the value of secrecy. In the 1980s, when the company Swiss Reinsurance regularly used the regulatory allowance to the full, it justified it on the grounds that publishing sooner would give competitors a greater chance of working out its strategies and responding more quickly. While other Swiss companies reported promptly in response to market pressure for timelier and frequent information, Swiss Re stuck with the delays, reporting its results for the year ended 31 December only in mid-November the following year.

But delaying publication had a cost as well as a benefit: investors worried about what problems might have occurred in the meantime. That risk – that lack of trust – meant they were willing to pay less for shares in Swiss Re. Did its bankers demand greater insight into its finances? Did that mean that banks, which controlled large numbers of shares in the company, either directly or for clients, knew more than other investors? Was this an invitation for insider trading?

Trading shares in the company based on insider information wasn't illegal in Switzerland at the time. But the law changed, as did the rules about disclosure, bringing Swiss practice in line with other highly developed markets. In the years that followed, Swiss Re developed one of the most thorough programmes of publishing results and giving the public access to what its senior managers told investment analysts.

Financial reporting

Financial reporting was the earliest form of disclosure that corporations faced because it was probably the most important for investors. Bookkeeping principles have existed for centuries. Something like what is in use today has been found in the records of twelfth-century Islam (Labib, 1969), though most western scholars trace its roots to Italy in the late fifteenth century, when the Italian monk Luca Pacioli published a detailed description of a system of double-entry accounting. Accounting entries are still subject to definitions, including one on quite basic matters. One example will suffice. When does the business achieve revenue? Is it on handshake, when the invoice was sent, when the goods were shipped or received, or when the payment arrived? Agreeing these matters is important for the banks and financiers who fund the business, so over time accounting standards developed. With the growth of public capital markets came the need not just for publication of the information, but also for public audits of the accounts to attest to their reliability.

How financial disclosure works

Audited accounts are typically published only once a year, but investors came to want information more frequently, to make sure that the company was still on the right course. First came half-year results, called 'interims' in the UK, unaudited but with almost as much detail concerning the financial accounts as the full-year figures. Then we got advanced notice of the full-year results, before the auditors had finished their work. Called 'preliminary results' in Britain, these figures were the ones investors came to rely upon, rather than waiting several weeks until the annual report came out.

Even in America, which Fukuyama had called a high-trust society, there are limits to investors' trust. They demanded and got from the regulatory bodies and the stock exchanges a requirement that listed corporations would have to report their results on a quarterly basis. While some countries, among them Sweden and – by encouragement rather than regulation – Germany, followed the US lead. Even in countries that opposed quarterly reporting, some companies followed the practice: their investors had begun to expect it. But others resisted, citing the incessant focus that quarterly reporting brought on management's ability to meet short-term targets (Tonello, 2006). Which is better: seeing how well senior managers and boards perform against quarterly targets for sales and profits, or giving them breathing room to engage in strategic investments? Which is worse: demanding quick fixes or letting problems go undisclosed for months and months?

Convergence in accounting standards

Agreeing to publish results is one step in the process, but the content of the publication is important too, especially in a global market for capital. Before 2005, accounting standards were set on a country-by-country basis – but not now. The demands of global investment markets are just too strong. The European Union and many other countries around the world have adopted international financial reporting standards, or IFRS, for all companies that offer equity or debt to trade on public markets. Despite doubts that authorities and auditors in some countries might be lax about enforcing them, the system rolled out with only minor hitches in most major countries, with the notable exceptions of Canada, Japan and the United States.

IFRS draws many of its features from the principles-based approach used in UK accounting. Instead of giving detailed interpretations of how to account for specific transactions, it leaves much discretion in the hands of the accountants and auditors. In effect it asks them to explain how they had interpreted the standards rather than complying with a set of rules. The emphasis of the system is to make accounts useful for investors – that is, to have the accounts reflect as much as possible the economic value that the company represents. By contrast, some national accounting systems in continental Europe worked on the principle that financial reporting should correspond to tax accounting. As a result the accounts might be expected to show less flattering profits and choose conventions for describing assets that fail to show the value they bring to production in the future.

The problems that arose at WorldCom, as well as a string of other companies, persuaded the Securities and Exchange Commission that generally accepted accounting principles in the US would benefit from an overhaul. Using the PCAOB's position to oversee the accountancy profession, the SEC set off on a course of action that would make US accounting less rule-oriented and more principles-based. It instigated a dialogue between the US Financial Accounting Standards Boards and the International Accounting Standards Board aimed at harmonizing the regulations. In time, the SEC then allowed non-US companies that use IFRS and have securities trading on US markets to avoid having to reconcile their accounts with US GAAP, and set plans to allow US companies to adopt IFRS instead of US GAAP. In mid-2008 it published a 'roadmap' that would have the US eventually adopt IFRS instead of having its own system, a controversial move that caused disagreement among the five commissioners themselves and met opposition in Congress.

Having comparable accounting standards makes it easier for investors to compare the value of a pharmaceutical company in France with another based in Japan or New Jersey. With companies increasingly competing with global rivals, and investors increasingly holding shares of companies irrespective of national boundaries, the usefulness of national accounting standards has diminished.

Problems with financial reporting

But then there's an old saying about accounting: judging a company's future based on the financial results is like driving a car while looking in the rear-view mirror. Financial accounting gives a pretty good impression of where you have been. It does not tell you where you are going.

A look at financial accounts and stock market valuations of companies shows us why they are important. At the height of the dot-com boom in 1999–2000, the stock market in its wisdom or wishful thinking thought that companies were worth on average more than twice the value of net assets shown on their balance sheets in many countries around the world. Some new businesses with, for all intents, no assets achieved market valuations of a billion dollars or more. This was clearly a case of an asset price bubble, where valuations inflated far beyond what the substance of the investment could hope to deliver. But even after the bubble burst, market capitalization continued to exceed the accounting value by more than 50 per cent. The reason, even many accountants agree, is that accounting itself is wrong.

Investors seek to anticipate the future. They try to put a price on the net present value of future cash flows, not just the value of past cash flows based on whatever accounting principles have been applied to their valuation. For that, investors want – and are increasingly getting – a lot of information that goes beyond the finances and helps the investors anticipate the future.

Operational reporting

The origins of shareholder activism have involved asking companies to provide greater detail about what they are doing, and pressing governments and regulators to demand more disclosure when the companies do not do so voluntarily. Some operational details have found their way into the financial reporting requirements as well. For internal purposes, companies use a wide variety of management accounting techniques, comparative data, ratios and other analyses they are not required to produce. Some of the demand for operational reporting is to make this kind of information available to the public.

Many companies now report information that goes well beyond the requirements as a way of signalling openness, transparency and, in a word, trustworthiness. But operational reporting goes beyond accounting figures. Company annual reports contain statements from the board, the CEO and sometimes from other corporate officers, on their view of the company's performance and the outlook for the future. They often give an assessment of the markets for the company's product, the nature of the competition it faces, how the strategy can create value in the future, or the actions underway concerning supply chain management or customer relationships.

Some financial analysts consider this information at least as valuable as financial reports. Even when not specifically forward-looking, it allows those outside the boardroom a chance to get a sense of what the directors and senior managers are thinking and feeling. Not surprisingly, official disclosure regulations have gradually expanded over the years to require that more operational information is included in official company reports. The US has rules concerning publication of a 'management discussion and analysis', a formal section of the annual report in which the company must describe non-financial information that may be relevant to future profitability. In the European Union, companies must now publish an annual business review, giving a narrative account of the business. Less prescriptive than the MD&A in the United States, the business review nonetheless asks companies to comment on circumstances in its markets and supply chain, in the general business environment and internally, that may have a material impact on the business. European regulations also require the immediate disclosure of changes in those circumstances that could affect the financial performance of the company. Important matters should not wait until the next results announcement.

Reporting on intangibles

Another aspect of non-financial reporting involves disclosure of aspects of the business that can be very important but which are hard to express in a narrative account of operations or to reduce to a simple financial statistic: things like brands, patents and other intellectual property, or the value of key employees and customer or supplier relationships.

The value of brands has been particularly important. Some companies' market capitalization depends far more on the value of their brands than any other component of their business. Take the example of Coca-Cola. According to its 2008 annual report, the company had net assets (that is, 'shareholder equity' or 'book value' in US accounting parlance) of £20.5 billion. Its market capitalization, however, was more than $100 billion. Accountants valued the business at less than a fifth of what investors felt it was worth. According to an analysis by Interbrand, a specialist brand consultancy, the Coca-Cola brand itself was worth more than $66 billion (Interbrand, 2008). Like most things concerned with intangible assets, what that means is a little hard to pin down. Interbrand's formula for calculating it may be disputed. But other studies using different methodologies still suggest that a lot of the value of the company arises from investors believing that the brand is important.

But brand value can be easily destroyed as well. The French water bottling company Perrier shows how operational problems (in this case, contaminated product) combined with poor management of communications (denying the problem first, before admitting it was true) caused the share price to collapse, destroying value for investors and permanently damaging its position with customers (Kurzbard & Siomkos, 1992). The Swiss food giant Nestlé subsequently acquired Perrier at a bargain price compared with its capitalization before the crisis. But was it really a bargain? The scandal had clearly affected consumers' attitude to the company and its product, affecting its future profitability.

This fragility is one of the reasons why financial analysts are sceptical about going too far with the notion of capitalizing brands – placing them officially on the balance sheet as an asset – or for that matter other intangible assets (consider Clarke & Dean, 2007). That has not stopped keen interest – in the investment community, as well as among marketers – in information like the Interbrand study or in corporations disclosing their own assessments of intangible assets.

Governance reporting

With increased concern over corporate governance reporting has come interest in having corporations disclose the governance policies and processes they use. Any governance code or law that gives the option of 'comply-or-explain' involves a demand that companies reveal what practices they have in place. Governance reporting often includes information about the organizational structure of the company as a whole, the board and its committees, and the shape of senior management. Increasingly, companies include information about the board's assessment of risks facing the business and how they deal with them.

Mandated by law in a growing number of countries is a requirement on disclosure of executive pay. The complex financial incentives given to senior managers led the US authorities to demand a simplified report that could be reduced to a simple table with a bottom line on how much these packages were worth. The US 'compensation analysis and discussion' contrasts with more loosely defined reports required in other places. This is an area in considerable flux, not least due to public and political pressure to end practices in incentive pay for those working in the financial services sector even well below board level in the organizational structure.

Social and environmental reporting

Initially in response to calls for 'social accountability' of corporations, disclosure practices have taken on some importance for investment markets as well, and not just among funds specifically involved in socially responsible investing, as discussed in Chapter 11. As the Perrier case shows, reputation is a valuable if fragile component of the business. Moreover, many industries are highly sensitive to these types of issues. Among the companies that get the highest ratings for their social and environmental reporting are those that structurally face the biggest social and environmental issues: mining, oil and gas, heavy industry, power generation and water supply.

Social policies of a mining company, for example, can be of strategic importance, not just public relations value. Working in southern Africa, for example, the company's contribution to fighting the infection of the population with HIV/AIDS may be an investment in keeping its workforce on the job and making sure there will be a workforce in the future.

Risk reporting

All businesses face risks, and those risks can be important, not just for the company's investors, but also for all those with whom it does business. They can be material to the health of the business and therefore to the value of the investment they represent. It is not surprising, therefore, that investors, regulators and others have placed increasing emphasis on risk reporting: if you cannot eliminate risk, then at least let investors, creditors and others know something about the extent of value at risk.

Some risks are fairly straightforward. Businesses can insure against commonplace hazards, like fire, flooding or accidental damage. Legal risks can be more subtle, but once a lawsuit has been filed it becomes a matter of public record. If large and potentially damaging to the business as a whole, regulators in many jurisdictions demand that the company include a discussion of those risks in their periodic reporting. Companies face financial risk from the markets for their raw materials and other inputs to the currency exposure they have when billing a customer in another currency, though possibilities exist to hedge such risks in commodity markets. In times of volatile oil markets, companies in industries like airlines, where fuel represents a large part of total costs, often report on their hedging activities as a way of demonstrating to investors that the risk is being managed, even if it cannot be completely controlled. Fraud and theft represent other financial risks. Operational risks, ranging from the failure of machinery to product recalls, the failure of a supplier to deliver and the departure of key members of staff to work for competitors can be very damaging as well, but reporting them can be difficult to do at all until the risk materializes. Then there is strategic risk – the chance that a business might fail, that a strategic alliance partner might not deliver the crucial expertise for the joint venture, or that the major decisions of management prove to be faulty, perhaps because of regulatory, social or environmental circumstances beyond the control of management.

But reporting on risk can often raise very serious operational and competitive issues. Often simply reporting about the risk can give a competitor an idea of how to inflict further damage by exploiting the company's weak points. Detailed disclosure could prove counterproductive for the investors whose interests disclosure is meant to protect. Gatekeepers like credit rating agencies can provide a buffer to some aspects of risk reporting. With their privileged access to detailed financial information, ratings agencies try to assess the danger that the company might not be able to meet its obligations on the various types of debt it has. Although not intended for any other purpose, credit ratings often find their way into the assessment of risk the equity investors make when buying shares or suppliers make when undertaking a major contract.

Issues in disclosure

Most disclosure takes place in writing, in company annual reports and interim financial statements, and on websites. But those are not the only channels of disclosure and the others present governance challenges of their own.

Investment briefings

It used to be common practice – and in many places it still is – that the senior management and chairman of public companies would follow up the announcement of financial results with a private briefing for financial analysts and what is often called a 'roadshow', in which senior company officials visit major institutional investors to discuss the results and the outlook for the business. In addition, company officials often give investment analysts 'guidance' about the company's view of the prospects for its earnings and revenues ahead of publication.

In 2000 the US Securities and Exchange Commission issued a rule known as Regulation FD (for 'fair disclosure') that required companies not to reveal any material, non-public information in such briefings, and if they did, even accidentally, they should also issue a formal statement, a news release, so that all investors would have equal access to the information. One of the effects of this was to lead companies to make many of their briefings available on the internet as webcasts, both simultaneously and with on-demand access, an audio and in some cases video records of what company officials had said in what had been private meetings, and to disclose officially the guidance they had been giving analysts confidentially and on a selective basis. These additional disclosures probably made analyst forecasts more reliable because more analysts had access to more data (Charoenrook & Lewis, 2009), but it remains in dispute how much value it adds for the corporation itself (Houston et al., 2008). The practice has spread to other countries, and especially among the larger companies which often had to comply with US rules because they had securities listed in the US or because their investors expected the same quality and range of information as their US rivals.

Face-to-face meetings between corporate officials and analysts or fund managers clearly offer something of value to the investors and analysts invited, even when the company does not – or is not allowed to – elaborate on comments already published and on the record. Participants in these meetings talk afterward about 'body language' or 'getting a feel' for the personalities, rather than that they received privileged access to important company information. But these methods of disclosure and the value investors put on them indicate that investment decisions and corporate valuation are often based, at least in part, on information that does not appear in financial statements.

These are matters of importance to the functioning of the financial markets in which the company's securities trade, and in the longer term how it can raise capital to fund its future investments. But these disclosure issues have further corporate governance effects too. They influence the way that senior management and the board perceive shareholder interests, and how they set policy as a result.

Fair value

Among the vagaries in financial disclosures is the issue of what value to place on the things that do appear in the balance sheet. In the post-Enron, post-WorldCom reforms in accounting, the profession has pushed hard for the use of *fair value* accounting whenever possible, a move that was controversial with many corporations at the start and became hotly debated by politicians as well as academics after the 2007–9 financial crisis seemed to have been aggravated by its effects.

The approach to valuation in accounting is in general to have the company's accounts reflect the economic value of the business. Traditionally, assets have been recorded at the price the company paid for them, and then depreciated at some rate depending on how long they were expected to last. During the period of high inflation in many developed countries during the 1970s and early 1980s, a new form of inventory accounting came into use, however, to provide some sort of recognition that newly purchased raw materials or semi-finished goods were more expensive that older ones.

This 'last-in, first-out' approach pointed the way to the idea and most – if perhaps not quite all – assets could be valued according to the current market price, rather than using historical prices as the basis. Had Enron or World-Com been forced to declare the current market value of many of the assets they had acquired – had they 'marked to market' – the problems with their accounting would have shown up much sooner. Investors would have been able to press for changes in strategy, and perhaps in management and on the board, at an earlier stage, before their investments had been so thoroughly destroyed.

Both international financial reporting standards and US GAAP post-2002 embedded the principle that the value of assets should be adjusted to reflect their current value, rather than left at the original purchase price. It might not capture all the value of intangible assets or investors' perceptions of their potential value. But it meant the assets reported in corporate financial statements would be a lot closer to the economic value those assets represented than they had previously shown using traditional accounting techniques. The accountancy profession – in America and throughout the world where IFRS had been adopted – were quite proud of what the new approach had achieved.

But the changes involved a dilemma, one that became quickly apparent when house prices in the United States started to fall in 2006. How do you account for the market value of assets for which no real market exists? The fall in real estate values, first in the US and later in other countries, gave a value for houses. Those valuations gave a basis for calculating the value of the mortgages on them, too. But many of those mortgages had been packaged into mortgage-backed securities – bonds that derived their value from the cash flow on a bundle of mortgages. So the value of mortgage-backed securities fell too, as did the value of the credit-default swaps that insurance companies and banks had written on them. In the panic, few of these instruments traded, so no one could be sure what the market price was, or whether the assets might be worthless. Who knew? Perhaps individual mortgages in the portfolios might still be fine, because the borrowers continued to make regular payments and the value of the houses was still higher than the value of the mortgages upon them.

These are, to be sure, accounting questions. But they have an impact on corporate governance as they affect the board's ability to judge what risks the company can afford to undertake and which it should avoid. In some cases they affect whether the business is even viable, that is, a 'going concern' – the ultimate corporate governance decision.

Impact of transparency

Polly Peck and WorldCom are far from the only cases in which companies manipulated their financial statements, bending and even breaking the accounting rules along the way. But the damage is not done by ignoring the rules alone. The losses for investors were disguised in the disclosures, working against the very principle of disclosure – to create trust between the company and investors, between investors and other investors, and between the market that their transactions create and the wider society.

The differing types of disclosures will be of varying interest to the different investors with their differing views on how the company can create and preserve value. Moreover, to build the trust that allows a liquid capital market to develop, stock market authorities have from the earliest days insisted that disclosures be made to *potential* investors and not just current shareholders. By so doing disclosures are made public, and made available all the corporation's publics, whether or not they are shareholders. That means the lobbying groups, non-governmental organizations, suppliers and customers have equal access to information about the company. Information will thus be available not only to the gatekeepers we discussed in Chapter 4, which the corporation pays to examine its performance, but also to the watchdogs who look out for the interests of other parties.

Of particular significance is the fact that if the public has access to the reports of public companies, competitors will too. As a consequence, disclosure regulations face a constant tension between asking companies to report in greater detail about their activities against the risk that such disclosure will undermine the competitiveness of the corporation against its rivals. Disclosure is good for investors, because it allows them to know better when the board ought to be applying the brakes through tougher monitoring and control. It harms investors, however, when it means that the enterprise will not get much acceleration from its engine when it steps on the gas.

Another effect of all these disclosures has been concern that users of information – whether individual or institutional investors, employees, suppliers, regulators, legislators or pressure groups – may simply lose the ability to digest it all. Even competitors – the users of corporate information with perhaps the greatest need and desire for the data – can get swamped in it all.

Corporate disclosure is meant to address one of the central problems identified in agency theory: information asymmetry (Gowthorpe, 2004; Hassink et al., 2007). Managers of the corporation have access to information unavailable to others. Boards of directors theoretically have access to all of it too, though in practice the flow of information to the board is controlled by the senior managers who select which portion of it reaches the board and which stays hidden along the way. Moreover, non-executive directors may lack the time to absorb all the information they receive. Shareholders have even less access to information and less time to process it, but public disclosure at least gives them access to more information with which to challenge the board.

One response to this has been calls for simplification of disclosures. Investors in some countries can choose to receive a short form on the annual report, with selected highlights, in effect. Selection of the highlights rests, of course, with management and such reports may not be audited to demonstrate the effectiveness of the selection, even if all the data have undergone an audit. Another approach has involved demanding that companies use simple language and avoid complex jargon and technical terms that might confuse the reader or obfuscate their meaning (Raiborn et al., 2008).

Another response is technological: take the accounting data in particular and wrap it at their origin in the accounting systems of corporations in a layer of computer code that will make it easier for investors to search databases not only for the company's information but for comparable data from alternative investment opportunities and analyse them. The development during the early 2000s of eXtensible Business Reporting Language, or XBRL, by the accounting profession holds the promise that investors will be able to get faster and more accurate information not only to guide their investment decisions but also with which to hold companies to account. Webcasting, too, has made important non-financial information accessible to the public, including to those analysts and institutional investors that were unable to attend events or were not invited. More recently, corporate contributions to social networking sites on the internet and other emerging communications channels has had the effect of further fragmenting the distribution of corporate information as well as increasing the volume.

Corporate disclosure risks becoming like the glare on bright day against the glass and steel of corporate headquarters. Transparency may be like sunlight and fresh air: distracting as well as antiseptic.

Further readings

Admati, A. R. & Pfleiderer, P. (2000). Forcing Firms to Talk: Financial Disclosure Regulation and Externalities. *Review of Financial Studies, 13*(3), 479–519.

Charoenrook, A. & Lewis, C. M. (2009). Information, Selective Disclosure, and Analyst Behavior. *Financial Management, 38*(1), 39–57.

Clarke, F. & Dean, G. (2007). *Indecent Exposure: Gilding the Corporate Lily*. Cambridge: Cambridge University Press.

Eccles, R. G., Herz, R. H., Keegan, E. M. & D.M.H., P. (2001). *The ValueReporting Revolution: Moving Beyond the Earnings Game*. New York: PricewaterhouseCoopers.

Gazdar, K. (2007). *Reporting Nonfinancials*. Chichester: John Wiley.

Hirshleifer, D. & Teoh, S. H. (2003). Limited Attention, Information Disclosure, and Financial Reporting. *Journal of Accounting and Economics, 36*(1–3), 337–86.

Hrasky, S. & Smith, B. (2008). Concise Corporate Reporting: Communication or Symbolism? *Corporate Communications: An International Journal, 13*(4), 418–32.

Nowland, J. (2008). The Effect of National Governance Codes on Firm Disclosure Practices: Evidence from Analyst Earnings Forecasts. *Corporate Governance: An International Review, 16*(6), 475–91.

Raiborn, C., Payne, D. & Pier, C. (2008). The Need for Plain English Disclosures. *Journal of Corporate Accounting & Finance, 19*(5), 69–76.

Reid, E. M. & Toffel, M. W. (2009). Responding to Public and Private Politics: Corporate Disclosure of Climate Change Strategies. *Harvard Business School Technology & Operations Mgt. Unit Research Paper No. 09-019*. Retrieved 26 June 2009, from http://ssrn.com/paper=1237982.

THIRTEEN

Governance beyond corporations

Cases: governing other types of organizations

The broad public discussion about governing the corporation has led to intro-spection and inspection of how other types of organizations are governed. If the corporate sector has issues of monitoring and control and of setting direction, perhaps there are lessons worth learning in how the public sector operates, how partnerships, mutual societies, charities and private companies work. The following vignettes give examples to offer a few insights into the issues.

Public sector: Financial Services Authority in the UK

Howard Davies had been a consultant at McKinsey, a civil servant in the Treasury and Foreign Office, and director general of the Confederation of British Industry, a grouping of the country's largest employers, before joining the Bank of England as deputy governor in 1995. With a change in government two years later came a new configuration in how the 'City', London's financial district, was governed, and Davies led it: a single, unified regulator for banking, insurance and securities, the Financial Services Authority. It combined the work of several focused regulators as well as the Bank of England's role in supervising the banking system itself. Davies was called executive chairman, the one man in charge of the one regulator, integrating its disparate arms, setting up new processes and then creating the framework to implement the sweeping new legal structures introduced with the Financial Services and Markets Act of 2000 and a wave of European Union regulation in the sector. Many other countries chose to emulate it as a solution to keeping track of the increasingly integrated, increasingly global market in banking, insurance and securities. Davies and the FSA became accountable to the Treasury department and its lead minister, the Chancellor of the Exchequer.

When he stepped down in 2003, the FSA was embroiled in controversy. Private investors had lost a lot of money on collective investment funds that did not do what the marketing literature had said they would. A parliamentary committee accused the FSA of 'being asleep on the job' (Steed, 2003). Under Davies, it had also pursued charges that UK news organizations had published leaked documents from a company quoted in Belgium, and their reports had created a false market. It had looked to some like an attempt to cage some of the watchdogs of corporate governance. Just before retiring, Davies dropped the investigation (Cave, 2003). It was a messy end to his six-year tenure.

In keeping with the principles of the Combined Code of corporate governance, his job was then split: Callum McCarthy became chairman, while John Tiner was named CEO. But the FSA was not a public corporation. Accountable to government, it did not have disparate, distant shareholders with the resulting agency problem. It already had something like a non-executive chairman in the person of a minister in the Treasury responsible for financial services. Perhaps we should not look at the decision through the lens of the Combined Code and its principles. Perhaps the thinking was that two people would do a better job than Davies had done on his own (Cole, 2003).

Four years later, CEO Tiner left the FSA, just a few weeks before Northern Rock, a mortgage bank, collapsed, requiring a rescue with public guarantees. It proved a vain attempt to put out the financial wildfire that year and eventually Northern Rock had to be nationalized. Chairman McCarthy stayed on another, painful year that saw the FSA once again accused of being 'asleep', this time 'at the wheel' (Gribben, 2008).

Non-profits: Dick Grasso at NYSE

For most of its history the New York Stock Exchange was a mutual association, an organization owned by its members, the firms that made markets in the shares of companies quoted on the exchange, buying shares when no one else was willing to part with shares, selling when no one else would make an offer. Members included individuals and partnerships who traded in very large volumes of shares with unlimited personal liability. Trust was essential. Trading in securities is a risky business, but it was the members' business. The exchange was a trading venue.

It was, nonetheless, one that received close scrutiny. In the complex and highly regulated world of financial services, the business of the exchange fell under the watchful eye of the Securities and Exchange Commission. NYSE also had a board of governors, which included powerful people from the world of politics and finance. Some came from the biggest customers of the exchange's members, the Wall Street investment banks and stockbrokers. It was, in effect, a stakeholder board.

For eight years starting in 1995, the role of chairman and CEO belonged to Richard Grasso, a rough-and-tumble trader with a shaved head. As he began to consider retiring came news that he had amassed a claim for deferred income of nearly $200 million. It was not a huge sum in the scale of CEO pay in America. But this was not a large corporation working in a highly competitive marketplace. NYSE was a still more of a club than company. Its open outcry method of traders shouting orders to each other on the exchange floor persisted even in the face of a global shift towards electronic transactions in securities. NYSE had, in some sense, slept through the computer revolution of the past quarter of a century. Its upstart arch-rival, Nasdaq, used the New York Stock Exchange's 200th anniversary in 1992 to launch an advertising campaign declaring Nasdaq the 'stock market for the *next* hundred years'. NYSE had not responded with any changes to its core model of trading.

The New York Attorney General sued the exchange over the pay package Grasso received. The SEC, embarrassed that it had not itself spearheaded the investigation, responded. Then chaired by William Donaldson – who had been chairman and CEO of NYSE just before Grasso – the SEC demanded board minutes and names of who had been involved in the decision to his successor so much money. CalPERS, the California public sector pension fund, sued NYSE and its member firms, alleging that they had overcharged institutional investors by some $155 million to pay Grasso (Thomas, 2006, provides an overview).

Grasso resigned in the end, and his severance arrangements rumbled in the courts for years, but he eventually got his full package of pension and deferred income in 2008. In the meantime, NYSE appointed a new interim chairman, who led the search to find a new CEO. The SEC pressed hard, as regulator, to ensure there was a separation of the roles of chairman and CEO, in accordance with principles of good corporate governance that only a minority of US corporations in fact followed.

Before long NYSE had become a public, for-profit company, with shares trading on its own exchange. It retained a non-executive chairman overseeing the work of the new CEO, modelled in part on the UK Combined Code.

Partnerships: Arthur Andersen partners, departed

'The day Arthur Andersen loses the public's trust is the day we are out of business.' This quote, from the managing partner of the accountancy firm Arthur Andersen in the US, comes from a CD-Rom of the firm's ethics standards in 1999. In 2002, Arthur Andersen, one of the Big Five global accountancy practices, imploded.

The story of its disintegration is a fascinating one, told well by Barbara Ley Toffler and her co-author, Jennifer Reingold. Toffler joined Andersen in 1995 to start up a line of business offering ethics services to the firm's corporate clients. An early warning of trouble ahead – in the first chapter of her book – she describes how a piece of work worth $75,000 came to be billed to the client at $400,000. 'This is Arthur Andersen,' her manager replied. 'That's the way we do it around here' (Toffler & Reingold, 2003, p. 3). Like all accountancy practices at the time, Arthur Andersen was a partnership. There were no shareholders.

Case

Equity in the firm belonged to those privileged few invited to become partners. Until 1991 in the United States and somewhat later in most other countries, partners carried unlimited liability for problems at the firm: they risked losing their homes, savings and pensions if something when wrong. It made partnerships – a common form for professional practices, including lawyers and doctors – structurally conservative, risk averse. One partner's misdeeds were every other partner's risk. Partners spend the firm's money as if it were their own – *carefully*, that is – because it is their own. As the size of the clients of accounting firms grew, so too did the risk of the audit, so the profession generally welcomed the move to limit their exposure to the capital in the business. They might still have a lot to lose, just not everything. That bargain also meant they could take more risks, and in larger firms take the risk with the backing of all the partners.

For Andersen, taking risks became a way of life, one that, according to Toffler's account, meant leaving behind the founder's famous intolerance for shady dealings. In June 2001, the firm settled a deeply embarrassing case brought by the SEC against its work with a client with the unfortunate name of Waste Management. Four Andersen executives and the firm stood accused of having failed to stop serious fraud at Waste Management. Andersen paid a $7 million fine without admitting wrong-doing. With a new CEO, elected by the partners, now in charge of the business, it was back to business as usual. But not for long.

In October 2001, one of Andersen's biggest clients, Enron Corp., reported a loss of $638 million in its third quarter, as it ended its connection with certain off-balance-sheet entities it had created, with the advice of Andersen, as we later learned. A few weeks later it restated its earnings for the years 1997–2000, recording a further loss of $591 million. Enron soon filed for bankruptcy. The SEC issued a statement – a warning in all but name – that it would investigate what had gone wrong. The Andersen partner who managed the account, apparently with the knowledge of some people at headquarters, set about shredding most of the documents Andersen had concerning its work with Enron.

A few months later, WorldCom collapsed under the weight of a fraud of around $11 billion. Like Enron, Andersen had been the auditor there. Like Enron, WorldCom paid Andersen even more for consulting services than it had for the audit. The US government then indicted the firm for fraud. Clients lost trust in the firm and began first to drift, then to run away. Then staff jumped ship. Then partners all around the world began to take their clients and staff to other accounting practices. Even before Andersen's CEO could negotiate a sale of the business to its rival Deloitte, the firm has disintegrated, burying all the equity the partners had had in the rubble.

Private companies: big trouble at tiny businesses

These are the stories of two small companies, owned and operated by private individuals and a small circle of investors. These are not real cases, but many real companies have problems something like these.

Robbins Communications   A marketing agency, let's call it Robbins Communications, built up a business turning over about $600,000 a year. After 20 years running it the founder, Jack Robbins, aged 51, knew that two large clients of long standing planned to cancel their contracts. Perhaps it was time to retire, sell the company, or even just close it down. It had not made much more money than he might have earned in salary at someone else's company, so perhaps there was not much point in trying to find a buyer. Jack owned 90 per cent of the business, with the rest held by friends who had given him money to start the business, and then more when it had financial trouble a while back.

Instead he decided to give it one more go. He invited investment from business angels, private investors who would provide new capital, perhaps even take control once the business was firing on all cylinders again. Two investors came on board. One wanted a more passive role, attending board meetings but leaving management of the business to Jack. The other wanted an executive position, perhaps eventually as CEO when Jack retired. It sounded a rather grand title in such a small company, Jack thought.

Before investing, the new shareholders undertook formal due diligence, hiring a firm of accountants to audit the books and even spending most of the working week in the office while the negotiations were underway. Jack created a new board, too. His new investors would join him on it, together with an independent chairman, a lawyer Jack had known for years but not a close friend. Jack still had a majority of the shares, but the chairman and the two new investors could outvote him at the board meeting. The decisions were consciously modelled on the Combined Code of corporate governance in the UK, because one of Jack's clients had been deeply involved in promoting the code. The Robbins board had separated the roles of chair and CEO and had a majority of independent directors. It met monthly, had detailed board papers to consider, and published minutes for the company's official records. Despite some strains everyone was committed to making the company work again.

When the new funds finally came, the company moved into larger offices with a new telephone system, extra desks and elegant meeting rooms, in anticipation of growth. Within three months it was insolvent, put into administration. The external auditor – indeed the founder himself – had failed to notice that for a year or so a part-time bookkeeper had been making systematic mistakes, booking as revenue invoices the company had received from suppliers.

Petal Publishing   Three friends from a major advertising agency decided to break away to form a new publishing company. It would specialize in cookbooks, but not just any cookbooks. Theirs would be produced for individual chefs at elegant, small restaurants. The chefs would commission the books, paying their production costs up front and helping with distribution by making copies available for sale to their guests. Petal Publishing would take the photographs, write the text, create the layouts and organize the printing. Petal Publishing would also work on getting the titles into bookshops and on internet book sites. Petal Publishing would sell to banks and corporations, who might use the books as client gifts, use the restaurants as meeting venues, and encourage the bankers to take their clients there as well. The three friends, David, George and Petal herself, all three in their late twenties, had all the talent they needed: David was a salesman, through and through; George had expertise in production; Petal was the writer, photographer and herself a trained chef. What they did not have was any money. Though Petal lent her name to the venture, David was the driving force – and majority shareholder.

They offered shares to friends and relatives and got a few takers for small amounts. It was not a revolutionary idea or technologically very exciting, so getting venture capital seemed out of the question. To convince a bank to grant them loans or government to provide guarantees for start-ups, they needed investors to demonstrate their confidence first. Eventually, through an introduction organized by their accountant, they found three private individuals they'd never met before who liked the idea – and liked the three partners.

The new investors demanded a shareholders' agreement. The three founders would be on the board, but so too would the three new investors, who reluctantly agreed that David could serve as chairman. Board meetings would take place every two months at the latest. Accounts would be sent to shareholders every month to keep track of the progress. Such a small company did not have to have an audit under law, but this one would. The executive directors could not take a salary increase of more than inflation without agreement of at least two-thirds of the board. Signed, sealed and delivered. Petal Publishing was born, with $100,000 in the bank.

Early successes came, but within a year, the strain of getting customers led the partners to fall out. Petal resigned and sold her shares to David for next to nothing. A year later George left too, unwilling to put up with David's increasingly bossy approach, one now backed by a 60 per cent shareholding. David was determined to keep going. He outsourced their work to freelancers.

The board never met. Not once. David as chairman never called a meeting. Accounts went out to shareholders about twice a year. The shareholders' agreement proved unenforceable because none of the outside investors felt it was worth the time or cost of taking the company to court. One by one they resigned from the board, fearing their own reputations might be damaged if the company did something seriously wrong.

It did not, but neither did it succeed. Petal Publishing struggled on for five years. David's polish as a salesman meant it achieved enough business to be credible, and he used the credibility to sell more shares to new investors, albeit at a much lower price. But in the end it just could not keep going. The cash had run out.

Questions arising

These examples highlight just a few of the many different types of organizations that have looked, in one way or another, at lessons that might be learned from the governance of corporations. But charities, not-for-profit and mutual organizations are not like corporations in that their purpose does not involve a profit motive, or an obligation to maximize the wealth of owners. Public sector bodies have obligations and responsibilities that reach beyond the organization and its members to the public at large.

1 To whom are boards of each of these types of organizations accountable?
2 How does their accountability differ from corporations with shares traded on public markets?
3 What benefits might structures like board committees bring to each type? What pitfalls might they face?
4 What types of individuals might be needed by each type of organization, and how might the requirements of board composition differ those of corporations?
5 What similarities are there between corporations, private companies, not-for-profits and public sector bodies that might affect the roles and responsibilities of their boards?

What makes a corporation different

Corporations are legal persons, devised to protect investors from the risks of full liability for the business. With the ability to sell shares to a wide and dispersed investing public they can become, in effect, ownerless, with no one minding the shop. This is the agency problem, and it is the reason, as we have seen, why various mechanisms of corporate governance have come into existence. Before the corporation emerged as a way of structuring economic activity, there was little need for these governance mechanisms. Entrepreneurs looked after their money, taking as much risk as they felt they could. Some failed. Others grew wealthy. Meetings of boards of directors were like having Sunday lunch with the family.

In the wake of the corporate governance scandals of the 1990s and 2000s, however, many other types of organizations looked to the reforms in corporate governance for possible lessons. How might these governance mechanisms help other types of business work better?

Private companies

The sole-trader or the single-person company is often said to have fewer governance problems. The risk is the individual's, a matter of personal responsibility, not one of society at large. Though more centralizing governments (like France, for example) may require sole-traders to register and get official sanction to do business, more liberal economies merely try to ensure the individuals pay their taxes. With incorporation as a company, however, comes a limit to liability, and most governments see a need for some registration and formal processes – to give comfort to suppliers and customers, not to protect the business. But many private companies raise outside capital, as we have seen in the cases of Robbins Communications and Petal Publishing. For them, access to a board of directors and more direct access to details of the business are often used as the mechanism of corporate governance.

The move towards board independence that we see in the corporate sector has been tried in private companies too, as have auditing the accounts and requiring any transactions between the company and its large shareholder to undergo special approval. Shareholder agreements can force the company's executives to channel any money they earn from any activity through the company, rather than letting them accept funds privately or use another company in ways that might create a conflict of interest.

Outside investors often demand a seat on the board to make sure they can inspect what's happening. This type of governance is used widely in the private equity and venture capital industries, where often large amounts of money are involved. In many of these situations, the managers of a business may come in from the outside, taking a stake in the business that will pay off only if they are successful. Some private equity deals involve buying a division of another company or taking an entire listed corporation private. That may mean leaving the existing management in place, who then report to a board made up of the venture capital or private equity firm. Keeping management interests aligned with shareholders' interests is relatively easy. Moreover, disagreements between shareholders over direction are minimized. Private companies, in short, rarely face an agency problem, at least at the top of the company. Stewardship is the rule, rather than the exception. This suggests that many of the other mechanisms of corporate governance may be a distraction.

Governance issues arise, however, when the founder of a company decides to retire, perhaps passing direction of the company along to a child or other family member. To what extent does 'Dad' stay involved? How much discretion is afforded to the new management? If an outsider is brought in to run the business, agency issues may arise, and with them the need for additional mechanisms of governance.

Partnerships

Partnerships arise when two or more individuals join together to own a firm but without issuing shares. Traditionally this is a very conservative approach, and trust between the partners can suffer if they do not all pull their weight.

One result is that many traditional partnerships – small accountancy practices, law firms – stay small and leave very little value in the business itself. Revenues are often billed by partners in the firm's name but then credited to their own internal accounts. The value of the business is often little more than the value of the accounts receivable.

But as partnerships grow, issues akin to those of corporations can arise. Firms like Arthur Andersen can reach to the thousands of partners, each with a say in how the business is run and with a vote about how it is organized. While Andersen, like other larger partnerships, had a CEO, such posts are often more involved in coordination and infrastructure than in consistent implementation of strategy throughout the firm. In partnership, the partner is, at least in theory, his own boss.

The managing partner of a mid-sized, 37-partner accountancy practice once denied being CEO of the firm. 'We have 37 CEOs,' he said. 'I'm just in charge of ordering coffee.' Partnerships struggle with governance issues, and structures like boards and committees can help. But their role is different, because it is the partner who is liable even if that liability is now limited in law. And the partner has direct, inside knowledge of the firm and its workings in ways that distant shareholders of a corporation cannot.

Running a large business often conflicts with the partnership mentality. Legal ownership of client relationships is not straightforward. Spending on information systems, buildings and marketing reduce the amount of money that partners take home in a year. Large businesses run as partnership can build equity value, too. The Andersen brand, for example, was once thought to be worth several billion dollars, a factor that came into play in 2000, just before the tempest hit, when its technology and strategy consulting arm broke away from the parent to become Accenture, a corporation. A court ordered the former consulting business to pay Arthur Andersen just $1 billion for its freedom, but it refused to let the new corporation use the valuable Andersen name. When it listed on the New York Stock Exchange, Accenture achieved a market capitalization of $25 billion, and was soon grateful it had not paid extra for the sake of retaining the name of Andersen Consulting.

Non-profit organizations

Both mutual associations and charities normally share the characteristic of being not-for-profit. As such they share the difficulty of creating the resilience that a for-profit corporation can by retaining profits. The two types differ in structure and purpose from each other, and the rules for each – and not least the tax laws – vary from jurisdiction to jurisdiction. But their broader purposes raise similar governance issues irrespective of the details of the law. We will look briefly at each.

Mutual associations

A feature that distinguishes mutual associations and cooperatives from corporations is the simple fact that their purpose does not involve the generation of profits. Any surpluses they achieve are intended to be invested in the business or returned to members in lower prices or fees. In the financial crisis of 2007–9 some mutual savings institutions stepped up their marketing campaigns to demonstrate they were *not* banks, and so not subject to the greed and risky practices that had endangered the stability of the global economy as well as the payments system. Owned by their 'members', who may be customers, suppliers, employees or just people who associate with the cause, mutuals have been a way of doing business for centuries. Farmers pool their crops through mutual associations and cooperatives, to spread the costs of storage and shipping. These mutuals give rise to savings institutions that handle the transactions, act as a repository of cash and lend money back to the farmers to fund them until the harvest season. Similar vehicles arose within large industrial districts as ordinary workers pooled their savings to provide loans for those in need and then for those seeking mortgages.

But mutuals are not risk-free. Memories of the savings and loans crisis in the United States in the late 1980s and early 1990s have faded somewhat. But it involved nearly a decade of trouble, in which one institution after another failed, about 2,000 in all, with the cost of the rescue to taxpayers estimated at more than $100 billion (Seidman, 1996). While the CEOs in the S&L industry might not have had stock options or other equity-based incentives to increase their personal gains, cash incentives led to increasingly speculative lending. An early form of bundling the loans into packages and selling them on to transfer risk foreshadowed the securitization that led to the 2007 collapse of the sub-prime mortgage market, too. William Siedman, who was chairman of the US Federal Deposit Insurance Corp. at the time of the S&L crisis, reflected later on lessons learned. Most concerned banking practice and the failure of regulators, but some pointed back to corporate governance: internal control, and 'full disclosure and total transparency' (Seidman, 1996, p. 62).

In governance terms, mutuals can look a lot like the 'modern corporation' described by Berle and Means (1932/1991), with the resulting principal/agent problem. Instead of widely dispersed shareholders (principals), none large enough to justify the cost of monitoring management (their agents), mutuals can grow to having large numbers of widely dispersed members (principals), none remotely large enough to justify the cost of monitoring management. Mutuals often have no members with a stake in the association even close to the positions that institutional investors now have with listed companies.

It is not surprising, therefore, that scholars find the governance issues in the mutual and cooperative sector as having large similarities to listed companies, but with fewer obvious solutions than those institutional investors can create for them. Cornforth (2004), for example, describes three key tensions in the practice of governance in mutual organizations:

- Board members may act as representatives for particular membership groups or as 'experts' charged with driving the performance of the organization forward. (This is a challenge in the corporation as well.)
- Boards have two roles, driving forward organizational performance against the need to ensure the organization behaves in an accountable and prudent manner. (This is the tension between the accelerator and the brake.)
- The simultaneous need to control and support management. (Here it is the dynamic in the boardroom that is important. How does someone challenge management judgements while still supporting management aims?)

Charities

Charities are non-profit organizations with a special purpose, one that serves some larger public good. As a result, they tend to get special tax status, perhaps even become tax exempt or face reduced tax rates for some of their activities. Legal frameworks can vary from country to country in ways that affect the governance structures and processes.

This is an area that calls out for us to examine governance from a steward-ship, rather than an agency, perspective. In the UK, for example, charity boards are required by law not to include any employees of the charity itself, so the executive versus non-executive distinction falls away. It is an extra layer of protection to prevent charitable funds being diverted to private use. Executives may still attend, but without voting on matters before the board. Moreover, board members cannot receive payment for their services – it is a voluntary role. So self-serving would seem on the surface almost completely excluded by design.

One study from a small but growing body of literature suggests that certain factors influence the performance of charity boards. Cornforth (2001) studied UK charities, finding that effectiveness depended most on whether the board has a clear understanding of its role and responsibilities. The other important factors: having the right mix of skills and experience, having the time, sharing a vision, and reviewing their own performance. As profit is by definition excluded, performance in charities typically has a lot to do with fundraising, though the Cornforth study looked at 17 factors in all.

But the agency problem cannot be ignored. Full-time managers of charities can steer the board's agenda even though they may not vote on its outcomes. A US study (Fisman & Hubbard, 2005) showed that organizations with governance structures that involved relatively poor oversight tended to pay their managers a higher proportion of donations, while allocating less to future expenditures. Better governance, it concluded, would give donors the confidence to allow the charities to build up their endowments and therefore improve their resilience.

Lacking other mechanisms of governance that we see in the corporate sector, it is not surprising to see guidelines for charitable organizations encouraging policies on ethics and whistle-blowing, and statements of board duties that emphasize exercising due diligence and transparency. In some cases charities are forbidden from conducting any business whatsoever with members of their boards or any organization they control.

Public sector

The governance of public sector organizations has undergone a serious debate – both in theory and practice – about the extent to which they can draw inspiration from developments in the commercial world. Sometimes called 'new public management', the practice of using private sector mechanisms in the public sector argues that the responsiveness of commercial organizations brings benefits to recipients of public services as well. Sometimes it leads to a separation of organizational governance from the government that created it (Greer & Hoggett, 2000). Critics argue that it opens the door to 'managerialism', in which managers themselves become the focal point of decision-making and the public service element of working in the public sector is correspondingly diminished.

Evidence of new public management can be seen in the UK, where the Office of Public Management and the Chartered Institute of Public Finance and Accountancy issued guidelines for the governance of public sector bodies (OPM & CIPFA, 2004) with strong similarities to the Combined Code for listed companies. Its emphasis was on independence for the boards achieved through non-executives sitting on a board of governors, with a chair independent of management. Senior managers may also be governors, depending on the type of organization. The governors share collective responsibility, as does the board of a corporation. The governing board also has functions parallel to those we see in corporate governance: allocating resources; monitoring executive performance; overseeing appointment and contractual arrangements for senior executives; and understanding and managing risk. Because accountability is to the public, rather than a subset of owners, 'ensuring that the voice of the public is heard in decision making' plays a more central role (OPM & CIPFA, 2004, p. 9). While it does not explicitly use the language of 'comply or explain' the same intent is there in a call to report publicly on how they live up to the standard, and explain why and how they have adapted its principles.

But how similar is the public sector? In 1980 Graham Allison analysed the differences in a seminal study of the problems, grouping the differences in three categories: environment factors, transactions between the organization and its environment, and internal structures and processes. His view was that very strong differences separate the public and private spheres. The public sector was much less exposed to markets and as a result to signalling information like the right prices for services. It faced greater constraints from courts and legislatures, and stronger political influence. Public expectations and scrutiny were higher too, and internal structures were more complex, leaving less autonomy for individuals (Allison, 1980).

Because such differences existed did not mean they needed to, however, and that became the thrust of the new approach. George Boyne (2002), for example, analysed 34 empirical studies for evidence of 13 hypotheses concerning the difference between public and private sector administration. Only three were supported by a majority of the studies: public organizations are more bureaucratic; public managers are less materialistic; and public managers have weaker organizational commitment than their private sector counterparts. It argued, therefore, that the public-service model of public sector organization left something to be desired. But critics of the approach (e.g. Kickert, 1997) argue that a managerial approach is one-sided and ill-suited to the public sector. While such comments focus on management, rather than board-level studies, there is some evidence that public sector boards that followed the route of corporate governance towards a more knowledgeable and active range of independent governors benefited in terms of better control and responsiveness (Ferlie et al., 1995).

In emerging markets, the World Bank has tried to promote better corporate governance alongside better governance in the public sector. Here the focus is often on seeking solutions to the agency problem frequently identified as corruption (for an example of its studies, see Shah, 2007).

Agents or stewards?

If the corporate sector is prone to the agency problem and requiring special mechanisms of corporate governance to control them, perhaps we might expect other types of organizations to take a different direction. Private companies, even large ones withdrawn by private equity firms with the intention of floating them again after a restructuring, often use structures that emphasize management's commitment to a common set of goals with the owners and intensive owner engagement with day-to-day operations. Perhaps even more so than private companies, partnerships involve structures and processes that point, if not to a common purpose, then at least to divisions of the proceeds that align with partners' contributions. In the non-profit and public sectors we might expect to see less greed and more voluntary spirit, as making a contribution to society plays a larger role. Stewardship, with its sense of a greater purpose, often features in the minds of the individuals involved.

As the discussion in this chapter has indicated, however, we might wish to be more tentative about concluding too strongly that the benefits – the virtues, even – of these forms of organization are preferable to those of the corporate sector. Each is open to self-dealing. Private companies frequently invite outside capital with the founder–manager in a position to use company resources as though they were his own. Partnerships struggle to grow and keep the agency problem in check. Non-profits often have distant principals. While the in-house agents may be scrupulous in not using the organization's resource for private purposes, the possibility is always present that they might bend the organization's direction towards their own notions of what its purpose should be.

Public sector organizations are accountable to the public as a whole, yet that very clear sense of accountability runs the risk of making them accountable to no one at all. That lack of accountability is what drove public sector theorists and practitioners to institute private sector mechanisms in the first place, even to the point of some public bodies calling those who seek assistance their 'customers'.

This brief discussion of a large and complex field suggests that – as in corporate governance – there is a constant tension: between agency and stewardship; between monitoring and control on the one hand and value creation on the other. The determination of which it will be depends very much on the people involved, and the solutions most often explored in corporate governance concern the structures and processes. Could it be that the solutions do not match the problems?

Further readings

Allison, G. T. (1980). *Public and Private Management: Are They Fundamentally Alike in All Unimportant Respects?* Paper presented at the Public Management Research Conference. Retrieved (date) From http://www.apubb.ro/Documents/Hintea/Public_Management/PublicAndPrivateManagement.pdf.

Boyne, G. A. (2002). Public and Private Management: What's the Difference? *Journal of Management Studies, 39*(1), 97–122.

Cornforth, C. (2001). What Makes Boards Effective? An Examination of the Relationships between Board Inputs, Structures, Processes and Effectiveness in Non-profit Organisations. *Corporate Governance: Aan International Review, 9*(3), 217–227.

Cornforth, C. (2004). The Governance of Cooperatives and Mutual Associations: a Paradox Perspective. *Annals of Public & Cooperative Economics, 75*(1), 11–32.

Dellaportas, S., Gibson, K., Hutchinson, M., Leung, P. & Van Homrigh, D. (2005). *Ethics, Governance and Accountability: A Professional Perspective.* Milton, Queensland: Wiley.

Desai, M. A. & Yetman, R. J. (2005). Constraining Managers without Owners: Governance of the Not-for-profit Enterprise. *NBER Working Paper 11140*. Retrieved 12 Jan. 2010, from http://www.nber.org/papers/w11140.

Ferlie, E., Ashburner, L. & Fitzgerald, L. (1995). Corporate Governance and the Public Sector: Some Issues and Evidence from the NHS. *Public Administration, 73*(3), 375–92.

Fletcher, L. B. & Miles, M. P. (2004). The Law of Unintended Consequences: The Effects of the Sarbanes–Oxley Act on Venture Funding of Smaller Enterprises. *Journal of Private Equity, 8*(1), 70–5.

Greenwood, R., Suddaby, R. & Hinings, C. R. (2002). Theorizing Change: The Role of Professional Associations in the Transformation of Institutionalized Fields. *Academy of Management Journal, 45*(1), 58–80.

Greer, A. & Hoggett, P. (2000). Contemporary Governance and Local Public Spending Bodies. *Public Administration, 78*(3), 513–29.

Hodges, R., Wright, M. & Keasey, K. (1996). Corporate Governance in the Public Services: Concepts and Issues. *Public Money & Management, 16*(2), 7–13.

Kickert, W. J. M. (1997). Public Governance in the Netherlands: An Alternative to Anglo-American 'Managerialism'. *Public Administration, 75*(4), 731–52.

McNulty, T. & Ferlie, E. (2002). *Reengineering Health Care: The Complexities or Organizational Transformation*. Oxford: Oxford University Press.

Parker, L. D. (2007). Boardroom Strategizing in Professional Associations: Processual and Institutional Perspectives. *Journal of Management Studies, 44*(8), 1454–80.

Rost, K., Inauen, E., Osterloh, M. & Frey, B. S. (2010). The Corporate Governance of Benedictine Abbeys: What Can Stock Corporations Learn from Monasteries? *Journal of Management History, 16*(1), 90–115.

FOURTEEN

An unsettled and unsettling future?

With fits and starts, the current governance crisis has been 30 years in the making. The decline in performance of the over-diversified, over-staffed corporation in the 1980s was marked, and blamed on management that was essentially ungoverned. A round of firings of management followed, accompanied by the creation of independent, active boards of directors . . . No more was the imperial Chief Executive Officer (CEO) to be criticized for ignoring the rightful returns of investors; but the scandals of Enron and others, and the bursting of the bubble of stock prices of Internet, telecom and energy company shares, has caused those of us involved with corporate enterprise to take another look. While we thought governance had reached an inevitable pinnacle of excellence, at least in form, we came to realize that it had not, in substance. . . . The substance of reform lies in the actual performance of boards in properly carrying out their responsibilities to shareholders and the public. This substance requires more than proper structure and process, and more can be done. Unfortunately, that 'more' is not in place. (MacAvoy & Millstein, 2003, p. 1)

* * *

On the first point, corporate governance: no need to repeat the story of events earlier in the decade, the bankruptcies and subsequent regulatory frenzies. In the US it was politicians, going very fast, very far. In Europe a mixture of politicians, lawyers, professors and the usual group of not necessarily business-friendly advocacy groups seized the opportunity to air their pet issues. This produces many trends and restrictions, but no clear direction. . . . For business, this specialisation, or responsibility for that which one can do best, is increasingly being called into question. Part of this trend is extending governance to new subject areas, to the so-called 'corporate social responsibility', including everything from public healthcare to global human rights. Another part of this trend are concepts based on mistaken analogies: the extensive debate, particularly but not exclusively in Europe, about alleged risks of the double mandate – one person acting both as CEO and chairman – often refers explicitly or implicitly to the organisation of our states. . . . We must urgently bring back some pragmatism to corporate governance that facilitates the choice for the best option under given circumstances. And if we want governance schemes that actually work in a real business environment, they must be based on principles, not detailed rules that try to pre-empt all the eventualities a lawyer can think of . . .

The second point of my considerations: 'giving something back to society'. This wrongheaded idea that companies incur a debt to society by virtue of being successful is based upon some fallacious assumptions. (Brabeck-Letmathe, 2005)

Case: Enron – emblem or anomaly?

Throughout this book, the name Enron has appeared along with glimpses of the case. What is this story that thrust corporate governance from being of parochial interest to a handful of management scholars and asset managers into the glare of public policy debate? How could one company so transform the way the general public thinks about corporations, their roles in society, and how society ought to oversee their actions?

Enron had been everyone's success story. Its revenues grew from $13.3 billion in 1996 to $100.8 billion five years later, rising by 150 per cent in its last full year, 2000. Earnings, which had taken a one-time hit in 1997, grew, but not nearly at the blistering pace of revenues. It share price, too, had climbed from $21 at the end of 1996 to over $80 at the end of 2000. Its letter to shareholders with the annual results began: 'Enron's performance in 2000 was a success by any measure, as we continued to outdistance the competition' (Enron, 2001, p. 2). As we have learned, that annual report did not tell the whole story. It made no mention of the off-balance-sheet 'limited liability partnerships' in which much of the bad business had been parked. The previous annual report (Enron, 2000c) disclosed them in a footnote, without recording the financial details or clearly identifying that the 'partner' was in fact Enron's own chief financial officer, Andrew Fastow.

Corporate malfeasance and misdemeanours have been present since the beginnings of the corporation. Even in the period in which it happened, 2000–2, the Enron collapse was not the first or the largest to fall. What distinguished this case was its shock value, the swing from top to bottom, the suddenness of it all, and how the company's own symbols become icons of irony.

- In December 2000, *Fortune* magazine and the Great Place to Work Institute named Enron the 22nd best place to work in America, up two notches from a year earlier (Levering & Moskowitz, 2000). It would not be around for the next year's survey, and its workforce would have seen their pension savings squandered with their jobs. Enron sent out press releases noting the fact, and that *Fortune* had also named it the 'Most Innovative Company' for five consecutive years, the top company for 'Quality of Management' and the second best company for 'Employee Talent' (Enron, 2000a).
- Its 'vision' statement read: 'Enron's vision is to become the world's leading energy company – creating innovative and efficient energy solutions for growing economies and a better environment worldwide' (Enron, 2001).

- It proclaimed its 'values' to be 'Communication, Respect, Integrity, Excellence'. Communication: 'We have an obligation to communicate. Here, we take the time to talk with on another . . . and to listen. We believe that information is meant to move and that information moves people.' Respect: 'We treat others as we would like to be treated ourselves. We do not tolerate abusive or disrespectful treatment. Ruthlessness, callousness and arrogance do not belong here.' Integrity: 'We work with customers and prospects openly, honestly and sincerely. When we say we will do something, we will do it; when we say we cannot or will not do something, then we do not do it.' Excellence: 'We are satisfied with nothing less than the very best in everything we do. We will continue to raise the bar for everyone. The great fun here will be for all of us to discover just how good we really can be' (Enron, 2001, p. 53).
- In its Code of Ethics (Enron, 2000b), Chairman Kenneth Lay wrote: 'As officers of Enron Corp, its subsidiaries, and its affiliated companies, we are responsible for conducting the business affairs of the companies in accordance with all applicable laws and in a moral and honest manner . . . We want to be proud of Enron and to know that it enjoys a reputation for fairness and honesty and that it is respected'.
- The corporate logo, adopted during its ascent to the top flight of American business, was known throughout the corporation as the 'crooked E'.

The details of the case became among the most widely discussed in the business media (for an overview see Sherman, 2002) and among academics (including Brickley et al., 2003; Coffee, 2002; Healy & Palepu, 2003) seeking to explain what went wrong. It became a case study in accounting, finance, human resources management, strategy and regulation. But it was as corporate governance that it had perhaps its greatest effect: it brought to an end for many in America the sense that the American way of organizing a corporation was the best.

Enron's board was, by all accounts, pretty well structured. It had 17 members, not small, but not all that large. It was dominated by non-executive directors who seemed to qualify as independent. Kenneth Lay had been chairman and CEO during its heyday, but stepped back after the 2000 year end to allow Jeffrey Skilling, already a board member, to become CEO. Neither Skilling nor Lay sat on board committees involved in monitoring and control.

The audit committee was made up of independent directors and chaired by an accounting professor who had been dean of the Graduate School of Business at Stanford, one of America's most prestigious universities. Nearly all the other directors had experience in related industries, and many had run large corporations themselves. The board had one female member, the wife of a prominent politician. But no one considered Wendy Gramm a 'trophy' director: she had a doctorate in economics and had previously been chairman of the Commodities Futures Trading Commission, which regulated much of Enron's trading activities. She served on the audit committee, which approved all the financial manoeuvrings that led to its downfall.

According to Ronald Sims and Johannes Brinkmann (2003, p. 243), the expression 'Enron Ethics' as entered the vocabulary of business and it 'reads like the new catchword for the ultimate contradiction between words and deeds, between a deceiving glossy facade and a rotten structure behind, like a definite good-bye to naive business ethics'. In Enron's case, and probably others, they argue, culture matters more than codes.

The public policy response was swift – and hastened by the collapse of WorldCom in June 2002, barely nine months later. The Sarbanes–Oxley Act rushed through both houses of Congress in July 2002 and was signed into law the first week of August. It imposed personal *and criminal* liability on CEOs and CFOs whose companies publish financial statements that turn out to be false. It made them directly responsible for the internal control systems throughout the company, and introduced a new regulatory regime for auditors of all public companies. What it did not do was to address in any way the use of off-balance-sheet entities that had allowed Enron to disguise the growing problems in its business. Similar problems would emerge in banking as the subprime mortgage crisis unfolded in 2007 and 2008. Waste makes haste; haste makes waste (Nordberg, 2008b).

Questions arising

Enron clearly was not a one-off case. Too many instances of governance failures emerged – in America and other countries around the world – in its wake. But the problems its investors, customers, suppliers and employees suffered were not commonplace either.

1   To what extent was Enron a sign of a systemic crisis, something requiring an overhaul of how businesses govern themselves?
2   What does Enron tell us about the balance of power between the layers of governance mechanisms, from markets, law and regulation, shareholders, gatekeepers, and the board itself?
3   How might a different balance of governance controls better serve corporations at different times and in different circumstances?
4   In what circumstances might mechanisms of supposedly good corporate governance interfere with the role of the business – and the board – in creating value?
5   What are the tradeoffs, therefore, between monitoring and control on the one hand and value creation on the other?

A balancing act?

A tidal wave of change swept around the world of corporate governance after Enron disintegrated in the final months of 2001; Sarbanes–Oxley in America, Cromme in Germany, Higgs in the UK, Tabaksblat in the Netherlands, Lippens in Belgium, Horwath in Australia, King II in South Africa. Major countries had already had corporate governance codes of some sort before that. Their requirements and recommendations would be strengthened. Smaller countries with emerging capital markets would create codes for the first time. Corporate executives and even fund managers would joke about how the fastest growing industry in the world was the corporate governance industry.

The quotation from Paul MacAvoy and Ira Millstein that begins this chapter indicates the frustration that many people felt in the aftermath of Enron. The two men, a distinguished academic and a top lawyer specializing in corporate law and governance, bemoan the 'recurrent crisis in corporate governance' in the title of their book (MacAvoy & Millstein, 2003). It was a crisis, not crises, suggesting that the problems they explored and that we continue to explore are symptoms of a larger problem that the solutions so far have failed to address. Their view was, in essence: structures and mechanisms are not enough to solve the agency problem in corporate governance.

The second quotation comes from a speech given in the United States by Peter Brabeck-Letmathe, at the time chairman and CEO of Nestlé, the multinational food company. (He subsequently gave up the CEO role to concentrate on his board Chairmanship.) Brabeck-Letmathe faced regular criticism – in the news media and from many of the UK-based institutional investors on his shareholder register – for refusing to give up the chairmanship to an independent outsider in keeping with the doctrine of the Combined Code in the UK and the other codes it inspired. Brabeck-Letmathe was concerned as well about the legal strictures of the Sarbanes–Oxley Act in the US, where Swiss-based Nestlé's equity trades over the counter. And he was annoyed at the clamour arising from the new corporate governance agenda of social responsibility, with its calls for an even wider circle of accountability. His view was, in essence: these structures and mechanisms are themselves the cause of a different problem in corporate governance. They get in the way of creating value.

The two comments underscore the issue we see throughout the debate on how to govern the corporations that dominate economic life in much of the developed world and increasing proportions of the emerging markets as well. Taken together they suggest that boards can face a struggle to keep the demands on their time and agenda in balance.

Tradeoffs?

A recurrent theme we have seen is that the recipes for addressing the 'recurrent crisis' in corporate governance are far from being panaceas. The legal scholar-turned-fund adviser Simon Wong puts it this way: 'while conventional governance mechanisms can be highly effective in many situations, they are not appropriate remedies in all contexts' (Wong, 2009, p. 2). Moreover, even in the situations where they are effective, they involve compromises, tradeoffs between the using the accelerator and the brake pedal, between value creation on the one hand and monitoring and control on the other. Some of the key elements we have examined, with their benefits and drawbacks, are summarized in Table 4. What emerges from this discussion is a sense that the directors of a corporation – and indeed organizations other than corporations – are constantly seeking to establish a

Table 4   Tradeoffs in corporate governance

Control	Benefit	Danger
Chair–CEO separation	Check on power	Loss of entrepreneurship
No former CEO on board	Freedom to change strategy; less commitment to incumbent policies, people	Loss of expertise, knowledge, including of regulators
Majority independent directors	Potential to overrule executives; greater shareholder alignment	Lack of expertise, knowledge
Audit independence	Incentive to challenge management	Loss of wise counsel of knowledgable people
Board committee independence	Improved oversight of key decisions	Board cohesion could falter
Remuneration disclosure	Gives shareholders ability to see, react to excesses	Leads to pay ratchet by making public comparators that then set a baseline for others
Non-financial reporting	Shows focus on value drivers	Gives competitors insight; risk that disclosures will be limited to boilerplate
Transparency	Lets shareholders judge performance	Information overload

balance, between competing demands on the resources of the company and competing approaches to corporate governance itself.

An imbalanced agenda?

As we explored in Chapter 7, boards fulfil four main roles: setting direction, marshalling resources, controlling and reporting, and evaluating and enhancing so as to refine how the direction is set. Most of their deliberations take place in private, owing to the confidentiality required for the commercial sensitivity of deliberations over strategy and the personal sensitivity of matters concerning the management of human resources. Only with the creation of the public company came the need to publish the outcomes of some of those deliberations: financial statements, at first just annually, then half-yearly, now increasingly quarterly. Here it is the outcomes of the financial controls that reach the public view through reporting (see Figure 7).

As we have seen, however, in the face of malfeasance and misdemeanours, corporations and the authorities have demanded increasing transparency as one of the means of creating trust – that more than just the tip of this iceberg should be exposed to public view. As a consequence, financial accounting disclosures have grown more revealing. In addition to consolidated accounts, accounting rules increasing specify and financial analysts increasingly demand even more detailed disclosures of regional breakdowns and results by line of business for corporations with complex businesses. Where corporations (with

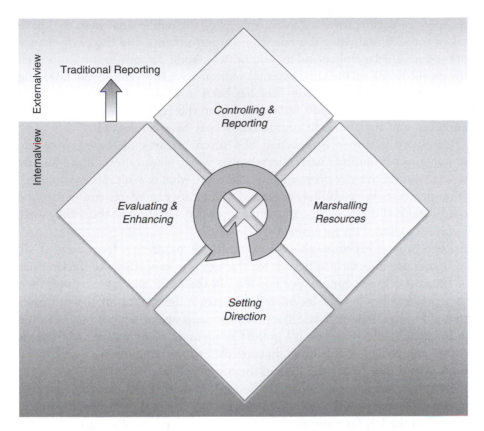

Figure 7 Transparency through reporting (Nordberg, 2007b, used with permission)

or without the knowledge of their auditors) might precisely have sought to keep sensitive matters confidential, the pressure of transparency is bringing them into public view.

Nor is this enhanced financial reporting the only development. Corporations face growing demands from investors for assessment of operational matters and how the intangible resources of the corporation are put to work. These reports allow outsiders to assess better which resources are being marshalled and to evaluate how they contribute to the business outcomes, to value creation.

At the same time, reporting on governance structures and mechanisms has become more articulated. We know increasingly not just about which individuals serve as directors of a company, but also their professional profiles, any business dealings they have had with the company, and even occasionally what personal connections they share with other members of the board – information to let shareholders and would-be investors ascertain in what ways the independence of the directors might be compromised. We know about board structures and processes, about board committees, how often they meet, who attended, and who did not. Codes of corporate governance, with their comply-or-explain provisions, ask boards to tell the public what steps they have taken towards evaluating the board's own performance and the performance of the individual members and the committees. Audit committees now often tell the public how long the same external auditors have been employed, how long the same partner in the audit firm has been in charge of the account, and exactly how much the audit firm earned from the company – not just for the audit but also any non-audit consultancy it may have conducted.

Corporate governance reporting also often involves discussing how the nominations committee has undertaken its work, what criteria it set for any new non-executive directors or senior managers, what consultants it employed, what processes the consultants adopted to identify candidates and ensure the candidates had the requisite skills and experience – in short to show they were not just cronies of the incumbent CEO.

Reporting on executive pay, for example, has progressed from none at all, to figures for directors, to figures for the top few executives, to declarations of the cost of stock options as a line item in the profit and loss account; then to a published policy for incentive-based pay, a description of the processes that led to its adoption, a statement in plain language of what it means to the individuals involved; and even – in the Compensation Discussion and Analysis for US companies – reducing all that complexity to a simple table with a single bottom line: How much did each of the top people earn?

Risk, too, has taken a higher profile in the range of information that corporations make public. The simple requirements of the Turnbull Review (1999) in the UK for a statement that the board has actually considered risk forced changes in board behaviour – some discussed risk for the first time. The Sarbanes–Oxley Act with its Section 404 on internal controls turned up the heat on companies around the world with any connection to US capital markets. Now many corporations report about their investments in risk technologies and outline the processes they follow to evaluate the information those technologies generate.

Social and environmental reporting has swelled too, now often rivalling the financial reports themselves in the level of detail given to the public. Once seen by many companies as merely a public relations exercise, such reporting is taken increasingly seriously by companies and their publics (Gill et al., 2008; Hasseldine et al., 2005; Rawlins et al., 2008; Reid & Toffel, 2009). The expanded reporting has come not least in response to increased shareholder activism, whether from traditional asset management firms, hedge funds, or specialist investors seeking detailed information for either negative or positive screening on ethical, social or environmental concerns.

One danger that this presents, however, is the sentiment expressed by Brabeck-Letmathe: that the board will concentrate too much on monitoring, control and reporting, worry too much about meeting the new legal requirements and satisfying the increasing public calls for more disclosure concerning the impact of

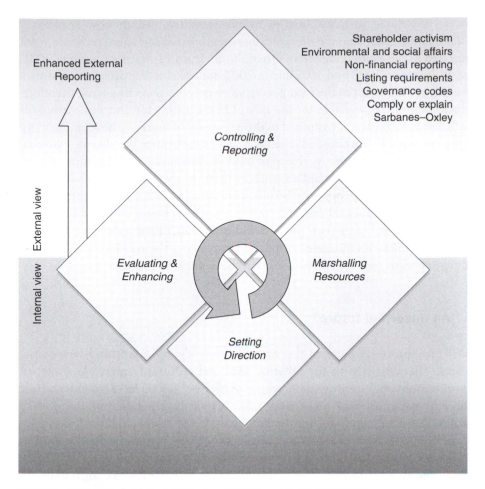

Figure 8 An imbalanced agenda? (Nordberg, 2007b, used with permission)

climate change on business operations. With such an expansion of what the board must consider for public consumption, there will be less time available for the rest of the board's agenda. If this sentiment is right, and the fear is shared by other corporate executives and directors, then the board's agenda can get out of balance (see Figure 8). This portrait may be more of an impression than a statement of reality in the boardroom, of course.

In the immediate aftermath of the post-Enron reforms, boards of listed companies in the United States and most other countries no doubt found they had to adjust their activities to take account of the increased requirements for monitoring and processes to place greater emphasis on independence. The result, logically, would mean a reduction in emphasis on setting direction, marshalling resources, evaluating and enhancing performance, as the board's agenda gets squeezed, and reporting to its various publics increases. Since Enron's failure, the time non-executive directors spend working on board business has certainly risen. According to global studies by the executive search firm Korn/Ferry (2003, 2008), the time the average non-executive director spent on board work jumped in the immediate aftermath of Enron, from 11 hours a month in 2001, to 15 hours in 2002 and 19 hours in 2003, before drifting back to 16 hours a month by 2007, just as the next governance crisis hit. Directors have, therefore, made more time available for the task of being a director. But in time boards will also have grown accustomed to the new ways of working, developing more efficient ways of working and creating a new equilibrium. We also see evidence of this in analyses of the workload of independent non-executive directors.

If the balance of the board's agenda has been somewhat slow to adjust after the shock of Enron, corporate boards were soon to undergo a further, deeper shock with the financial crisis of 2007–9, in which lapses in corporate governance played at least a part. Much is still unsettled, much unsettling. So when we contemplate the future of corporate governance, the most we can expect is tentative ideas, not conclusions, and far fewer answers than questions.

An unsettled future?

Will the future be more of the past? There is clearly a tension between the inertia that comes with the differing legal and cultural frameworks in which corporations operate around the world. Mark Roe (2003) has argued forcefully that the path corporate governance takes is heavily dependent on the starting point. German corporate governance would not simply follow the Anglo-American approach even if the experiences of corporations in the US and UK had been exemplary. Too much depends on the legal frameworks and traditions, the custom and practice within societies, and the relationships between corporations and the political forces that shape governance.

Convergence or persistence?

But there are also powerful forces pushing towards convergence in corporate governance, at least among the top-flight of globally active, large companies.

- *Institutional investment*: The data we have seen suggest that institutional investors – including traditional mutual funds, pension funds and insurers on the one hand, and alternative approaches used by hedge funds, private equity and sovereign wealth funds on the other – look set to continue and perhaps even strengthen their influence. They have developed because of:
- *Demographic shifts*: The ageing of the population in most of the developed economies has limited the power of states to provide pensions, while the increased longevity of individuals has meant that retirement savings have to be stretched over longer periods. One policy response has been to extend the normal working life to delay the date when individuals retire. But the demographics still suggest that the younger generations will have to save even more for their retirements, as state funding diminishes. That means, in

all likelihood, greater involvement in equity markets and increased expectations on the performance of corporations.

- *Globalization of product markets*: Another factor behind the importance of institutional investment has been the growth of global markets for goods and services in general. Businesses facing competition for their products seek to copy each other's approaches to efficiency while seeking ways to differentiate their products, which then get copied by competitors. In global markets, that means companies benchmark themselves against global rather than national peers. They will pursue global supply chains, albeit with heightened awareness now of the risk of disruption to them. The financial crisis of 2007–9 has shown how sensitive supply chains of all descriptions can be to the availability of credit. Global corporations will also seek to raise capital – from whatever sources, irrespective of nationality – that hold out the promise of a lower cost of capital.

- *Globalization of asset markets*: Asset managers, meanwhile, seek to diversify portfolios 1) to spread risk and 2) to invest in markets likely to show disproportionate gains. That means asset managers working on behalf of pension funds in relatively mature, slow-growth economies will seek to boost returns by investing in fast-growing economies. To mitigate against the agency costs of being distant shareholders, these asset managers seem likely to press for greater transparency and growing convergence in corporate governance practices, a judgement reinforced by a McKinsey study (Newell & Wilson, 2002) on the value of good governance.

- *Board membership*: Global businesses increasingly demand international backgrounds of the non-executive directors they bring onto the board, to help the board achieve the perspective of the business itself. The cadre of global directors seems likely to cross-pollinate board practices that seem to work well, at least in terms of the efficiency for the directors themselves.

- *Language*: The widening use of the English language in international businesses, combined with the depth and liquidity of US and UK capital markets seems likely to reinforce trends that have made American and British modes of corporate governance the benchmarks against which other systems are assessed.

These influences logically apply more to large, internationally active businesses, and other trends in the economy push in different directions. In a much-cited 'trends' analysis (Davis & Stephenson, 2006), consultants at McKinsey saw many industries moving away from a pyramid structure to something resembling a barbell. At one end we would see a handful of very large, global players, while at the other small, niche operators would drive innovation. The middle ground, of medium-sized, nationally oriented companies, would tend to be hollowed out. If this is true, corporate governance might separate into three streams: First, would be further articulation of a global standard for the large companies, supported and perhaps even driven by large asset management firms seeking a clear shareholder orientation to board decisions. The new governance agenda of corporate responsibility would get a look in, not least because those asset managers also cater to socially responsible investing. Second, we could see experimentation among private companies with new governance models, built on private equity models, acceptance of enhanced roles for entrepreneurs, and built specifically in the knowledge that exit – in the form of a takeover by a large corporation – is the most likely endgame. Third, with the hollowing out of the mid-market, the mid-capitalization listed companies, which struggle now to attract the attention of large asset managers, will turn increasingly to individual investors – high net-worth individuals and employee shareholders. Here national systems of corporate governance paying special attention to issues of self-dealing and related party transactions could well stay in place.

One of the industries where McKinsey sees the barbell structure already taking shape is the asset management industry, which has been so significant in the development of corporate governance codes and practices. A separate study (McKinsey, 2006) showed how the large, general asset management firms were growing larger, while the proliferation of boutique hedge funds and private equity firms with different investment styles has spearheaded innovative practices. The implications for corporate governance are rather harder to discern, but the rise in hedge fund activism we have discussed in Chapter 10, which has not been confined in any sense by national boundaries, suggests there may be pressure for convergence in governance practices outside the boundaries of large, global companies.

Globalization of trade in goods and services and in the equity of the companies that produce them may be putting pressure on the practices of corporate governance and even on lawmakers in different jurisdictions to learn from each other and adapt. Such pressures no doubt run counter to the inertia of established legal frameworks and custom and practices that have created current arrangements in corporations and slow the pace of change induced from the outside (Gilson, 2004; Gordon, 2004). Inertia is a powerful force, especially when it is backed by the force of law. But the recurrent crisis in corporate governance – one not constrained to a single system of governance – suggests that an impetus for change remains.

The case of Enron seems to have provided what the institutional theorist Royston Greenwood and his colleagues (2002, p. 60) have in a different context called a 'precipitating jolt' that destabilized the existing order, allowing change to take place. This was clearly true in America, where any hint of complacency about having the best form of corporate organization disappeared. Because Enron was followed not just by further governance lapses in the United States but also Parmalat and Ahold in Europe, HIH in Australia and others, many people saw cause to seek changes.

In the European Union, already striving to achieve the efficiencies and consumer choice associated with an integrated, single market in financial services, the jolt also pushed forward reform of corporate governance, though not sufficiently that it could overcome the inertial forces of national systems. One share, one vote, for example, could not gain traction. Britain, even under a left-oriented Labour government, could not be persuaded that requiring boards to adopt a stakeholder orientation added value. Germany was sure a single-tier board of directors of the Anglo-American variety provided less social stability than the division between supervisory and management boards.

A return to state capitalism?

The financial crisis of 2007–9 gave the global system another precipitating jolt, however. It was one that showed just how interconnected the world's different financial systems had become, and how interdependent their economies – even the 'real' economies of trade in goods and services – had become too. The ominous clouds that gathered from the subprime mortgage crisis in the United States sent their first lightning bolt crashing down on two relatively small banks in Germany. They had leapt into the market for securitized home loans with both feet, with both assets and liabilities. The wildfire that spread engulfed virtually every country, and spread from the financial system to ordinary corporations, private companies and even the voluntary and public sectors.

Moreover, in some countries the crisis brought an uncomfortable return to the practice of state capitalism, with implications for corporate governance as well. In the US, bailouts did not stop with the banks and insurance companies that had created mortgages-backed securities and credit default swaps. Soon the famous General Motors would be dubbed 'Government Motors' after a partial nationalization and brief spell in the bankruptcy courts in 2009. GM, which had until only a year earlier been the world's largest carmaker, was forced to sell its European arm Opel, only to find the governments of Germany, Belgium and the UK squabbling over which factories would get how much of a subsidy to stay open. The squabble ended in GM – now under control of the US government and its trade unions – keeping hold of Opel, a less than clear triumph for private sector capital.

It the UK, Northern Rock was nationalized and two of the four largest banks required rescues that left the government in nominal control of their businesses. Even Switzerland, perhaps the least socialist-leaning of all continental European countries, was forced to buy a large stake in UBS, the country's largest bank, to prevent a collapse of the financial system on which its economy is largely based. UBS too had rushed to participate in the global excitement around mortgage-backed securities. (The Swiss government managed to sell its shares for a profit, of $1.1 billion, after only a few months.)

This was, for most governments outside the old Soviet bloc, an undesired return to the type of state capitalism they had discarded through the first wave of privatizations in the West during the 1980s. For the former communist countries, it felt like an unhappy return to state control from before the disintegration of the Soviet Union in 1991.

State involvement in ownership of major banks and corporations raises complex questions about the way in which governments could or should be involved in corporate governance. How should they vote their shares? Should the boards they elect adopt a dominantly agency stance, reining in managers with tight monitoring and control, or allow them to pursue aggressive strategies to create value? Should they instruct the banks to lend at unprofitable rates to achieve social aims, running the risk that such lending would exacerbate their shortage of capital? Would banks operating now with the explicit backing of the state be able to compete unfairly against those operating with a merely implicit guarantee that they, too, would be bailed out?

And more questions: Should governments be involved in other board decisions, such as setting the level of executive pay? Would limiting the pay of senior managers at state-controlled banks mean that they would end up paying too little, with the loss of competitiveness that would entail? Or, should governments take this once-in-a-lifetime chance, use this once-in-a-lifetime 'precipitating jolt', to force through a new set of institutional arrangements that would put banking – and perhaps other industries as well – onto a new direction in corporate governance? Or, had the globalization of markets in goods and services, including financial services, become so integrated and interdependent that no one government could act on its own, or that even a network of governments might falter (Nordberg, 2009a)?

Alternatives?

The 'recurrent crisis' in corporate governance, as MacAvoy and Millstein (2003) called it after Enron, caused many changes in both how boards operate and how we think about corporate governance. But the financial crisis of 2007–9 and the role that corporate governance failings seems to have played in it suggest that the principles, guidelines, recommendations, codes and legal changes have not entirely addressed the underlying issues. So what alternatives might we have? We look first at the issues that arise in the interplay of those concerned with corporations in general, and then at possibilities that occur for specific corporations and specific settings.

Remedies through the layers of governance?

Let's review the six layers of relationship that affect corporate governance by boards: 1) law and regulation, 2) relations within the board, 3) relations between boards and management, 4) relations between boards and owners, 5) relations between owners, and 6) relations between the corporation and its publics.

Law and regulation?   If codes of conduct have not worked, is it time for a new legal framework for corporations and a stronger role for regulation of corporations and the role in society? If so what should it be?

Agenda point 18: The case for regulatory inaction

Call it a manifesto for the impossible: doing nothing while the house seems to burn down. When the financial crisis hit in 2007 and then intensified for the next 18 months, it was, simply, for political reasons impossible to do nothing. But when it comes to the regulatory response perhaps the impossible was precisely the right thing to do. That view emerges from an analysis of the crisis by a self-confessed reluctant regulator, Luca Enriques of the Italian securities commission Consob. Enriques is also a law professor at the ancient and great university in Bologna, a combination that makes for thoughtfulness and practicality. He sees perils and mistakes ahead, as a wave of re-regulation sweeps through financial markets. '[L]eaving aside the necessary overhaul of banking regulation, maintaining a pretence of doing something while actually innovating very little may in fact be the best course of action for policymakers who care about the effectiveness of financial market regulation in the long run.'

'When the going gets tough … everyone gets going': Look at what happened in the crisis, he explains. Regulators around the world introduced bans on short-selling in the shares of financial firms. That was 'not only very easy to sell to public opinion as something both intuitively right and sufficiently bold, but also hard to enforce in an interconnected world in which trade orders can come from any jurisdiction via chains of intermediaries.' If he's right, then here's the implication: it was a policy that made politicians look good, created a lot of paperwork for banks and brokers, and did nothing to affect the share prices of the institutions it was meant to save. He doesn't blame supposedly independent regulators for bowing to political pressure. No, they were merely protecting their image 'in a world dominated by the mass media'. Indeed, after more than a decade of concern about corporate governance, perhaps we ought to be concerned about regulatory governance. We have learned a lot about corporate governance, but 'there is less debate on whether all steps have been taken by individual jurisdictions to have the best possible regulators' governance mechanisms in place,' he adds. Turning from theory to practice, he notes:

US regulatory governance: The Securities and Exchange Commission is almost entirely governed by political processes: presidential appointment subject to Senate approval, annual funding debates in Congress, a government body – the General Accountability Office – scrutinizing the books, and transparency through the Sunshine Act (note: that law even prevents two commissioners from discussing policy with each other in the corridor).

British regulatory governance: The UK Financial Services Authority is a corporation, limited by guarantee, and makes itself subject to much of the Combined Code of corporate governance. Non-executives directors often maintain their employment elsewhere and staff the nomination and audit committees of the company. The chair and CEO roles are split, and there's even a lead non-executive director.

(Cont'd)

Who's to say which is better? Not Enriques. 'A well-functioning political arena can make the marginal contribution of corporate governance mechanisms in the absence of market constraints absolutely trivial,' he writes. 'On the other hand, in countries where politicians have a strong clout on formally independent regulators, governance mechanisms granting voice to constituencies such as industry, practitioners and consumer representatives can help avoid excessive regulation and hyper-sensitivity to public image concerns, at least in circumstances not as extreme as the ones we have experienced in the early Fall of 2008.'

So what to do? Enriques asserts that regulators and legislators should have the courage to do almost nothing. The capital adequacy framework for banks needs attention. 'But in many areas, the best course of action will be to stay idle, not least for the very simple reason that markets themselves are already self-correcting, and regulators are intensifying their action,' he concludes (see Enriques, 2009). (*The BoardAgenda*, 9 Oct. 2009; http://www.edgevantage.co.uk/categories/article.asp?i=4792.)

The answers are not easy to find: Sarbanes–Oxley represented a legalistic approach to solving the problems of corporate governance in the US, backed with a wave of intrusive regulation of corporations, corporate executives, audit firms, and gatekeepers like credit rating agencies. Yet the global financial crisis that followed had its roots in the American economy, and in one of the most tightly regulated industries in the world. Financial regulation in the US has been complex, allowing banks in particular to play one regulator off against another, quite unlike the systems at work in much of the rest of the world. But the banking crisis in the UK was perhaps just as severe as in America, despite having unified financial regulation under a single authority a decade before the crisis.

Relations within the board?   How can we reconfigure that work of boards so they are better able to perform the tasks of monitoring management and creating value?

Here, too, the answers are not easy. The post-Cadbury reforms in the UK and around the world put an emphasis on ever-greater independence of boards. The UK code warns against having boards become too independent; however, it urges that boards have the right range of skills and experience and to avoid having power too concentrated in the hands of certain individuals, and that 'there should be a strong presence on the board of both executive and non-executive directors' (Financial Reporting Council, 2008, p. 7). Was the Enron board perhaps *too* independent?

Relations between boards and management?   The financial crisis showed that directors had not understood the nature of the risk their banks and insurance companies in particular were taking. Is there a case for challenging the notion that management runs the business and the board sets the direction, provides the resources, monitors performance and evaluates outcomes? Should boards be even more hands-on?

We have seen a hint of this in the UK inquiry into the governance of major financial institutions (Walker, 2009a), with the suggestion that board members be more engaged in the business and that the definitions of independence – the line, in effect, between boards and management – might need to change. Officials in countries around the world took pains throughout the crisis to point out that banks are different from other types of organizations because of the central role they play in the economy. So perhaps the case made in the Walker Review is a special one. In a closely regulated industry, and one where the cost of the implicit state guarantee has become explicit, do bank boards serve a purpose? Might a combination of regulation and boards made up of seasoned executives suffice?

Relations between boards and owners?   The financial crisis, like the other governance crises that preceded it, has served to underscore how great the costs of the agency problem can be. Have banks – or indeed all major corporations, all 'modern' corporations in the sense of Berle and Means (1932/1991) – become in effect 'ownerless corporations' (UK Parliament, 2009)? If this is right, what alternatives are there to a 'capitalism without owners', as Robert Monks and Allen Sykes (2002) have called it, a model they thought was doomed to fail?

The remedy of the more activist-minded investors to the agency problem and ownerless corporations has been for shareholders to act like owners and engage with the businesses whose equity they own. That involves shareholders 1) taking part in the voting rights they have, and 2) seeking through law and regulation to expand those rights. Engagement of this type is already in evidence in companies like the many in continental Europe where a single, large shareholder is still evidence, though it presents the danger that the single, large shareholder will run roughshod over the interests of smaller ones. Taking the more common situation in the US and UK, a sizeable number of institutional investors, each with sizeable but not controlling interests, could become engaged, the recipe offered by many activists (e.g. Davis et al., 2006).

Institutional investors sometimes worry about conferring too much with each other, lest they run afoul of regulations and market conventions concerning 'in concert' actions that might trigger a demand that they mount a takeover bid. Relaxing 'in concert' rules is one of the possible solutions suggested as a solution to the problem of the 'ownerless corporation'. Putting more matters to a shareholder vote is another (Bebchuk, 2005): the 'say on pay' debate in the US after such rules came into effect in Europe is a case in point. But what about allowing shareholders to nominate directors, and having contested elections for directorships? Would such steps make boards better, or just more contentious?

Let us leave to one side the observation that many shareholders – think of the index-tracking fund seeking to operate at the lowest possible cost – do not want to spend the time and resources it takes to conduct engagement. Even some proponents of shareholder rights worry that the notion can go too far and prove counterproductive. Ira Millstein, the Weil Gotshal Manges attorney who has long been a strong voice for shareholder activism, views calls for greater shareholder empowerment with some alarm. Writing with colleagues from his firm during the financial crisis, he addressed the issues of shareholder engagement in these terms:

> it may be time for a dialogue on the limits of shareholder power. Where is the legitimate boundary? Long ago owners gave up rights to control the joint stock company in return for limited liability – and directors took on the fiduciary liability. If shareholders insist on ever-greater say in corporate decision-making, at what point do we need to rethink director liability? We may well miss the opportunity to achieve lasting balance in the corporate power structure if shareholders fail to recognize and respect that there are limits on the issues that are appropriate for shareholder initiatives – limits that are in keeping with both the duty of the board to direct and manage the affairs of the corporation and the limited liability that has been granted to shareholders. (Millstein et al., 2008, p. 3)

When do greater shareholder rights bring with them greater shareholder liability for corporate wrongs?

Relations between owners?   Nor is it clear that greater shareholder engagement will result in clearer direction for corporations. Even if the legitimacy of corporate decisions might be enhanced by improved shareholder democracy, what can we do to ensure the competing and conflicting shareholder interests avoid perverse effects?

Most of the time, in most circumstances, shareholders share an interest in seeing the corporation do well. Most of the time, in most circumstances, their opportunities to voice their specific interests are limited as well, so the broader notion of creating shareholder value takes over at the level of the board. But the complexities of trading in equities have created a greater divergence between the interests of individual shareholders. Greater engagement in corporate decision-making suggests that such divergence would gain greater prominence in the decision-making by boards. The benefits of short-selling and stock lending are considerable, so few authorities and fewer market participants seem interested in banning it. Moreover, the short-sellers are in the main at least tacitly supported by those they put at a disadvantage – the stock lenders. So is not the Latin warning *caveat emptor* – let the buyer beware – equally applicable as *caveat venditor* – let the seller beware – when market conduct rules allow both equal access to information?

Relations between corporations and their publics? The financial crisis has highlighted – perhaps even more than Enron, Maxwell, or the others – that cases of corporate governance gone wrong have implications for society at large. Is it not time society did something?

If 'society' means government, then does 'something' mean something other than law and regulation? Some societies have enacted laws that give directors explicit duties to bear in mind the interests of employees, suppliers, customers and the community. That has not prevented cases of corporate excess, managerial greed or self-seeking actions on the parts of shareholders. Moreover, pressure groups already mount campaigns that put pressure on managements to respond those groups' agendas, even when they might compete. Viewed as a system of politics and power, such actions can prove quite forceful in changing the public's perception of a corporation and changing the decisions those corporations – those boards – have made. Legitimacy matters, and so therefore does reputation. Is the focus, then, wrongly put on the *corporation* and more correctly put on the people who manage and direct the business?

Gatekeepers and watchdogs?

Perhaps there are additional solutions to be found in strengthening the role – and the internal governance – of the gatekeepers and watchdogs that provide some external and perhaps reasonable independent check on the business. Credit rating agencies face more intense regulation following their combined failings in the run-up to the crises at Enron and WorldCom and then in the financial crisis of 2007–9 (European Commission, 2009; Joint Forum, 2009; SEC, 2009). In both cases the business model, in which the organization issuing securities pays to have the ratings done, was found wanting. The agencies not only rated the instruments, but they took another fee for advising on how to reshape the issue to make it more acceptable. Like other professional advisers, they had only their reputation to lose, and in a highly concentrated, global market with only a small number of global providers, reputation might matter less than it once did. Alternatives like having the users of ratings information pay have not succeeded in the past, however, as that suffers from a large problem of free-riding where only a handful of investors might pay but all would seek to benefit. This conundrum has proved intractable, so rather than seeking a solution, regulators and the investment industry have chosen so far just to seek to mitigate the risk through tighter processes, closer scrutiny of them, and a large dose of transparency, the universal antiseptic. They have also taken steps to make credit ratings a more competitive market by lowering barriers to entry, despite at least some evidence that greater competition could lead to poorer-quality ratings (Becker & Milbourn, 2009).

Auditors have witnessed large changes in their business since Enron. Not only did the implosion of Arthur Andersen reduce the competition for global services to just four firms, all those firms and the large number of much smaller ones met with more intrusive regulatory oversight. Governments in various countries stepped up surveillance and in some cases constrained qualitatively what non-audit services they could offer. Other mechanisms – like requiring companies to change the audit firm every so often to prevent relationships from becoming too cosy – have proved unpopular and were perhaps unworkable in a market with so little competition. Creating greater competition has proved difficult as well, as few practising professionals seemed likely to choose the dangers associated with trying to crack into the business of the Big Four firms when they can lead a comfortable life without the stress. Putting quantitative limits on the degree of non-audit work the audit firm can undertake risks unduly limiting the range of services a board can call upon in an emergency.

Other professional advisers face conflicts of interest when they do work for boards as well as the managers the boards are seeking to monitor. Lawyers in adversarial legal systems like the US and UK have a duty of care to the client that can prevent them from disclosing information concerning wrong-doing. One of the solutions proposed, post-Enron, was to encourage whistle-blowing by lawyers through a series of channels designed to minimize the conflicts if not to eliminate them. Codes of corporate governance in other countries encourage corporations to give board committees the right to hire their own professional advisers, independently of the executive.

Outsiders, including the news media, face seemingly intractable and inter-related problems in how they conduct their business. Scrutinizing corporate disclosures requires people with expertise and in large numbers. People who are really good at it are hard to find and costly to train, and they can earn a lot more working as investment analysts.

Specific remedies?

So far we have discussed the issues that appear for all corporations, whatever their circumstances and from whatever jurisdiction they hail. But perhaps the lessons to draw from the 'recurrent' crisis is that corporate governance might better be focused on other factors than board size, composition, and processes; shareholder rights, and stakeholder privileges. We will consider several in outline:

Industry models?   The financial crisis raises a specific question: are banks, and perhaps insurance companies, different from other corporations? Should different mechanisms of governance apply?

The question arose specifically in the case of the Walker Review (2009a, 2009b) in the UK and more generally in other countries as the crisis unfolded. But the steep recession that following the squeeze on bank liquidity showed that corporations in other industries (automotive, especially) were also too big, too interconnected with the rest of the economy to be allowed to fail. Put another way, these industries operate with an unstated assumption that a government guarantee underpins their contracts, making contracts with them more valuable than ones with competitors. How does society, government, recover that value? Should those 'too big to fail' pay higher taxes? Doing so would make the tacit guarantee explicit, with serious implications for competition.

Life-cycle governance? We have discussed (especially in Chapter 13) how different types of organizations may have different forms of governance and seen where the lessons of *corporate* governance might not always apply. But what of corporations at different stages in their development?

The main codes of corporate governance acknowledge a difference between large and smaller listed companies. The Sarbanes–Oxley Act allowed the US Securities and Exchange Commission to set different rules for different sizes of company, too. But size is not the only distinction. Newly listed, fast-growing companies may be better served with corporate governance mechanisms, both inside the board and in dealings with shareholders, differing from those mature companies need. Corporations in decline, perhaps facing a life-threatening crisis, might benefit from yet another type of governance. These are issues that the focus in codes on structures and processes may overlook. Should we use a corporate life-cycle approach to governance? (For an interesting study, see Filatotchev et al., 2006.)

Governance for the business?

Underpinning much of the discussion about corporate governance have been the issues involved in agency theory. What constellation of structures, processes, laws and regulations can we put in place so that the corporation can go about its tasks of creating value without running wild, out of control? In some ways, the board at Enron – in its composition, structure and processes – seemed in a formal sense quite a good example of how to governance a corporation. It did not work. Layers of corporate governance – from the constraints that markets for its goods and services apply to the non-market mechanisms of boards and their committees – seek to keep managers in check, apply the brakes when there's a danger of going too fast to make the next turn along the road ahead.

The corporation is in business to do something, not just not to do something wrong. The work of boards of directors – and corporate governance, then – is about creating value from the resources at the company's disposal, interacting with suppliers, customers and other business partners, interacting as well with the communities in whose vicinity it operates and with the natural environment its processes affect.

Directors could look at their business as though it were a legal person, with rights and duties described in and prescribed by the law. They could think of it as a 'nexus of contracts' (Coase, 1937), a mechanism through which people wishing to buy and sell from each other do so with less friction and at a lower cost than they would by writing individual contracts for each transaction.

There is another way to think about the corporation, however one that affects how directors approach their work: Imagine that the legal person has a personality. Companies have cultures that arise from the people who work there, and especially the people who guide and direct them. They contract with each other, yes, and on occasion they contract a disease. The English word 'corporation' shares its roots with 'corporeal', the *corpus* – a body. The thing the French call a *Société Anonyme* is first and foremost a *société*, what the Germans call an *Aktiengesellschaft* is last but not least a *Gesellschaft*; a society. Irrespective of what weight any individual might place on the merits of stakeholder theory to describe or prescribe director duties, let us recall that these things we call corporations are made up of people.

Board meetings are gatherings of people too, people charged with a common purpose, whatever that purpose might be. The decisions they make come with pressures from a wide variety of directions, making multiple demands upon the resources at the corporation's disposal, not all of which they can hope to satisfy. More than anything else, the job of the board of directors is to make the tough choices, when resources are the most constrained and contested. Studies that have looked inside boards of directors (Arcot & Bruno, 2007; Clarke & Dean, 2005; McNulty & Pettigrew, 1996; Pettigrew & McNulty, 1998; van den Berghe & Baelden, 2005) often find something other than 'mechanisms' of corporate governance. They find people dealing in complex power relationships with each other, a collection of personalities seeking the right mix of supporting and challenging approaches to the items on the board's agenda.

Because people make those decisions, because they interact with each other and the problems in complex ways, it is perhaps understandable that all the mechanisms of corporate governance can seem, well, too mechanical. Is that why, often, the answers to the public policy questions surrounding corporate governance often come before we have heard the questions? Is that why the corporate governance community embraced as its standard the principle of 'comply-or-explain' rather than the straitjacket of rules – to give the people in corporations some room to breathe? If so, why is the crisis a recurrent one?

References

ABI (2009). ABI Response to FSA Remuneration Guidance. *Association of British Insurers News Release*. Retrieved 17 Aug. 2009, from http://www.abi.org.uk/Media/Releases/2009/08/ABI_response_to_FSA_remuneration_guidance_.aspx.

Achleitner, A.-K., & Kaserer, C. (2005). Private Equity Funds and Hedge Funds: A Primer. *Center for Entrepreneurial and Financial Studies, Technische Universität München.* Retrieved 21 June 2008, from http://ssrn.com/paper=1109100.

Adams, R. B. & Ferreira, D. (2009). Women in the Boardroom and their Impact on Governance and Performance. *Journal of Financial Economics, 94*(2), 291–309.

Admati, A. R. & Pfleiderer, P. (2009). The 'Wall Street Walk' and Shareholder Activism: Exit as a Form of Voice. *Review of Financial Studies, 22*(7), 2645–85.

Albert-Roulhac, C. (2009, March 10). Corporate Governance Report 2009: Boards in Turbulent Times. *Heidrick & Struggles Biennial Survey of Corporate Governance in Europe.* Retrieved 23 Dec. 2009, from http://www.heidrick.com/NR/rdonlyres/A03A8F3A-A676-43FC-BBBA-06105F43B034/0/CorporateGovernance2009Europe.pdf.

Allianz. (2005, Sept. 11). Conversion of Allianz AG into a European Company (SE). Retrieved 2 Jan. 2009, from http://www.allianz.com/en/allianz_group/press_center/news/financial_news/stakes_and_investments/news29.html.

Allison, G. T. (1980). *Public and Private Management: Are They Fundamentally Alike in All Unimportant Respects?* Paper presented at the Public Management Research Conference. Retrieved 19 July 2010, from http://www.apubb.ro/Documents/Hintea/Public_Management/PublicAndPrivateManagement.pdf.

Anson, M., White, T. & Ho, H. (2003). The Shareholder Wealth Effects of CalPERS' Focus List. *Journal of Applied Corporate Finance, 15*(3), 102–11.

Aoki, M., Jackson, G. & Miyajima, H. (eds) (2007). *Corporate Governance in Japan*. Oxford: Oxford University Press.

Arcot, S. R. & Bruno, V. G. (2007). One Size Does Not Fit All, After All: Evidence from Corporate Governance. *1st Annual Conference on Empirical Legal Studies*. Retrieved 21 March 2008, from http://ssrn.com/paper=887947.

Baker, G. P. & Hall, B. J. (2004). CEO Incentives and Firm Size. *Journal of Labor Economics, 22*(4), 767–98.

Balkin, D. B. & Gomez-Mejia, L. R. (1990). Matching Compensation and Organizational Strategies. *Strategic Management Journal, 11*(2), 153–69.

Barber, B. M. (2006). Monitoring the Monitor: Evaluating CalPERS' Activism. *SSRN eLibrary*, Retrieved 19 July 2010 from http://ssrn.com/paper=890321.

Bassen, A., Prigge, S. & Zöllner, C. (2008). Behind Broad Corporate Governance Aggregates: A First Look at Single Provisions of the German Corporate Governance Code. Retrieved 28 Jan. 2009, from http://ssrn.com/paper=965355.

Bebbington, J., Gray, R., Hibbitt, C. & Kirk, E. (2001). Full Cost Accounting: An Agenda for Action. *Association of Chartered Certified Accountants*. Retrieved 24 December 2008, from http://www.accaglobal.com/pubs/publicinterest/activities/research/research_archive/acca_rr73_001.pdf.

Bebchuk, L. A. (2005). The Case for Increasing Shareholder Power. *Harvard Law Review, 118*(3), 833–914.

Bebchuk, L. A. & Fried, J. M. (2004a). *Pay without Performance: The Unfulfilled Promise of Executive Compensation*. Cambridge, MA: Harvard University Press.

Bebchuk, L. A. & Fried, J. M. (2004b). Stealth Compensation via Retirement Benefits. *Berkeley Business Law Journal, 1*(2), 291–326.

Bebchuk, L. A., Grinstein, Y. & Peyer, U. C. (2009). Lucky CEOs and Lucky Directors. *Journal of Finance*. Retrieved 24 July 2009, from http://ssrn.com/paper=1405316.

Bebchuk, L. A. & Roe, M. J. (1999). A Theory of Path Dependence in Corporate Ownership and Governance. *Stanford Law Review, 52*, 127–70.

Bebchuk, L. A. & Spamann, H. (2009). Regulating Bankers' Pay. *Harvard Law and Economics Discussion Paper 641*. Retrieved 19 July 2010 from http://ssrn.com/paper=1410072.

Becht, M., Bolton, P. & Röell, A. A. (2002). Corporate Governance and Control. Retrieved 13 October 2008, from http://ssrn.com/paper=343461.

Becht, M., Franks, J., Mayer, C. & Rossi, S. (2009). Returns to Shareholder Activism: Evidence from a Clinical Study of the Hermes UK Focus Fund. *Review of Financial Studies, 22*(8), 3093–129.

Becker, B. & Milbourn, T. (2009, 8 July). Reputation and Competition: Evidence from the Credit Rating Industry. *Harvard Business School Working Paper 09-051*. Retrieved 3 Aug. 2009, from http://www.hbs.edu/research/pdf/09-051.pdf.

Benn, S. & Dunphy, D. (eds) (2007). *Corporate Governance and Sustainability: Challenges for Theory and Practice*. London: Routledge.

Berle, A. A. & Means, G. C. (1932/1991). *The Modern Corporation and Private Property* (rev edn). New Brunswick, NJ: Transaction Publishers.

Berry, L. (1983). *Relationship Marketing*. Chicago, IL: American Marketing Association.

Betts, P. (2009, 30 June). Porsche and VW are Spinning Out of Control. *FT.com*. Retrieved 29 July 2009, from http://www.ft.com/cms/s/0/de338592-65a4-11de-8e34-00144feabdc0.html.

Bhagat, S., Bolton, B. & Romano, R. (2007). The Promise and Peril of Corporate Governance Indices. *European Corporate Governance Institute*. Retrieved 14 October 2008, from http://www.wlrk.com/docs/The promiseandPerilofCorporateGovernanceIndices.pdf.

Blair, M. M. & Stout, L. A. (1999). A Team Production Theory of Corporate Law. *Virginia Law Review, 85*(2), 247–328.

Boatright, J. R. (2002). Contractors as Stakeholders: Reconciling Stakeholder Theory with the Nexus-of-Contracts Firm. *Journal of Banking & Finance, 26*(9), 1837–52.

Bogle, J. (2003). Owners' Capitalism. Speech to the National Investor Relations Institute annual conference. Retrieved 28 June 2009, from http://www.vanguard.com/bogle_site/sp20030611.html.

Borden, M. (2007). The Role of Financial Journalists in Corporate Governance. *Fordham Journal of Corporate & Financial Law, 12*, 311–69.

Borrus, A. (2002, 8 April). The Credit-Raters: How They Work and How They Might Work Better. *Business Week*.

Bovensiepen, N. & Blechschmidt, P. (2005). Müntefering kritisiert Manager: Bei manchen Unternehmern stimmt die Ethik nicht. *Süddeutsche Zeitung*. Retrieved 19 July 2010 from http://www.sueddeutsche.de/deutschland/artikel/468/51417/.

Bowie, N. E. (1999). *Business Ethics: A Kantian perspective*. Oxford: Blackwell.

Bowie, N. E. (2000). Business Ethics, Philosophy, and the Next 25 Years. *Business Ethics Quarterly, 10*(1), 7–20.

Boyne, G. A. (2002). Public and Private Management: What's the Difference? *Journal of Management Studies, 39*(1), 97–122.

Brabeck-Letmathe, P. (2005, 8 March). Corporate Governance – A European Vantage Point. Retrieved 5 July 2008, from http://www.nestle.com MediaCenter SpeechesAndStatements/AllSpeechesAndStatements/03_08_2005.htm.

Brandeis, L. D. (1913–14). Other People's Money. *Louis D. Brandeis Collection, Louis D. Brandeis School of Law, University of Louisville.* Retrieved 10 November 2009, from http://www.law.louisville.edu/library/collections/brandeis/node/191.

Branson, D. M. (2006). *No Seat at the Table: How Corporate Governance and Law Keep Women Out of the Boardroom.* New York: New York University Press.

Breeden, R. C. (2003). Restoring Trust: A Report on Corporate Governance for the Future of MCI, Inc. Retrieved 15 Oct. 2006, from http://www.ecgi.org/codes/documents/breeden_cg_report.pdf.

Brickley, J. A., Smith, C. W., Jr. & Zimmerman, J. L. (2003). Corporate Governance, Ethics, and Organizational Architecture. *Journal of Applied Corporate Finance, 15*(3), 34–45.

Browne, J. (1997, 17 May). Speech at Stanford University. Retrieved 4 Aug. 2009, from http://www.bp.com/genericarticle.do?categoryId=98&contentId=2000427.

Burgess, K. (2009, 30 December). Hermes sends out message of renewal. *FT.com.* Retrieved 31 Dec. 2009, from http://www.ft.com/cms/s/0/20354774-f564-11de-90ab-00144feab49a.html#.

Cadbury, A. (1992). The Financial Aspects of Corporate Governance. Retrieved 9 April 2007, from http://www.ecgi.org/codes/documents/cadbury.pdf.

Cadbury, A. & Millstein, I. (2005). A New Agenda for the ICGN. Retrieved 9 April 2007, from http://www.icgn.org/conferences/2005/documents/cadbury_millstein.pdf.

CalPERS (2009). Global Principles of Accountable Corporate Governance. *California Public Employees' Retirement System.* Retrieved 27 July 2009, from http://www.calpers-governance.org/docs-sof/marketinitiatives/2009-04-01-corp-governance-pub20-final-glossy.pdf.

Capgemini, & Merrill Lynch. (2009, 24 June). World Wealth Report 2009. Retrieved 3 Aug. 2009, from http://www.capgemini.com/resources/thought_leadership/2009_world_wealth_report/.

Caprasse, J.-N., Clerc, C. & Becht, M. (2007). Report on the Proportionality Principle in the European Union. Retrieved 27 June 2008, from http://ec.europa.eu/internal_market/company/docs/shareholders/study/final_report_en.pdf.

Cave, A. (2003, 15 Sept.). Davies Drops Interbrew Inquiry Controversial Investigation into Document Theft Hits Dead End but Belgian Probe Continues. *Daily Telegraph.*

Chandler, A. D., Jr. (1990). *Scale & Scope: The Dynamics of Industrial Capitalism.* Cambridge, MA: Belknap Press.

Charkham, J. (1994). *Keeping Good Company: A Study of Corporate Governance in Five Countries.* Oxford: Oxford University Press.

Charkham, J. (2005). *Keeping Better Company: Corporate Governance Ten Years On.* Oxford: Oxford University Press.

Charny, D. (1997, 17–18 May). The German Corporate Governance System. *Sloan Project on Corporate Governance: Cross-Border Views.* Retrieved 24 June 2008, from http://ssrn.com/paper=125188.

Charoenrook, A. & Lewis, C. M. (2009). Information, Selective Disclosure, and Analyst Behavior. *Financial Management, 38*(1), 39–57.

Cioffi, J. W. (2002). Restructuring 'Germany Inc': The Politics of Company and Takeover Law Reform in Germany and the European Union. *Law & Policy, 24*(4), 355.

Clarke, F. & Dean, G. (2005). Corporate Governance: A Case of 'Misplaced Concreteness'? In C. R. Lehman (ed.), *Corporate Governance: Does One Size Fit Any? Advances in Public Interest Accounting* (pp. 15–39). London/Amsterdam: Elsevier.

Clarke, F. & Dean, G. (2007). *Indecent Exposure: Gilding the Corporate Lily*. Cambridge: Cambridge University Press.

Coase, R. H. (1937). The Theory of the Firm. *Economica, 4*(16), 386–405.

Coffee, J. C., Jr. (2002). Understanding Enron: It's About the Gatekeepers, Stupid. Retrieved 7 November 2007, from http://ssrn.com/paper=325240.

Coffee, J. C., Jr. (2006). *Gatekeepers: The Professions and Corporate Governance*. Oxford: Oxford University Press.

Cole, R. (2003, 2 April). Internal Workings at FSA in Spotlight. *The Times*.

Cornforth, C. (2001). What Makes Boards Effective? An Examination of the Relationships between Board Inputs, Structures, Processes and Effectiveness in Non-profit Organisations. *Corporate Governance: An International Review, 9*(3), 217–27.

Cornforth, C. (2004). The Governance of Cooperatives and Mutual Associations: A Paradox Perspective. *Annals of Public & Cooperative Economics, 75*(1), 11–32.

Crooks, E. (2009, 9 June). BP's Most Senior Woman Executive to Retire. *FT.com*. Retrieved 4 Aug. 2009, from http://www.ft.com/cms/s/0/e0321b8a-548b-11de-a58d-00144-feabdc0.html.

Crowther, D. & Rayman-Bacchus, L. (eds) (2004). *Perspectives on Corporate Social Responsibility*. Aldershot: Ashgate.

Crystal, G. S. (1992). *In Search of Excess: The Overcompensation of American Executives*. New York: W W. Norton.

Davis, I. & Stephenson, E. (2006). Ten Trends to Watch in 2006. *McKinsey Quarterly*. Retrieved 21 Jan. 2006, from http://www.mckinseyquarterly.com/Strategy/Globalization/Ten_trends_to_watch_in_2006_1734.

Davis, J. H., Schoorman, F. D. & Donaldson, L. (1997). Toward a Stewardship Theory of Management. *Academy of Management Review, 22*(1), 20–47.

Davis, S., Lukomnik, J. & Pitt-Watson, D. (2006). *The New Capitalists: How Citizen Investors are Reshaping the Corporate Agenda*. Boston: Harvard Business School Press.

DesJardins, J. R. (2007). *Business, Ethics, and the Environment*. Upper Saddle River, NJ: Pearson Education.

Dittmann, I., Maug, E. G. & Schneider, C. (2008). Bankers on the Boards of German Firms: What They Do, What They are Worth, and Why They are (Still) There. Retrieved 22 March 2008, from http://ssrn.com/paper=1093899.

Donaldson, L. & Davis, J. H. (1991). Stewardship Theory or Agency Theory: CEO Governance and Shareholder Returns. *Australian Journal of Management, 16*(1), 49–64.

Donaldson, T. & Preston, L. E. (1995). The Stakeholder Theory of the Corporation: Concepts, Evidence, and Implications. *Academy of Management Review, 20*(1), 65–91.

Eccles, R. G., Herz, R. H., Keegan, E. M. & D.M.H., P. (2001). *The Value Reporting Revolution: Moving Beyond the Earnings Game*. New York: PricewaterhouseCoopers.

Economist (2008a). Fuld Again. *Economist.com*. Retrieved 14 Aug. 2009, from http://www.economist.com/businessfinance/displayStory.cfm?story_id=12209384.

Economist (2008b, 14 Oct.). The Guilty Men of Wall Street. *Economist.com*. Retrieved 14 Aug. 2009, from http://www.economist.com/businessfinance/displayStory.cfm?story_id=12410288.

Economist (2008c). Nightmare on Wall Street. *Economist.com*. Retrieved 15 Sep. 2009, from http://www.economist.com/businessfinance/displayStory.cfm?story_id=12231236.

Edmans, A. (2009). Does the Stock Market Fully Value Intangibles? Employee Satisfaction and Equity Prices. Retrieved 30 Dec. 2009, from http://ssrn.com/paper=985735.

Elkington, J. (1999). *Cannibals with Forks: The Triple Bottom Line of 21st Century Business*. Oxford: Capstone.

Enriques, L. (2009). Regulators' Response to the Current Crisis and the Upcoming Reregulation of Financial Markets: One Reluctant Regulator's View. *University of Pennsylvania Journal of International Economic Law, 30*(4), 1147–55.

Enriques, L. & Volpin, P. F. (2007). Corporate Governance Reforms in Continental Europe. *Journal of Economic Perspectives, 21*(1), 117–140.

Enron (2000a, 14 July). Enron Broadband Services announces expansion to Europe. *PR Newswire*. Retrieved 18 Aug. 2009, from http://www.prnewswire.co.uk/cgi/news/release?id=49653.

Enron (2000b, July). Enron Code of Ethics. *TheSmokingGun.com*. Retrieved 18 Aug. 2009, from http://www.thesmokinggun.com/graphics/packageart/enron/enron.pdf.

Enron (2000c). Enron Corporation 1999 Annual Report. Retrieved 18 Aug. 2009, from http://picker.uchicago.edu/Enron/EnronAnnualReport1999.pdf.

Enron (2001). Enron Corporation 2000 Annual Report. Retrieved 18 Aug. 2009, from http://picker.uchicago.edu/Enron/EnronAnnualReport2000.pdf.

European Commission (2009, 23 April). Approval of New Regulation Will Raise Standards for the Issuance of Credit Ratings Used in the Community. Retrieved 24 April 2009, from http://europa.eu/rapid/pressReleasesAction.do?reference=IP/09/629&format=HTML&aged=0&language=EN&guiLanguage=en.

Evan, W. M. & Freeman, R. E. (1993). A Stakeholder Theory of the Modem Corporation: Kantian Capitalism. In T. L. Beauchamp & N. E. Bowie (eds) *Ethical Theory and Business* (4th edn). Upper Saddle River, NJ: Prentice Hall.

Fabrikant, G. (2002, 6 Sep.). G.E. Expenses For Ex-Chief Cited in Filing. *New York Times*. Retrieved 24 July 2009, from http://www.nytimes.com/2002/09/06/business/ge-expenses-for-ex-chief-cited-in-filing.html.

Fama, E. F. (1970). Efficient Capital Markets: A Review of Theory and Empirical Work. *Journal of Finance, 25*(2), 383–417.

Fear, J. (1997). German Capitalism. In T. K. McCraw (ed.), *Creating Modern Capitalism: How Entrepreneurs, Companies, and Countries Triumphed in Three Industrial Revolutions* (pp. 133–82). Cambridge, MA: Harvard University Press.

Ferlie, E., Ashburner, L. & Fitzgerald, L. (1995). Corporate Governance and the Public Sector: Some Issues and Evidence from the NHS. *Public Administration, 73*(3), 375–92.

FESE & ESC (2008, Dec.). Share Ownership Structure in Europe 2007. *Federal of European Stock Exchanges and Economics and Statistics Committee*. Retrieved 19 August 2009, from http://www.fese.eu/_lib/files/Share_Ownership_Survey_2007_Final.pdf.

Filatotchev, I., Toms, S. & Wright, M. (2006). The Firm's Strategic Dynamics and Corporate Governance Life-cycle. *International Journal of Managerial Finance, 2*(4), 256–279.

Filatov, A., Tutkevich, V. & Cherkaev, D. (2005). Board of Directors at State-Owned Enterprises (SOE) in Russia. Retrieved 27 June 2008, from http://www.oecd.org/dataoecd/9/44/35175304.pdf.

Financial Reporting Council (2008). Combined Code on Corporate Governance. Retrieved 11 Aug. 2008, from http://www.frc.org.uk/documents/pagemanager/frc/Combined_Code_June_2008/Combined%20Code%20Web%20Optimized%20June%202008(2).pdf.

Financial Reporting Council (2009, 1 Dec.). Consultation on the Revised UK Corporate Governance Code. Retrieved 1 Dec. 2009, from http://www.frc.org.uk/documents/ page-manager/frc/Combined_Code_2009/Web_changes_to_2009_REview_of_the_Combined_Code_July_2009/Combined%20Code%20review%20progress%20report%20July%202009.pdf.

Finkelstein, S. & Hambrick, D. C. (1996). *Strategic Leadership: Top Executives and Their Effects on Organizations*. Minneapolis: West Publishing Co.

Finkelstein, S., Hambrick, D. C. & Cannella, A. A., Jr. (2009). *Strategic Leadership: Theory and Research on Executives, Top Management Teams, and Boards.* Oxford: Oxford University Press.

Finkelstein, S. & Mooney, A. C. (2003). Not the Usual Suspects: How to use Board Process to Make Boards Better. *Academy of Management Executive, 17*(2), 101–13.

Fisman, R. & Hubbard, R. G. (2005). Precautionary Savings and the Governance of Nonprofit Organizations. *Journal of Public Economics, 89,* 2231–43.

Fiss, P. C. & Zajac, E. J. (2004). The Diffusion of Ideas over Contested Terrain: The (Non) Adoption of a Shareholder Value Orientation Among German Firms. *Administrative Science Quarterly, 49*(4), 501–34.

Fletcher, L. B. & Miles, M. P. (2004). The Law of Unintended Consequences: The Effects of the Sarbanes–Oxley Act on Venture Funding of Smaller Enterprises. *Journal of Private Equity, 8*(1), 70–5.

Franks, J. R., Mayer, C. & Rossi, S. (2004). Spending Less Time with the Family: The Decline of Family Ownership in the UK. Retrieved 6 Feb. 2004, from http://ssrn.com/paper=493504.

Freeman, R. E. (1984). *Strategic Management: A Stakeholder Approach.* Boston: Pitman Publishing.

Freeman, R. E. (1994). The Politics of Stakeholder Theory: Some Future Directions. *Business Ethics Quarterly, 4*(4), 409–22.

Freeman, R. E. & Evan, W. M. (1990). Corporate Governance: A Stakeholder Interpretation. *Journal of Behavioral Economics, 19*(4), 337–59.

Friedman, M. (1962/2002). *Capitalism and Freedom* (40th anniversary edn). Chicago, IL: University of Chicago Press.

Friedman, M. (1970, Sep. 13). The Social Responsibility of Business is to Increase its Profits. *The New York Times Magazine,* 122–6.

Frost, C. A. (2007). Credit Rating Agencies in Capital Markets: A Review of Research Evidence on Selected Criticisms of the Agencies. *Journal of Accounting, Auditing & Finance, 22*(3), 469–92.

Fukuyama, F. (1995). *Trust: The Social Virtues and the Creation of Prosperity.* New York: Free Press.

Gallagher, J. G., Lauchlan, J. & Steven, M. (1996). Polly Peck: The Breaking of an Entrepreneur? *Journal of Small Business and Enterprise Development, 3*(1), 3–12.

Gill, D. L., Dickinson, S. J. & Scharl, A. (2008). Communicating Sustainablity: A Web Content Analysis of North American, Asian and European firms. *Journal of Communication Management, 12*(3), 243–62.

Gillan, S. & Starks, L. (2007). The Evolution of Shareholder Activism in the United States. *Journal of Applied Corporate Finance, 19*(1), 55–73.

Gilson, R. J. (2004). Globalizing Corporate Governance: Convergence of Form or Function. In J. N. Gordon & M. J. Roe (eds), *Convergence and Persistence in Corporate Governance* (pp. 128–58). Cambridge: Cambridge University Press.

Gompers, P., Ishii, J. & Metrick, A. (2003). Corporate Governance and Equity Prices. *Quarterly Journal of Economics, 118*(1), 107–55.

Gordon, J. N. (2004). The International Relations Wedge in the Corporate Governance Debate. In J. N. Gordon & M. J. Roe (eds), *Convergence and Persistence in Corporate Governance* (pp. 161–209). Cambridge: Cambridge University Press.

Gordon, J. N. & Roe, M. J. (eds) (2004). *Convergence and Persistence in Corporate Governance.* Cambridge: Cambridge University Press.

Gowthorpe, C. (2004). Asymmetrical Dialogue? Corporate Financial Reporting via the Internet. *Corporate Communications: An International Journal, 9*(4), 283–93.

Graafland, J. J. (2002). Profits and Principles: Four Perspectives. *Journal of Business Ethics, 35*(4), 293–305.

Graham, J. R., Lemmon, M. L. & Wolf, J. G. (2002). Does Corporate Diversification Destroy Value? *The Journal of Finance, 57*(2), 695–720.

Grayson, D. & Hodges, A. (2004). Corporate Social Opportunity! Seven Steps *to* Make Corporate Social Responsibility Work for your Business. Sheffield: Greenleaf Publishing.

Grayson, D., Lemon, M., Slaughter, S., Angel Rodriguez, M., Jin, Z. & Tay, S. (2008). A New Mindset for Corporate Sustainability. Retrieved 17 Feb. 2008, from http://www.bigger-thinking.com/docs/en/a_new_mindset_white_paper.pdf.

Greenbury, R. (1995). Directors' Remuneration: Report of the Study Group. *European Corporate Governance Institute* Retrieved 27 Oct. 2008, from http://www.ecgi.org/codes/documents/greenbury.pdf.

Greenwood, R., Suddaby, R. & Hinings, C. R. (2002). Theorizing Change: The Role of Professional Associations in the Transformation of Institutionalized Fields. *Academy of Management Journal, 45*(1), 58–80.

Greer, A. & Hoggett, P. (2000). Contemporary Governance and Local Public Spending Bodies. *Public Administration, 78*(3), 513–29.

GRI (2006). G3 Reporting Framework. Retrieved 29 July 2008, from http://www.globalre-porting.org/ReportingFramework/G3Guidelines/.

Gribben, R. (2008). 'Red' Adair's Task to Prove the FSA isn't Asleep at the Wheel. *Daily Telegraph*. Retrieved 30 May 2008, from http://www.telegraph.co.uk/finance/markets/2790840/Lord-Turners-task-to-improve-the-FSA-isnt-asleep-at-the-wheel.html.

Guerrera, F. (2009, 12 March). Welch Condemns Share Price Focus. *Financial Times Big Debate: The Future of Capitalism*. Retrieved 28 July, 2009, from http://www.ft.com/cms/s/0/294ff1f2-0f27-11de-ba10-0000779fd2ac.html.

Gumbel, A. & Woolf, M. (2003, 23 Jan.). Beyond Petroleum, or Beyond the Pale? BP Left Out in the Cold. *The Independent*. Retrieved 4 Aug. 2009, from http://www.indepen-dent.co.uk/environment/beyond-petroleum-or-beyond-the-pale-bp-left-out-in-the-cold-602666.html.

Gummesson, E. (2002). *Total Relationship Marketing*. Oxford: Butterworth-Heinemann.

Hambrick, D. C. & Abrahamson, E. (1995). Assessing Managerial Discretion Across Industries: A Multimethod Approach. *Academy of Management Journal, 38*(5), 1427–41.

Hambrick, D. C. & Mason, P. A. (1984). Upper Echelons: The Organization as a Reflection of Its Top Managers. *Academy of Management Review, 9*(2), 193.

Hamilton, R. W. (2000). Corporate Governance in America 1950–2000: Major Changes But Uncertain Benefits. *Journal of Corporation Law, 25*(2), 349.

Hampel, R. (1998). Committee of Corporate Governance – Final Report. Retrieved 25 April 2008, from http://www.ecgi.org/codes/documents/hampel.pdf.

Hampson, S. (2007, 30 Jan.). Why Values Must Still Matter to Tomorrow's Companies. *Financial Times*. Retrieved 20 June 2007, from http://www.tomorrowscompany.com/uploads/hampsonarticle.doc.

Hasseldine, J., Salama, A. I. & Toms, J. S. (2005). Quantity versus Quality: The Impact of Environmental Disclosures on the Reputations of UK Plcs. *The British Accounting Review, 37*(2), 231–48.

Hassink, H., Bollen, L. & Steggink, M. (2007). Symmetrical Versus Asymmetrical Company-Investor Communications via the Internet. *Corporate Communications: An International Journal, 12*(2), 145–60.

Hawkes, S. & Costello, M. (2008, 2 April). Sir Richard Greenbury Slams Investors over M&S Row. *TimesOnline*. Retrieved 27 April 2008, from http://business.timesonline.co.uk/tol/business/industry_sectors/retailing/article3666035.ece.

Hayes, R. M. & Schaefer, S. (2008). CEO Pay and the Lake Wobegon Effect. *Journal of Financial Economics*. Retrieved 23 July 2009, from http://ssrn.com/paper=966332.

Healy, P. M. & Palepu, K. (2003). The Fall of Enron. *Journal of Economic Perspectives, 17*(2), 3–26.

Hendry, J., Sanderson, P., Barker, R. & Roberts, J. (2007). Responsible Ownership, Shareholder Value and the New Shareholder Activism. *Competition & Change, 11*(3), 223–40.

Hermes (2006). Hermes Corporate Governance Principles. *Hermes Investment Management.* Retrieved 27 July 2009, from http://www.hermes.co.uk/files/pdfs/Hermes_Corporate_Governance_Principles_web_030306.pdf.

Hewlett-Packard (2002, 11 March). HP Issues Letter to Shareowners Highlighting ISS Support, the Case for Change. *HP News Release.* Retrieved 16 Aug. 2009, from http://h30261.www3.hp.com/phoenix.zhtml?c=71087&p=irol-newsArticle&ID=267507&highlight=

Higgs, D. (2003). Review of the Role and Effectiveness of Non-Executive Directors. Retrieved 15 Oct. 2006, from http://www.ecgi.org/codes/documents/higgsreport.pdf.

Hillman, A. J. & Dalziel, T. (2003). Boards of Directors and Firm Performance: Integrating Agency and Resource Dependence Perspectives. *Academy of Management Review, 28*(3), 383–96.

Hillman, A. J., Nicholson, G. & Shropshire, C. (2008). Directors' Multiple Identities, Identification, and Board Monitoring and Resource Provision. *Organization Science, 19*(3), 441–56.

Hofstede, G. (1980). *Culture's Consequences: International Differences in Work-related Values.* Beverly Hills, CA: Sage.

Hopt, K. J. (2006). Comparative Company Law. In M. Reimann & R. Zimmermann (eds), *The Oxford Handbook of Comparative Law* (pp. 1161–91). Oxford: Oxford University Press.

Hopt, K. J. & Leyens, P. C. (2004). Board Models in Europe – Recent Developments of Internal Corporate Governance Structures in Germany, the United Kingdom, France, and Italy. Retrieved 19 July 2010, from http://ssrn.com/paper=487944.

Houston, J. F., Lev, B. I. & Tucker, J. (2008). To Guide or Not to Guide? Causes and Consequences of Stopping Quarterly Earnings Guidance. Retrieved 15 Nov. 2008, from http://ssrn.com/paper=1280693.

Hu, H. T. & Black, B. S. (2006). Empty Voting and Hidden (Morphable) Ownership: Taxonomy, Implications, and Reforms. *The Business Lawyer, 61*(3), 1011–70.

IBFD (2003, Sept.). Survey on the Societas Europaea. Retrieved 2 Jan. 2009, from http://ec.europa.eu/taxation_customs/resources/documents/survey.pdf.

ICGN (2005). Statement on Global Corporate Governance Principles. Retrieved 2 March 2009, from http://www.icgn.org/organisation/documents/cgp/revised_principles_jul2005.pdf.

IFC (2005). The Irresistible Case for Corporate Governance. *International Finance Corp.* Retrieved 26 April 2009, from http://ifcln1.ifc.org/ifcext/corporategovernance.nsf/AttachmentsByTitle/The_Irrisistible_Case_Text/$FILE/IrresistibleCase4CG.pdf.

IFC (2006). Case Studies of Good Corporate Governance Practices: Companies Circle of the Latin American Corporate Governance Roundtable. Retrieved 3 March 2009, from http://www.ifc.org/ifcext/corporategovernance.nsf/attachmentsbytitle/case+studies_eng/$file/case+studies+eng.pdf.

IFC (2007). Corporate Governance Manual: Belgrade. Retrieved 3 March 2009, from http://www.ifc.org/ifcext/cgf.nsf/AttachmentsByTitle/CorporateGovernance_manual_Belgrade2007/$FILE/Corporate_Governance_Manual_New.pdf.

IIF (2003). Policies for Corporate Governance in Emerging Markets: Revised Guidelines. Retrieved 3 Feb. 2009, from http://www.iif.com/download.php?id=XNo9ruLxjnY=

IIF (2004). Corporate Governance in Brazil: An Investor Perspective. Retrieved 3 March 2009, from http://www.iif.com/download.php?id=I3LV1/E9vpQ=.

Interbrand (2008). Best Global Brands Rankings 2008. Retrieved 10 August 2009, from http://www.interbrand.com/best_global_brands.aspx?year=2008&langid=1000.

Investor AB (2009). Annual Report 2008. *Investor Aktiebolaget* Retrieved 27 July 2009, from http://ir.investorab.com/files/press/investor/200903092125-3.pdf.

Janis, I. J. (1972). *Victims of Groupthink: A Psychological Study of Foreign Policy Decisions*. Boston: Houghton Mifflin.

Jensen, M. C. (1993). The Modern Industrial Revolution, Exit, and the Failure of Internal Control Systems. *Journal of Finance, 48*(3), 831–80.

Jensen, M. C. (2001). Value Maximization, Stakeholder Theory, and the Corporate Objective Function. *Journal of Applied Corporate Finance, 14*(3), 8–21.

Jensen, M. C. & Meckling, W. H. (1976). Theory of the Firm: Managerial Behavior, Agency Costs and Ownership Structure. *The Journal of Financial Economics, 3*(4), 305–60.

Johnson, S., Porta, R. L., Lopez-de-Silanes, F. & Shleifer, A. (2000). Tunneling. *The American Economic Review, 90*(2), 22–7.

Johnston, J. & Phillips, L. (2005). Male, Pale and Stale. *Directors & Boards, 29*(4), 48–50.

Joint Forum (2009, 15 June). Stocktaking on the Use of Credit Ratings. Retrieved 15 June 2009, from http://www.iosco.org/library/pubdocs/pdf/IOSCOPD291.pdf.

Kahan, M. & Rock, E. B. (2006). Hedge Funds in Corporate Governance and Corporate Control. Retrieved 21 June 2008, from http://ssrn.com/paper=919881.

Kaplan, R. S. & Norton, D. P. (1992). The Balanced Scorecard – Measures That Drive Performance. *Harvard Business Review, 70*(1), 71–9.

Kickert, W. J. M. (1997). Public Governance in the Netherlands: An Alternative to Anglo-American 'Managerialism'. *Public Administration, 75*(4), 731–52.

Korn/Ferry (2003, 10 Nov.). 30th Annual Board of Directors Study. *Korn/Ferry Institute.* Retrieved 18 Aug. 2009, from http://www.kornferryinstitute.com/files/pdf1/30th_Annual_Board_of_Directors_Study-FINAL.pdf.

Korn/Ferry (2008, 17 Dec.). 34th Annual Board of Directors Study. *Korn/Ferry Institute.* Retrieved 18 Aug. 2009, from http://www.kornferryinstitute.com/files/pdf1/Board_Study07_LoRez_FINAL.pdf.

Kroll, M., Wright, P., Toombs, L. & Leavell, H. (1997). Form of Control: A Critical Determinant of Acquisition Performance and CEO Rewards. *Strategic Management Journal, 18*(2), 85–96.

Kurzbard, G. & Siomkos, G. J. (1992). Crafting a Damage Control Plan: Lessons from Perrier. *Journal of Business Strategy, 13*(2), 39–44.

Labib, S. Y. (1969). Capitalism in Medieval Islam. *The Journal of Economic History, 29* (1), 79–96.

Lane, C. (2003). Changes in Corporate Governance of German Corporations: Convergence to the Anglo-American Model? *Competition & Change, 7*(2/3), 79–100.

Langdon, J. (2008). Travels with Cap'n Bob: A Review of the Life and Travels of Robert Maxwell [Radio]. UK: BBC Radio 4.

Leblanc, R. (2004). Preventing Future Hollingers. *Ivey Business Journal, 69*(1), 1–9.

Lee, P. (2002). Not Badly Paid But Paid Badly. *Corporate Governance: An International Review, 10*(2), 69–75.

Levering, R. & Moskowitz, M. (2000, Dec.). 100 Best Companies to Work for in America. *Great Place to Work Institute and Fortune.* Retrieved 18 Aug. 2009, from http://www.greatplacetowork.com/best/list-bestusa-2000.htm.

Library of Congress (2002). H.R.3763, The Sarbanes–Oxley Act. Retrieved 15 Oct. 2006, from http://frwebgate.access.gpo.gov/cgi-bin/getdoc.cgi?dbname=107_cong_bills&docid=f:h3763enr.txt.pdf.

Lipton, M. & Lorsch, J. W. (1992). A Modest Proposal for Improved Corporate Governance. *Business Lawyer, 48*(1), 59–77.

Listokin, Y. (2007). Management Always Wins the Close Ones. *National Bureau of Economic Research.* Retrieved 1 Jan. 2009, from https://nber15.nber.org/c/2007/si2007/LE/listokin.pdf.

Lysandrou, P. & Stoyanova, D. (2007). The Anachronism of the Voice–Exit Paradigm: Institutional Investors and Corporate Governance in the UK. *Corporate Governance: An International Review, 15*(6), 1070–78.

MacAvoy, P. & Millstein, I. (2003). *The Recurrent Crisis In Corporate Governance.* Basingstoke: Palgrave Macmillan.

Mackay, C. (1852/1995). *Memoirs of Extraordinary Popular Delusions and the Madness of Crowds.* Ware, Hertfordshire: Wordsworth Editions.

Marlow, J. (2009, April 10). Restructuring in the Face of Climate Change. *Green Inc. NYT. com.* Retrieved 4 Aug. 2009, from http://greeninc.blogs.nytimes.com/2009/04/10/restructuring-in-the-face-of-climate-change.

Maslow, A. H. (1943). A Theory of Human Motivation. *Psychological Review, 50*(4), 370–96.

Maslow, A. H. (1954). *Motivation and Personality.* New York: Harper & Row.

McCraw, T. K. (ed.), (1997). *Creating Modern Capitalism: How Entrepreneurs, Companies, and Countries Triumphed in Three Industrial Revolutions.* Cambridge, MA: Harvard University Press.

McKinsey (2006). The Asset Management Industry in 2010: Bigger, Sometimes Better – And the Best Pulling Away. *McKinsey & Co.* Retrieved 21 Aug. 2009, from http://www.mckinsey.com/clientservice/bankingsecurities/latestthinking/The_Asset_Management_Industry_in_2010.pdf.

McNulty, S. (2006, 13 Oct.). Manzoni Holiday Hit by BP Explosion. *Financial Times.* Retrieved 4 Aug. 2009, from http://www.ft.com/cms/s/0/d427ab34–5a56-11db-8-f16-0000779e2340.html.

McNulty, S. (2009, 31 Oct.). BP fined record $87m over Texas City. *FT.com* Retrieved 31 Oct. 2009, from http://www.ft.com/cms/s/0/9b5383a0-c560-11de-8193-00144 feab49a.html.

McNulty, T. & Pettigrew, A. (1996). The Contribution, Power and Influence of Part-time Board Members. *Corporate Governance, 4*(3), 160–79.

McNulty, T. & Pettigrew, A. (1999). Strategists on the Board. *Organization Studies, 20,* 47–74.

Micklethwait, J. & Wooldridge, A. (2003). *The Company: A Short History of a Revolutionary Idea.* London: Phoenix.

Miller, G. S. (2003). The Press as a Watchdog for Accounting Fraud. Retrieved 15 June 2007, from http://papers.ssrn.com/sol3/Papers.cfm?abstract_id=484423.

Millstein, I., Gregory, H. J. & Grapsas, R. C. (2008, Jan.). Rethinking Board and Shareholder Engagement in 2008. Retrieved 22 March 2008, from http://www.weil.com/files/Publication/5c443ec5–4732-4988-bb2c-b757c207d291/Presentation/PublicationAttachment/a9c9ed8e-f7b1-4b87-8010-c58e024c2834/Corporate_Governance_Advisory_Memo_Jan_2008.pdf.

Millstein, I. & MacAvoy, P. (1998). Active Board of Directors and Performance of the Large Publicly Traded Corporation. *Columbia Law Review, 98*(5), 1283–1322.

Milne, R. (2005, 19 Oct.). Investors Open Fire on VW's Deal with Porsche. *Financial Times.*

Milne, R. (2006, 18 Dec.). A Chairman with No Desire to Leave Office. *Financial Times.*

Milne, R., Williamson, H., & Tait, N. (2008, 28 May). Bitter Fight for Control of VW Moves to the Courts. *Financial Times.*

Monks, R. A. G. & Minow, N. (2003). *Corporate Governance* (3rd edn). London: Blackwell.

Monks, R. A. G. & Sykes, A. (2002). *Capitalism Without Owners Will Fail: A Policymaker's Guide to Reform.* London: Centre for the Study of Financial Innovation.

Montier, J. (2007). *Behavioural Investing: A Practitioner's Guide to Applying Behavioural Finance.* Oxford: Wiley.

Morgenson, G. & McGeehan, P. (2002, 14 Nov.). Wall St. and the Nursery School: A New York Story. *NYT.com.* Retrieved 8 August 2009, from http://www.nytimes.com/2002/11/14/business/wall-st-and-the-nursery-school-a-new-york-story.html?scp=11&sq=jack%20grubman&st=cse.

Nasdaq (2002). Summary of NASDAQ Corporate Governance Proposals. Retrieved 3 Nov. 2002, from http://www.nasdaq.com/about/Corp_Gov_Summary101002.pdf.

Nasdaq (2008). Listing on NASDAQ. Retrieved 8 May 2008, from http://www.nasdaq.com/about/listing_information.stm.

New York Stock Exchange (2003). Final NYSE Corporate Governance Rules. Retrieved 15 Oct. 2006, from http://www.ecgi.org/codes/documents/finalcorpgovrules.pdf.

Newell, R. & Wilson, G. (2002). A Premium for Good Governance. *McKinsey Quarterly.* Retrieved 28 May 2007, from http://www.mckinseyquarterly.com/article_abstract.aspx?ar=1205&L2=39&L3=3.

Nordberg, D. (2005). Governance Lesson as Heads Roll at Deutsche Börse. Retrieved 9 May 2005, from http://www.edgevantage.co.uk/categories/article.asp?i=2457.

Nordberg, D. (2007a). News and Corporate Governance: What Dow Jones and Reuters Teach Us About Stewardship. *Journalism: Theory, Practice and Criticism, 8*(6), 718–35.

Nordberg, D. (2007b). Rebalancing the Board's Agenda. *Journal of General Management, 33*(2), 13–23.

Nordberg, D. (2008a). The Ethics of Corporate Governance. *Journal of General Management, 33*(6), 35–52.

Nordberg, D. (2008b). Waste Makes Haste: Sarbanes–Oxley, Competitiveness and the Subprime Crisis. *Journal of Financial Regulation and Compliance, 16*(4), 365–83.

Nordberg, D. (2009a). Return of the State? The G20, the Financial Crisis and Power in the World Economy. Retrieved 9 April 2009, from http://ssrn.com/paper=1375387.

Nordberg, D. (2009b). Some are More Equal: The Politics of Shareholder Activism. Retrieved 28 June 2009, from http://ssrn.com/paper=1150130.

Nordberg, D. (2010a). The Politics of Shareholder Activism. In H. K. Baker & R. Anderson (eds), *Corporate Governance: A Synthesis of Theory, Research, and Practice.* New York: John Wiley & Sons.

Nordberg, D. (2010b). Unfettered Agents? The Role of Ethics in Corporate Governance. In H. K. Baker & R. Anderson (Eds), *Corporate Governance: A Synthesis of Theory, Research, and Practice.* New York: John Wiley & Sons Inc.

Nordhaus, W. (2007). The Challenge of Global Warming: Economic Models and Environmental Policy. Retrieved 19 Dec. 2008, from http://nordhaus.econ.yale.edu/dice_mss_072407_all.pdf.

OECD (1999). OECD Principles of Corporate Governance. Retrieved 8 Jan. 2008, from http://www.ecgi.org/codes/documents/principles_en.pdf.

OECD (2003). Experiences from the Regional Corporate Governance Roundtables. Retrieved 27 June 2008, from http://www.olis.oecd.org/olis/2003doc.nsf/LinkTo/NT0000469E/$FILE/JT00152151.PDF.

OECD (2004). OECD Principles of Corporate Governance, Revised. Retrieved 15 Oct. 2006, from http://www.oecd.org/dataoecd/32/18/31557724.pdf.

OPM & CIPFA (2004). Good Governance Standard for Public Services. *The Independent Commission on Good Governance in Public Services.* Retrieved 14 Aug. 2009, from http://www.cipfa.org.uk/pt/download/governance_standard.pdf.

Paley, A. R. & Hilzenrath, D. S. (2008, 24 Dec.). SEC Chief Defends His Restraint. Retrieved 19 June 2009, from http://www.washingtonpost.com/wp-dyn/content/article/2008/12/23/AR2008122302765.html.

Penrose, E. (1959). *The Theory of Growth of the Firm.* New York: Wiley.

Peston, R. (2009, 1 Aug.). Interview with Paul Myners. *Leading Questions programme, BBC News Channel*. Retrieved 1 Aug. 2009, from http://news.bbc.co.uk/1/hi/business/8179024.stm.

Pettigrew, A. & McNulty, T. (1998). Sources and Uses of Power in the Boardroom. *European Journal of Work & Organizational Psychology, 7*(2), 197–214.

Pfeffer, J. & Salancik, G. R. (1978). *The External Control of Organizations: A Resource Dependence Perspective*. New York: Harper & Row.

Porter, M. E. (1980). *Competitive Strategy*. New York: Free Press.

Porter, M. E. & Kramer, M. R. (2006). Strategy & Society: The Link Between Competitive Advantage and Corporate Social Responsibility. *Harvard Business Review, 84*(12), 78–92.

Porter, S. & Johnson, M. F. (1997). How Firms Responded to the New Tax Law Limiting the Deductibility of Certain Executive Compensation. *Ernst & Young Visiting Professor Paper.* Retrieved 24 July 2009, from http://www.taxfoundation.org/files/fb7e0c506b-f1edd5782aa96516c62c98.pdf.

Prahalad, C. K. & Hamel, G. (1990). The Core Competence of the Corporation. *Harvard Business Review, 68*(3), 79–91.

Pugliese, A., Bezemer, P.-J., Zattoni, A., Huse, M., Bosch, F. A. J. V. d. & Volberda, H. W. (2009). Boards of Directors' Contribution to Strategy: A Literature Review and Research Agenda. *Corporate Governance: An International Review, 17*(3), 292–306.

Raiborn, C., Payne, D. & Pier, C. (2008). The Need for Plain English Disclosures. *Journal of Corporate Accounting & Finance, 19*(5), 69–76.

Rappaport, A. (1986). *Creating Shareholder Value: The New Standard for Business Performance*. New York: Free Press.

Rawlins, B., Paine, K. & Kowalski, P. (2008). Measuring the Transparency of Environmental Sustainability Reporting Through Websites of Fortune 50 Corporations. Retrieved 24 Dec. 2008, from http://www.themeasurementstandard.com/Images/Environ SustainReport.pdf.

Reid, E. M. & Toffel, M. W. (2009). Responding to Public and Private Politics: Corporate Disclosure of Climate Change Strategies. *Harvard Business School Technology & Operations Mgt. Unit Research Paper No. 09–019.* Retrieved 26 June 2009, from http://ssrn.com/paper=1237982.

Reinhardt, U. E. (2009, 13 Feb.). Jack Welch and the Lone Ranger Theory. *Economix column, NYT.com.* Retrieved 24 August 2009, from http://economix.blogs.nytimes.com/2009/02/13/jack-welch-and-the-lone-ranger-theory/.

Roberts, J. (2005). Agency Theory, Ethics and Corporate Governance. In C. R. Lehman (ed.), *Corporate Governance: Does One Size Fit Any? Advances in Public Interest Accounting* (pp. 249–69). London/Amsterdam: Elsevier.

Roe, M. J. (2003). *Political Determinants of Corporate Governance: Political Context, Corporate Impact*. Oxford: Oxford University Press.

Rose, P. (2007). The Corporate Governance Industry. *Journal of Corporation Law, 32*(4), 887–926.

Sabherwal, S. & Smith, S. D. (2008). Concentrated Shareholders as Substitutes for Outside Analysts. *Corporate Governance: An International Review, 16*(6), 562–77.

Sampson, A. (1973). *The Sovereign State of ITT*. London: Hodder and Stoughton.

Schäfer, D. (2009, 23 July). Triumph for VW in Porsche battle. *FT.com.* Retrieved 29 July 2009, from http://www.ft.com/cms/s/0/349f8268-77ad-11de-9713-00144feabdc0.html.

Schäfer, D. & Mackintosh, J. (2009, 15 March). Hedge Funds May Sue Porsche Over VW. *Financial Times.* Retrieved 26 June 2009, from http://www.ft.com/cms/s/0/ac72c164-1188-11de-87b1-0000779fd2ac.html.

Schmidt, R. H. & Spindler, G. (2004). Path Dependency and Complementarity. In J. N. Gordon & M. J. Roe (eds), *Convergence and Persistence in Corporate Governance* (pp. 114–27). Cambridge: Cambridge University Press.

Schmolke, K. U. (2006). Institutional Investors' Mandatory Voting Disclosure – European Plans and US Experience. Retrieved 1 Jan. 2009, from http://lsr.nellco.org/cgi/view-content.cgi?article=1075&context=nyu/lewp.

Schumpeter, J. A. (1942/1976). *Capitalism, Socialism and Democracy*. New York: Harper & Brothers.

Schwed, F., Jr. (1940/1995). *Where are the Customers' Yachts? Or a Good Hard Look at Wall Street*. New York: Wiley.

Sealy, R., Vinnicombe, S. & Singh, V. (2008). The Female FTSE Report 2008: A Decade of Delay. *International Centre for Women Leaders*. Retrieved 24 July 2009, from http://www.som.cranfield.ac.uk/som/dinamic-content/research/documents/ft2008.pdf.

SEC (2003, 28 April). Ten of Nation's Top Investment Firms Settle Enforcement Actions Involving Conflicts of Interest between Research and Investment Banking. *SEC.gov*. Retrieved 29 April 2003, from http://www.sec.gov/news/press/2003-54.htm.

SEC (2009, 17 Sep.). SEC Votes on Measures to Further Strengthen Oversight of Credit Rating Agencies. *Securities and Exchange Commission news release*. Retrieved 20 Sep. 2009, from http://www.sec.gov/news/press/2009/2009-200.htm.

Seidman, L. W. (1996). The World Financial System: Lessons Learned and Challenges Ahead. *NIKKIN 7th Special Seminar on International Finance*. Retrieved 14 Aug. 2009, from http://www.fdic.gov/bank/historical/history/vol2/panel3.pdf.

Shah, A. (ed.) (2007). *Performance Accountability and Combating Corruption*. Washington: The World Bank.

Sharfman, B. S. (2010, 20 Jan.). When Shareholder Primacy Does Not Apply. *SSRN eLibrary*. Retrieved 27 Jan. 2010, from http://ssrn.com/paper=1518597.

Shekshnia, S. V. (2004). Roles, Responsibilities, and Independence of Boards of Directors. In D. J. McCarthy, S. M. Puffer & S. V. Shekshnia (eds), *Corporate Governance in Russia* (pp. 201–22). Cheltenham: Edward Elgar.

Sherman, S. (2002). Enron: Uncovering the Uncovered Story. *Columbia Journalism Review, 40*(6), 22–8.

Sims, R. R. & Brinkmann, J. (2003). Enron Ethics (Or: Culture Matters More than Codes). *Journal of Business Ethics, 45*(3), 243–56.

Singh, V. (2007). Ethnic Diversity on Top Corporate Boards: A Resource Dependency Perspective. *International Journal of Human Resource Management, 18*(12), 2128–46.

Smith, A. (1776/1904). *The Wealth of Nations*. Retrieved 19 July 2010 from http://www.econlib.org/library/Smith/smWNCover.html.

Smith, R. (2003). Audit Committees Combined Code Guidance. Retrieved 29 December 2008, from http://www.ecgi.org/codes/documents/ac_report.pdf.

Smith, T. (1992). *Accounting for Growth*. London: Century Business.

Sonnenfeld, J. (2004). Good Governance and the Misleading Myth of Bad Metrics. *Academy of Management Executive, 18*(1), 108–13.

Steed, A. (2003, 15 Feb.). MPs Take Tough Line on Splits. *Daily Telegraph*, p. 14.

Stern, N. (2006). Report on the Economics of Climate Change: The Stern Review. Retrieved 17 March 2008, from http://www.sternreview.org.uk.

Stiles, P. (2001). The Impact of the Board on Strategy: An Empirical Examination. *Journal of Management Studies, 38*, 627–50.

Stiles, P. & Taylor, B. (2001). *Boards at Work – How Directors View Their Roles and Responsibilities*. Oxford: Oxford University Press.

Strier, F. (2008). Rating the Raters: Conflicts of Interest in the Credit Rating Firms. *Business & Society Review, 113*(4), 533–53.

Swedish Corporate Governance Board (2008). Swedish Code of Corporate Governance. Retrieved 29 March 2008, from http://www.ecgi.org/codes/documents/swedish_cgc_jul2008_en.pdf.

Tambini, D. (2008). What is Financial Journalism For? Ethics and Responsibility in a Time of Crisis and Change. Retrieved 17 Nov. 2008, from http://www.polismedia.org/research/financialjournalism.aspx.

Teather, D. (2009, 28 July). BP Chief Defends Green Energy Record. *Guardian.co.uk*. Retrieved 4 Aug. 2009, from http://www.guardian.co.uk/business/2009/jul/28/bp-chief-defends-green-record.

Temin, P. & Voth, H.-J. (2004). Riding the South Sea Bubble. *American Economic Review, 94*(5), 1654–68.

Thomas, L., Jr. (2006). The Winding Road to Grasso's Huge Payday. *NYT.com* Retrieved 11 Aug. 2009, from http://www.nytimes.com/2006/06/25/business/yourmoney/25grasso.html?_r=1&scp=3&sq=grasso%20nyse&st=cse.

Thompson, T. A. & Davis, G. F. (1997). The Politics of Corporate Control and the Future of Shareholder Activism in the United States. *Corporate Governance: An International Review, 5*(3), 152.

Toffler, B. L. & Reingold, J. (2003). *Final Accounting: Ambition, Greed, and the Fall of Arthur Andersen*. New York: Broadway Books.

Tonello, M. (2006). Revisiting Stock Market Short-Termism. *The Conference Board Research Report No. R-1386-06-RR*. Retrieved 28 July 2009, from http://ssrn.com/abstract=938466.

Turnbull, N. (1999). Internal Control: Guidance for Directors on the Combined Code. Retrieved 15 Nov. 2008, from http://www.ecgi.org/codes/documents/turnbul.pdf.

Tyson, L. (2003). The Tyson Report on the Recruitment and Development of Non-Executive Directors, a Report to the UK Department of Trade and Industry. Retrieved 8 April 2007, from http://facultyresearch.london.edu/docs/TysonReport.pdf.

UK Parliament (2006). Companies Act. Retrieved 20 June 2007, from http://www.opsi.gov.uk/acts/acts2006/ukpga_20060046_en.pdf.

UK Parliament (2009, 15 May). Banking Crisis: Reforming Corporate Governance and Pay in the City. *House of Commons Treasury Committee: Ninth Report of Session 2008–9*. Retrieved 22 Aug. 2009, from http://www.publications.parliament.uk/pa/m200809/cmselect/cmtreasy/519/519.pdf.

van den Berghe, L. A. A., & Baelden, T. (2005). The Complex Relation Between Director Independence and Board Effectiveness. *Corporate Governance: The International Journal of Business in Society. 5*(5), 58–83.

Veniot (1995). The Boards of Directors of Listed Companies in France. Retrieved 30 July 2008, from http://www.ecgi.org/codes/documents/vienot1_en.pdf.

von Werder, A., & Talaulicar, T. (2006). Executive Summary, Umsetzung der Empfehlungen und Anregungen des Deutschen Corporate Governance Kodex. Retrieved 24 June 2006, from http://www.bccg.tu-berlin.de/main/publikationen/Kodex%20Report%202006_Executive%20Summary.pdf.

von Werder, A. & Talaulicar, T. (2007). Executive Summary, Umsetzung der Empfehlungen und Anregungen des Deutschen Corporate Governance Kodex. Retrieved 13 Nov. 2007, from http://www.bccg.tu-berlin.de/main/publikationen/Kodex%20Report%202007_Executive%20Summary.pdf.

von Werder, A. & Talaulicar, T. (2009). Kodex Report 2009: Die Akzeptanz der Empfelungen und Anregungen des Deutschen Corporate Governance Kodex. Retrieved 23 July 2009, from http://www.bccg.tu-berlin.de/main/publikationen/2009/Kodex-Report%202009.pdf.

Walker, D. (2009a, 16 July). A Review of Corporate Governance in UK Banks and Other Financial Industry Entities. *HM Treasury Independent Reviews*. Retrieved 16 July 2009, from http://www.hm-treasury.gov.uk/d/walker_review_consultation_160709.pdf.

Walker, D. (2009b, 26 Nov.). A Review of Corporate Governance in UK Banks and Other Financial Industry Entities: Final Recommendations. *HM Treasury Independent Reviews*.

Retrieved 26 Nov. 2009, from http://www.hm-treasury.gov.uk/d/walker_review_consul-tation_160709.pdf.

Wearing, R. (2005). *Cases in Corporate Governance*. London: Sage.

Wernerfelt, B. (1984). A Resource-based View of the Firm. *Strategic Management Journal, 5*(2), 171–80.

Williamson, O. E. (1985). *The Economic Institutions of Capitalism*. New York: Free Press.

Williamson, O. E. & Winter, S. G. (1993). *The Nature of the Firm: Origins, Evolution, and Development*. Oxford: Oxford University Press.

Wong, S. C. Y. (2009). Uses and Limits of Conventional Corporate Governance Instruments: Analysis and Guidance for Reform (Integrated Version). *Private Sector Opinion, Global Corporate Governance Forum*. Retrieved 13 Nov. 2009, from http://ssrn.com/paper=1409370.

Wright, P., Kroll, M. & Elenkov, D. (2002). Acquisition Returns, Increase in Firm Size, and Chief Executive Officer Compensation: The Moderating Role of Monitoring. *Academy of Management Journal, 45*(3), 599–608.

Zetzsche, D. A. (2007). An Ethical Theory of Corporate Governance History. Retrieved 14 Oct. 2008, from http://ssrn.com/paper=970909.

Zingales, L. (2000). In Search of New Foundations. *Journal of Finance, 55*(4), 1623–53.

Index

Research Methods Books from SAGE

Read sample chapters online now!

INTERPRETING QUALITATIVE DATA **THIRD EDITION**

DAVID SILVERMAN

Qualitative Research & Evaluation Methods

3 EDITION

Michael Quinn Patton

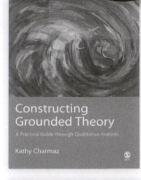

Constructing Grounded Theory

A Practical Guide through Qualitative Analysis

Kathy Charmaz

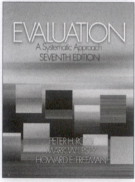

EVALUATION
A Systematic Approach
SEVENTH EDITION

PETER H. ROSSI
MARK W. LIPSEY
HOWARD E. FREEMAN

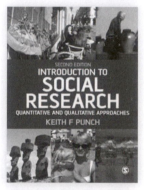

SECOND EDITION
INTRODUCTION TO SOCIAL RESEARCH
QUANTITATIVE AND QUALITATIVE APPROACHES
KEITH F PUNCH

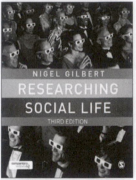

NIGEL GILBERT
RESEARCHING SOCIAL LIFE
THIRD EDITION

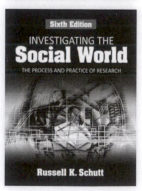

Sixth Edition
INVESTIGATING THE Social World
THE PROCESS AND PRACTICE OF RESEARCH

Russell K. Schutt

AN INTRODUCTION TO QUALITATIVE RESEARCH
UWE FLICK
EDITION 4

DEVELOPING EFFECTIVE RESEARCH PROPOSALS

Keith F Punch

SECOND EDITION

www.sagepub.co.uk

SAGE

Research Methods
Books from SAGE

Read sample chapters online now!

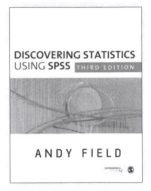

DISCOVERING STATISTICS USING SPSS THIRD EDITION

ANDY FIELD

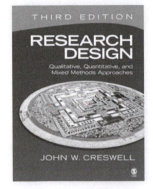

THIRD EDITION

RESEARCH DESIGN

Qualitative, Quantitative, and Mixed Methods Approaches

JOHN W. CRESWELL

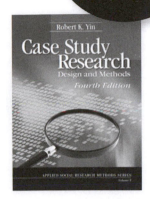

Robert K. Yin

Case Study Research
Design and Methods
Fourth Edition

APPLIED SOCIAL RESEARCH METHODS SERIES

Second Edition

QUALITATIVE INQUIRY & RESEARCH DESIGN
Choosing Among Five Approaches

John W. Creswell

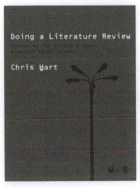

Doing a Literature Review

Chris Hart

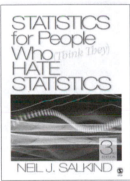

STATISTICS for People Who (Think They) HATE STATISTICS

NEIL J. SALKIND

SECOND EDITION

INTERVIEWS
Learning the Craft of Qualitative Research Interviewing

Steinar Kvale
Svend Brinkmann

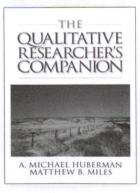

THE QUALITATIVE RESEARCHER'S COMPANION

A. MICHAEL HUBERMAN
MATTHEW B. MILES

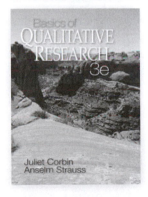

Basics of QUALITATIVE RESEARCH 3e

Juliet Corbin
Anselm Strauss

www.sagepub.co.uk

SAGE

The Qualitative Research Kit

Edited by Uwe Flick

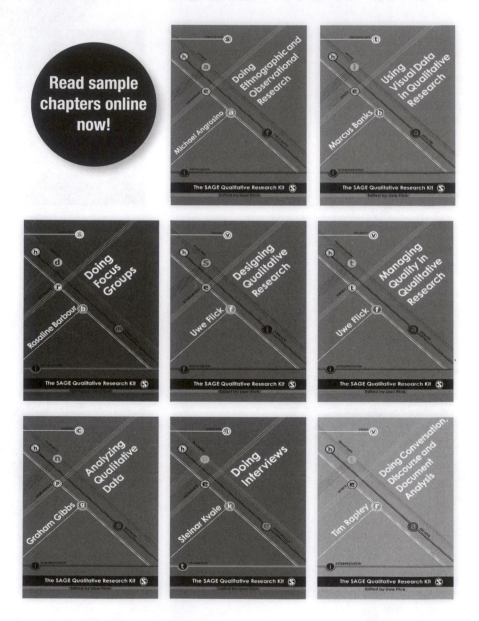

Read sample chapters online now!

Doing Ethnographic and Observational Research — Michael Angrosino — The SAGE Qualitative Research Kit — Edited by Uwe Flick

Using Visual Data in Qualitative Research — Marcus Banks — The SAGE Qualitative Research Kit — Edited by Uwe Flick

Doing Focus Groups — Rosaline Barbour — The SAGE Qualitative Research Kit

Designing Qualitative Research — Uwe Flick — The SAGE Qualitative Research Kit — Edited by Uwe Flick

Managing Quality in Qualitative Research — Uwe Flick — The SAGE Qualitative Research Kit — Edited by Uwe Flick

Analyzing Qualitative Data — Graham Gibbs — The SAGE Qualitative Research Kit — Edited by Uwe Flick

Doing Interviews — Steinar Kvale — The SAGE Qualitative Research Kit — Edited by Uwe Flick

Doing Conversation, Discourse and Document Analysis — Tim Rapley — The SAGE Qualitative Research Kit — Edited by Uwe Flick

www.sagepub.co.uk